Children, Food and Identity in Everyday Life

Studies in Childhood and Youth

Titles include:

Allison James, Anne Trine Kjørholt and Vebjørg Tingstad (*editors*)
CHILDREN, FOOD AND IDENTITY IN EVERYDAY LIFE

Studies in Childhood and Youth
Series Standing Order ISBN 978–0–230–21686–0 hardback
(*outside North America only*)

You can receive future titles in this series as they are published by placing a standing order. Please contact your bookseller or, in case of difficulty, write to us at the address below with your name and address, the title of the series and the ISBN quoted above.

Customer Services Department, Macmillan Distribution Ltd, Houndmills, Basingstoke, Hampshire RG21 6XS, England

Children, Food and Identity in Everyday Life

Edited By

Allison James
University of Sheffield, UK

Anne Trine Kjørholt
University of Trondheim, Norway

and

Vebjørg Tingstad
University of Trondheim, Norway

First published 2009 by
PALGRAVE MACMILLAN

Palgrave Macmillan in the UK is an imprint of Macmillan Publishers Limited,
registered in England, company number 785998, of Houndmills, Basingstoke,
Hampshire RG21 6XS.

Palgrave Macmillan in the US is a division of St Martin's Press LLC,
175 Fifth Avenue, New York, NY 10010.

Palgrave Macmillan is the global academic imprint of the above companies
and has companies and representatives throughout the world.

Palgrave® and Macmillan® are registered trademarks in the United States,
the United Kingdom, Europe and other countries

ISBN: 978-0-230-57599-8 hardback

This book is printed on paper suitable for recycling and made from fully
managed and sustained forest sources. Logging, pulping and manufacturing
processes are expected to conform to the environmental regulations of the
country of origin.

A catalogue record for this book is available from the British Library.

A catalog record for this book is available from the Library of Congress.

10 9 8 7 6 5 4 3 2 1
18 17 16 15 14 13 12 11 10 09

Printed and bound in Great Britain by
CPI Antony Rowe, Chippenham and Eastbourne

Contents

Illustrations

Tables

Figures

Acknowledgements

Grateful acknowledgement is made to Glenryck Foods for permission to reproduce the advertisement for Glenryck and Puffin pilchards.

Contributors

Kathryn Backett-Milburn is Professor of the Sociology of Families and Health in Community Health Sciences and the School of Health in Social Science at the University of Edinburgh, Scotland. She is also co-director of the Centre for Research on Families and Relationships (CRFR). Kathryn is a qualitative research specialist currently involved in research into children, families and work–life balance using qualitative longitudinal research methods (she is a PI and heading up the User Engagement strand for the ESRC Timescapes QLR Study); social class, family and the adolescent diet; work–life balance issues for women; qualitative understanding of demographic issues in Scotland; and research with ChildLine Scotland.

Helene Brembeck is Professor of Ethnology and co-director of the Center for Consumer Science (CFK) at Göteborg University, Sweden. The focus of her research interest encompasses parenthood and childhood in consumer culture, food, eating and ethnicity. She has published several books and anthologies in this field including *Little Monsters: (De) Coupling Assemblages of Consumption* (2007, LIT Verlag, co-edited with Karin M. Ekström and Magnus Mörck); and *Elusive Consumption* (2004, Berg, co-edited with Karin M. Ekström). Her most recent work is the book *Hem till McDonald's* [Home to McDonald's] (2007, Carlssons) about family dining at McDonald's.

Joseph Burridge is a part-time teacher in the School of Sociology and Social Policy at the University of Nottingham, a Sessional Tutor in Media and Communications at Nottingham Trent International College (Kaplan), and a Research Associate at the School of Nursing and Midwifery at the University of Sheffield. He was a Lecturer in Sociology at Nottingham Trent University, and before that he worked as a Research Associate on the *Changing Families, Changing Foods* Programme at the University of Sheffield, UK. Prior to that, he was an ESRC Postdoctoral Research Fellow in the Department of Social Sciences at Loughborough University, and spent several years at the University of Nottingham as an undergraduate and then postgraduate student.

Daniel Thomas Cook is Associate Professor of Childhood Studies and Sociology at Rutgers University, Camden, New Jersey, USA. He is editor of *Symbolic Childhood* (2002) and author of *The Commodification of Childhood* (2004) as well as a number of articles and book chapters on childhood, consumer society, leisure and urban culture. Cook serves as an Editor of *Childhood: A Journal of Global Child Research*.

Penny Curtis is a senior lecturer in the School of Nursing and Midwifery and Deputy Director of the Centre for the Study of Childhood and Youth at the University of Sheffield. Her research has included work on children and internal aspects of the built environment of the hospital, children food and eating, children's participation in everyday decision-making in the home, and children's experiences of obesity.

Nika Dorrer is research fellow in the Department of Applied Social Science at the University of Stirling, Scotland. Her research interests have been in the relationship between young people's well-being and identity in different socio-cultural contexts and in recovery approaches to mental health. Her background is in social psychology.

Caroline Dryden is a chartered social psychologist with particular interests in critical psychology, the family, gender relations and health. She obtained her PhD at Bristol and taught for a number of years in communication studies at Sheffield Hallam before coming to work as a lecturer in Health Care at the University of Sheffield. She specialises in qualitative methods and was a co-investigator on the Leverhulme Trust funded project 'Men, Children and Food'.

Katie Ellis joined the Department of Sociological Studies at The University of Sheffield, UK, in 2003, following the completion of her MSc in Sociology and Social Research. Whilst studying, Katie worked as a family support worker, forming close relationships with a range of children, all experiencing personal and social difficulties. Through her research, Katie champions young people's issues, and strives to listen to children's stories with a view to improving services and provisions for them. Katie is particularly interested in young people who are viewed as troubled or troublesome and is committed to research which enables young people to share their experiences. Katie is now working on a PhD looking at girl's experiences of secure accommodation.

Ruth Emond is a lecturer in Social Work at the University of Stirling and a social worker at the Family Change Project in Perth, Scotland working with children and their families who have experienced trauma. Her research and practice interests include children's experiences of residential care, children in care and their friendships and play therapy as a 'treatment' for childhood trauma.

Allison James is Professor of Sociology, Director of the Centre for the Study of Childhood and Youth and Director of the Interdisciplinary Centre of the Social Sciences at the University of Sheffield, UK. She is also Professor 2 at Norwegian Centre for Child Research, Trondheim. She has worked in the sociology/anthropology of childhood since the late 1970s and has helped pioneer the theoretical and methodological approaches to research with children which are central to the new childhood studies. Her latest books include *European Childhoods* (2008, London, Palgrave, co-edited with A. L. James) and *Key Concepts in Childhood Studies* (2008, London, Sage, with A. L. James).

Julia Keenan is a social and cultural geographer with interests in health, risk and governmentality perspectives, the new genetics and parenting cultures. She is currently working as a research assistant at the University of Leeds.

Anne Trine Kjørholt is Associate Professor and Director of Norwegian Centre for Child Research at the Norwegian University of Science and Technology in Trondheim, Norway. Research interests are discourses on childhood, children's rights and citizenship, early childhood education and care. Among publications are: *Beyond Listening. Children's Perspectives in Early Childhood Services* (co-edited with A. Clark and P.Moss); *Flexible Childhood? Exploring Children's Welfare in Time and Space* (co-edited with H. Zeiher, D. Devine and H.Strandell); *Global Childhoods: Globalization, Development and Young People* (co-edited with S. Aitken and R.Lund). She is Associate Editor of the *Journal of Irish Educational Studies*, General Editor of the Nordic journal *Barn*, and an Editorial Board Member of both *Childhoods Today* and *Childhood*.

Julia Lawton is a Senior Research Fellow in Community Health Sciences, which is part of the Medical School at the University of Edinburgh. Her background and training is in social anthropology and medical sociology. She is responsible for developing, coordinating and supervising an integrated programme of research in the area of health-related risk and lifestyle. Her specific research interests include people's experiences of disease self-management and disease prevention, particularly in relation to type 2 diabetes and other mutli-factorial conditions where lifestyle plays a key role.

Ian McIntosh is a senior lecturer in Sociology in the Department of Applied Social Science of English People in Scotland and the identities associated with place and neighbourhoods at Stirling University, Scotland. He has recently completed research into the experiences of

English people in Scotland and the identities associated with place and neighbourhoods.

Alan Metcalf has worked and written on a variety of topics, including home, the disposal of possessions and family, fatherhood and food practices Currently, he is working as a researcher on the ESRC funded project The Waste of the World (www.thewasteoftheworld.org). Central to each of these studies has been an interest in consumption, identities and material culture.

Jenny Owen is a sociologist, and is a senior lecturer in the Public Health section of the School of Health and Related Research, University of Sheffield. In addition to the research on families and food discussed in this volume, she also has research and teaching interests in public policy constructions of teenage pregnancy, in young people's experience of sexual health services, and in inter-professional learning about child welfare.

Samantha Punch is a senior lecturer in Sociology in the Department of Applied Social Science at Stirling University, Scotland. She is currently researching youth transitions and migration in rural Bolivia and Argentina; and household livelihoods in Asia. Other research interests include children's experiences of sibling relationships and birth order in Scotland.

Mei-Li Roberts is a Research Fellow at the University of the Highlands and Islands (UHI) Centre for Rural Childhood, UHI Millennium Institute and degree course leader for the BA (Hons) Child and Youth Studies, UHI Millennium Institute. She has previously worked at the University of Edinburgh and the University of St Andrews (in collaboration with the University of Dundee) and undertook her doctoral research at the University of St Andrews. Her research interests include conceptions of diet, weight, health and physical activity amongst children, young people and their families in Scotland and Christianity, missionaries, translation and identity in Melanesia.

Geraldine Shipton was a Senior Lecturer in Psychoanalytic Studies at the University of Sheffield and is now a psychoanalyst in full-time private practice in Sheffield. She has written a number of books including *Working with Eating Disorders: A Psychoanalytic Approach* (2004, London, Palgrave).

Helen Stapleton is a lecturer at the University of Sheffield, The University of Sheffield School of Nursing and Midwifery Centre for

Health & Social Care Studies and Service Development, UK. Her current research interests include qualitative methodologies, parenting cultures, the social context of sexuality and reproduction, the health and well-being of children, young people and families, and more recently, food and consumption practices in the context of family formation.

Vebjørg Tingstad is Associate Professor at the Norwegian Centre for Child Research at the Norwegian University of Science and Technology in Trondheim, Norway. Her current research interest involves childhood, media, consumption and food. Recent publications are *Children's Chat on the Net. A Study of Children's Social Encounters in Two Norwegian Chat Rooms* (2003), *Barndom under lupen* [Exploring Childhood-Growing up in a Changing Media Culture] (2006), and journal articles on childhood, commercial television and consumption. Tingstad is an editor of the Nordic journal *Barn*.

Wendy Wills is a Senior Research Fellow at the University of Hertfordshire's Centre for Research in Primary and Community Care (CRIPACC). She is a sociologist and also a public health nutritionist. She previously worked at the University of Edinburgh and before that undertook her doctoral research at the London School of Hygiene and Tropical Medicine (University of London). She works mainly with children, young people and families and the practitioners and professionals with whom they come into contact with, to undertake research on the social and cultural factors which drive everyday food and eating practices and lay perceptions of diet, health and weight. She co-convenes the British Sociological Association's food study group.

Introduction: Children, Food and Identity in Everyday Life

Allison James, Anne Trine Kjørholt, Vebjørg Tingstad

The relationship between children and food is currently high on the political agendas of many countries particularly in relation to matters such as school meals, childhood obesity and children's exposure to marketing (media discourses) of various kinds. Within these discourses, however, ideas of risk predominate as the main way in which children's relationship with food is constructed and as such this constitutes a largely problematic 'child' identity. It is against such a background, therefore, that this volume seeks to explore the significance of a range of food practices for childhood identities in the context of children's everyday lives in different cultural settings.

Our first focus is on children's everyday encounters with food. This makes it possible to understand not only how they are positioned as consumers by, for example, television and marketing, but also how, as social actors, they engage with parents through negotiations around food and eating or, alternatively through 'pester power', and how they influence and are influenced by their peers at school. Our second focus is on the ways in which childhood identities are constructed and mediated through particular foodstuffs and policy initiatives around children's food consumption in different societies. Thirdly, in drawing on empirical material, stretching from early babyhood through to middle childhood and adolescence, the volume also enables an understanding of the changing relationship between children, food and identity over time. Taken together, these perspectives are able to provide a more measured and insightful understanding of the various and subtle dimensions of the relationship between children, food and identity than is normally headlined in the press.

In sum, therefore, our concern is to explore those processes of identification in which food and eating practices are the material means through which children's identities *as children* are both reflected and refracted by asking a series of questions: What do particular kinds of foodstuffs and eating practices reveal about the nature of childhood and children's everyday experiences? Why do children eat particular foods? In what ways do children's food and eating practices differ from those of adults? What similarities might there be and how might we understand these? What do the kinds of food policies constructed by nation-states reveal about the place of children in particular societies?

Such questions are underpinned, however, by a particular understanding of identity, one that sees identity as neither fixed nor static. Rather, following Jenkins, we argue that 'identity can only be understood as process...[it] is never a final or settled matter' (1996:2). Moreover, it is this that makes our focus on an age-based category such as 'children' particularly interesting. The individuals who 'occupy' the status of 'child' in any historical moment are, through the inevitability of the ageing process, also poised to leave it as adulthood encroaches (Hockey & James 2003). This means, therefore, that, in exploring questions of identity in relation to food, we have to be attentive, not only to the kinds of social categories that are invoked – child, adult, girl, boy – but also to the temporality of the historical moment, the cultural context within which such processes are occurring and, importantly, to the individuals themselves. As Hockey and James argue, in respect of changing identities across the life course 'identities only become meaningful in terms of the individual's response to them' (2003:201). Thus, what this volume explores, across the various chapters, are the ways in which children's identities become enmeshed in ideas about food and eating, processes that reveal the ongoing nature of social identification.

The significance of this volume, aside from its timeliness in an era when there is a rapidly growing global and public interest in children and food consumption, lies also in the sociological and anthropological perspectives that frame the individual chapters. In endeavouring to tease out the links between children, food and identity, drawing on the theories and concepts of sociology and anthropology, this book represents the first of its kind, providing a counterweight to the more nutritionally and medically based materials that are currently available. Drawing on empirical research recently conducted in England,[1] Scotland, Norway, Sweden and the United States, the volume demonstrates, in different cultural settings, the ways in which children are positioned as food consumers and their response to this; the kinds of meanings that food can have for children; the popular assumptions about the impact that TV and marketing have on children's food-consumption practices;

and the ways in which children are culturally positioned vis-à-vis food and eating through a range of public policy discourses.

The study of children and food

It has long been demonstrated by social scientists that the importance of food is not simply a question of the nourishment it provides for the body. As the classical accounts of sociologists and anthropologists have shown, food and eating practices are deeply implicated in the structuring of social, political and economic relations (Goody 1982; Levi-Strauss 1983; Caplan 1997; Douglas 2002); in the ways good parenting is constituted (Coveney 2000); in the ways in which gender relations take place (Charles & Kerr 1988; Murcott 2000) and in the everyday making of family life (Murcott 1982; DeVault 1991). Indeed, food and eating habits have been described as a total social phenomenon with significant meanings for a variety of different aspects of human life (Døving 2002). From the moment children are born, their responses to food and eating practices are shaped by the ways in which they interact with others (Lupton 1998). Cross-cultural studies of food and eating practices, for example, reveal differences not only related to diet, but also in how eating practices and meals reflect and constitute intergenerational relations, discipline, the transmission of value and norms, morals, emotional expressions and so on. Thus, children's participation in common meals has a significant symbolic value as an assertion of belonging to a particular culture (Douglas 2002).

By introducing childhood studies into the field of cultural food research, this volume seeks to build on and extend this earlier research. With its twin foci on the ways in which childhood is socially constructed and children are social actors who participate in the social world – and indeed can affect change in it (see James & James 2004) – we suggest that new perspectives can be brought to bear and new insights into food and eating developed. While, as evidenced above, the cultural aspects of food consumption have been developed within the sub-fields of the sociology and anthropology of food (Beardsworth & Keil 1997; Warde 1997; Warde & Martens 2000) and food studies (Counihan & van Esterik 1997; Scholliers 2001; Belasco & Scranton 2002), relatively few scholars have focused on children and childhood. Exceptions such as van Esterik (1997), Lyngø (2001) and Bentley (2002) deal, however, mainly with historical discourses on baby food and nutrition, rather than engaging with children's activities as food consumers today, which is the focus of this volume.

Where attention has been given to the relationship between children and food this has almost exclusively been studied in relation to the private sphere of families, and here the focus has been principally on adult informants, rather than on children themselves (Lupton 1998; Coveney 2000). This is at odds with the fact that a growing part of children's food consumption, certainly in western contexts, is taking place outside of the family – in public institutions such as day care centres and schools and, to an increasing degree, in places like snack bars, fast-food restaurants and candy stores, that children visit on their own or together with friends at an early age (Brembeck & Johansson 1996). There is therefore a gap in our knowledge about children's activities as food consumers in public spaces, and hardly any work explores children's own experiences and perspectives (Tingstad 1996; Christensen 2002, 2003). Thus, although a lot of public concern in western contexts is currently being raised about children's exposure to media, advertisements and various market-related activities, and the possible links this has to eating disorders, obesity and distorted body images, very little is yet known about children's activities as food consumers in public spaces or indeed children's views on food more generally. Through this volume we seek to provide such information and, in doing so, draw attention to the importance of seeing children as active participants in relation to food-consumption practices in line with the paradigm common in childhood studies that attributes children with the status of social actors – people who do things and have things to say, people who can tell us about their lives as children (James & Prout 1990).

Thus, Dryden, Metcalfe, Owen and Shipton explore in Chapter 4 the ways in which English children draw on a variety of different discourses in their drawings of imagined lunch-boxes. Not only do their choices reflect and refract wider ideas, currently being promulgated in the media about nutrition, diet and healthy eating, but they also reveal the ways in which children engage with ideas of gender and age. Moreover, such processes of identification are, Dryden et al. suggest, indications of the ways in which small children may already be engaging with ideas of food moralities and self-worth. This, they argue, raises the question as to the potential implications for young people's sense of self and identity in relation to the current moralising about food and eating practices.

Food, identity and generational relations

As the chapters in this volume demonstrate, as is the case with adults, food consumption in children's everyday lives is changing. Increasing levels of fragmentation and individualisation, in terms of both the provision of food and where and how children's meals are consumed, are accentuating food choices and involving children in new kinds of identity formation. By identity formation we mean both the process of children growing into a particular society and the lifelong identity processes through which an individual acts reflexively in relation to the self and his/her surroundings (Jenkins 1996). In this respect, Taylor's (1991) theories of individualism in modern western societies are useful for understanding the powerful discourses and storylines that affect the construction of modern subjects – children as well as adults (Kjørholt 2005). In an earlier social order, individual life was to a large degree determined by 'fate' and by inhabiting particular positions serving the interests of a community grounded in the order of things or the will of God. Today, new moral positions hold that everyone has the right to have their own values and to develop their own ways of life grounded in individual choices about what is important. Taylor claims further that:

> This individualism involves a centring on the self and a concomitant shutting out, or even unawareness, of the greater issues or concerns that transcend the self, be they religious, political, historical. As a consequence, life is narrowed or flattened. (Taylor 1991:14)

In relation to the sphere of children, food and consumption, the kinds of changes described above would include children's negotiations and impact on family purchasing as well as parental worries about nutrition and children's health. This suggests that an important dimension of the relationship between children, food and identity has to be understood in terms of intergenerational relations. In this respect, Alanen (2001) argues for a concept of generation that does more than rely on externally derived definitional criteria such as age – for example, the idea that adults are older than children, and that therefore adults and children belong to different generations. Instead, for Alanen, the concept of generation refers to the *processes* through which 'the two generational categories of children and adults are recurrently produced...through relations of connection, and interaction, of interdependence' (2001:21). Central to this formulation is the idea that the exercise of power – or usually the lack of it in the case of children – because this is one of the ways in which children's agency is constrained by adults. Indeed, it is precisely this limitation on their exercise of power, in comparison to that of adults, which is central to the subject position of 'the child'.

Thus, if food is to be seen as an index of generational relations, then the power (symbolic or otherwise) which food has, in and through time and space, to mark out particular kinds of identities for children and young people must be central to the analysis.

This becomes clear in Chapter 1 by Keenan and Stapleton, which describes how new mothers in England, some of whom are obese, impute particular kinds of identities to their newborn children, identities that, for these mothers, become symbolised through their infants' suckling activities. While accepting current policy prescriptions that babies should be fed on demand, mothers nonetheless regulated feeding in important ways. Babies who were identified as being 'lazy' were often fed according to a schedule, rather than on demand, while babies who had colic might be fed before they cried for food – in this case, so that mothers' might assuage their anxieties about not being identified as a 'good mother'. These links between food, identity and intergenerational relations take on a different hue as babies grow older. As Keenan and Stapleton go on to show, mothers begin to identify their babies' agentic food-consumption practices in rather different terms – as signs of their infant's cleverness or, indeed, their jealousy and guile. And Cook's analysis (Chapter 6) of middle-class US mothers' efforts to guard against what they perceive as the 'bad' food promoted commercially for children also demonstrates the power relations that mediate child–adult relations around food. Through stealth, some of these mothers trick their children into eating 'healthy' food, albeit doing so 'for their own good'.

Children's food?

Any analysis of such intergenerational relations needs, of course, to be situated in historical and biographical time, in recognition of the fact that the ongoing reproduction of child–adult relations is a practical and everyday accomplishment of the different social identities of 'adult' and 'child'. It is a process that takes place and shape in and through people's everyday lives and experiences and has therefore to be contextualised in those lives. From this perspective, then, the idea of 'children's food', as a cultural category, is not simply a reference point for distinctions in relation to what people of different generations eat. Rather, it becomes a cultural classification that is continually shored up, disaggregated, reconstituted and fragmented in and across the shared histories and biographies of adults and children in different societies.

As this volume demonstrates, while there is a growing global interest – indeed anxiety – about what children are eating, what is needed in order to address these concerns properly, is – first and foremost – a thorough understanding of the meaning of food and eating practices for children and for adults in various cultural contexts. A first interesting question relates to the meaning of the concept 'children's food'. How is it conceptualised? By whom? And with what consequences? Without knowing this, any strategies designed to allay anxieties about what children are eating are unlikely to be successful since the term 'children's food' is not simply a descriptive one. On the contrary, it is a cultural construction that embraces sets of expectations about childhood and children's practices that are historically and culturally located. Moreover, as a cultural category – one that ostensibly distinguishes between the foods that adults and children eat – it is, necessarily, also involved in the ongoing structuring and restructuring of the everyday social relations that take place between adults and children both within families and elsewhere. It could be argued, then, that the food that children eat constitutes a lens through which adult–child relations can be explored as they unfold in daily life as a series of routines and rituals. And, if this *is* so, then it is clear that we need to understand how these generational relations actually transpire and the meanings they take on in the context of food and eating practices before making policies that are simply designed to change children's diets.

In this respect, Chapter 2 by James, Curtis and Ellis shows for example, that in the English context many families work hard to avoid children simply eating 'children's food' – that is food that is different from that which adults eat and classed as 'junk' food in England, such as pizza, chips, burgers and other types of fast food. Mothers in particular may go to considerable lengths to ensure that evening meals are eaten together, as family meals, by adapting menus or by discrete and devious processes of food substitution. However, the extent to which different families pursue such strategies is dependent upon the kinds of child–adult relations that characterise 'family life' in particular families. And this, in turn, reflects the kinds of social status that children have in the family. In some families, children and their parents appear to have almost equivalent status, with respect to the mundane routines and rituals of everyday family life. In others, by contrast, there is a strict hierarchy in operation and children's unequal status is symbolised in their ready consumption of 'children's food' in the place of adult/family food. And in a second chapter (Chapter 5), focused on the role of fathers and drawing on the same data set, Curtis, James and Ellis show that indeed, in some families, fathers and children come to occupy similar status positions in a family hierarchy where it is mothers who see themselves – and are in turn seen – as the moral guardians and practical managers of what the family eats.

Chapter 3 by Wills, Backett-Milburn, Lawton and Roberts contributes further to this discussion by showing the ways in which middle-class teenagers in Scotland comply with family food practices, even in contexts distant from parental gaze and control. They show that, in contrast to working-class young people interviewed in a previous research study, these teenagers remain bound by a family habitus that is critical about the consumption of fast food. There was a close fit between what teenagers ate at home and when out with their friends. Thus, while children's food is commonly taken to be 'fast food', these particular children and young people appeared, on the whole, to refrain from eating it.

However, as Chapter 6 by Cook details, the concept of children's food does not simply describe a range of commodities that are commercially produced for children. Rather, what he shows, in the context of the United States, are the ways in which children's subjectivities, both as children and as individuals, emerge through the negotiations that take place around such foodstuffs in the middle-class family context. He demonstrates the struggles that occur as mothers try to negotiate with their children about what they should eat and shows how, through trying to subvert the role that food advertising plays in denoting food as 'children's food', they unwittingly help consolidate these commercialised meanings.

In Chapter 7 by Brembeck, however, the concept of children's food takes on a rather different hue. In her study of Bosnian and Iraqi refugee families in Sweden, she explores the ways in which children take an active role in introducing new food practices to their families, thereby contributing to processes of cultural integration. For these children, so-called 'children's food' – hamburgers and pizzas – are symbols of identification and belonging. But this is not simply to the category of 'children'; rather, for these refugees, these foodstuffs provide a sense of belonging to 'Sweden' and to modernity itself. This is why meatballs also feature as 'children's food' in this context and why the Bosnian and Iraqi mothers, in contrast to those in the United States described by Cook (Chapter 6 of this volume), actively encouraged their children's consumption of such foodstuffs.

Institutional food and eating practices

If, as suggested above, food and meals can be studied as a lens for moral values, ideology and social change then the increasing emphasis in western countries on neoliberal discourses, constructing children as consumers and autonomous participants with the right to influence social matters, should be reflected in food-consumption practices, particularly in public spaces. Studies of meals and eating practices in day-care institutions in the Nordic countries in the 1990s demonstrated, for example, that common meals for everybody were abolished in some day-care centres, mainly because of declining budgets, but also based on an argument to increase children's rights to decide individually when to eat (Kjørholt, Tingstad & Brembeck 2005). Similarly, the former practices of a joint structured meal for everybody was abolished in a Danish day-care centre as part of a national project aimed at realising children as citizens with rights to have a say in their everyday lives (Kjørholt 2005). Thus, in Scandinavia, children's ability to decide when to eat seems to be an important part of neoliberal discourses constructing small children as citizens with the right to individual choice and self-determination (Kjørholt 2005). Such examples challenge prevailing discourses on traditional day-care pedagogy – and professional care both in Denmark and Norway, which value collective meals for everybody. These collective meals can be characterised as a time-structuring, ritual activity, affirming a particular cultural fellowship and making visible each and everybody's belonging to a specific community of children – *barnefellesskap*. Such traditional discourses emphasise a homelike, cosy atmosphere in the construction of the meal as a cultural practice for identification (Korsvold 1998). Flowers and candles, for example, create an aesthetic framework around a community of children in which cultural values are both reproduced and created, making such common meals both a central site for social interaction, friendship, care and humour, and an affirmation, for children, of belonging to a community of children.

Such themes are strongly evidenced in Chapter 8 by Punch, McIntosh, Emond and Dorrer that, in the Scottish context, explores how food works to provide such points of communal contact and belonging for those children who do not have homes and families. In their study of the food rituals that take place in the institutional context of children's homes, they show how food can be both a site of conflict and of togetherness. For children whose homes lives have been ruptured and who therefore find themselves living in residential care where many of the primary markers for familial identification are lacking, food becomes a medium charged with symbolism. For the staff it was one of the ways in which their care for the children could be expressed, albeit that meal times could also provoke conflict. However, food was also an important medium through which both staff and children could emphasise their personal, individual identities – for example, a preference for hot chocolate, rather than coffee or liking very milky tea – in an institutional context where more collective identities such as 'care worker' or 'child in care' might threaten to predominate.

Conclusion

As noted at the outset, the media – particularly TV advertising – is increasingly singled out in western countries as having a large role to play in current concerns about childhood obesity. Indeed as Chapter 9 by Tingstad shows, this is despite there being any hard evidence to support such claims. Rather, what her analysis of Norwegian discourses around childhood obesity argues is that the 'causes' of childhood obesity are complex and multi-faceted and that how children are positioned in a society must be understood as integral to that process. Thus, in Norway, where TV advertising has always been tightly regulated, childhood obesity is, nonetheless, on the rise and, she suggests, one aspect of this might be the transfer of responsibility from the state to the individual – a process that, in the Norwegian context, also includes children, since here children are viewed by the state as active members of a democratic society. This provides, she suggests, an ironic twist to the debates about the causes of childhood obesity; in Norway, the outcome of such discourses and ways of thinking might be that children themselves are to blame!

Such a message seems at odds with the protectionist discourses through which children and childhood are currently being viewed in many contexts (for a discussion of this in relation to England, see for example, James & James 2008) and in Chapter 10 by Burridge are some clues as to why this might be the case. In his analysis of the food adverts that appeared in women's magazines in England, during the 1950s and 1960s, he shows that healthy eating and food enjoyment were invariably counterpoised. Moreover, it was adults who were appealed to through messages relating to health, while children were, by contrast, encouraged simply to enjoy their food. The outcome of such duality is the message that 'healthy' food is somehow not enjoyable and that therefore children's nutrition has to be managed by their mothers. The message seems to be that left to their own devices children will make 'unhealthy' choices.

Thus, as this volume demonstrates, children's identities are variously and complexly mediated through food, whether in the context of the home, the family, the media or other institutional settings. Children's food practices are therefore a key research arena for childhood studies.

Note

1. Five of the chapters in this volume stem from research carried out at the University of Sheffield, UK, under the auspices of the research programme *Changing Families, Changing Food*, funded by The Leverhulme Trust, 2005–2008.

References

Alanen, L. (2001). 'Childhood as a generational condition: Children's daily lives in a central Finland town', in Alanen, L. & Mayall, B. (eds), *Conceptualizing Child–Adult Relations*. London: RoutledgeFalmer.

Beardsworth, A. & Keil, T. (1997). *Sociology on the Menu. An Invitation to the Study of Food and Society*. London: Routledge.

Belasco, W. & Scranton, P. (2002). *Food Nations. Selling Taste in Consumer Societies*. London: Routledge.

Bentley, A. (2002). 'Inventing baby food: Gerber and the discourse of infancy in the United States', in Belasco, W. & Scranton, P. (eds), *Food Nations. Selling Taste in Consumer Societies*. London: Routledge.

Brembeck, H. & Johansson. B. (1996). *Postmodern Barndom*. Göteborg: Etnologiska föreningen i Västsverige.

Caplan, P. (ed.) (1997). *Food, Heath and Identity*. London: Routledge.

Charles, N. & Kerr, M. (1988). *Women, Food and Families*. Manchester: Manchester University Press.

Christensen, P. (2002). *The Meaning of Food to Children and Young People from a Life-Course Perspective*. Paper presented at the Children, Families and Food Conference, Edinburgh University UK.

Christensen, P. (2003). 'Børn, mad og daglige rutiner'. *Barn* (21)2–3: 119–137.

Counihan, C. & van Esterik, P. (eds) (1997). *Food and Culture. A Reader*. London: Routledge.

Coveney, J. (2000). *Food, Morals and Meaning. The Pleasure and Anxiety of Eating*. London: Routledge.

DeVault, M. (1991). *Feeding the Family*. Chicago: University of Chicago Press.

Douglas, M. (2002). [1966]. *Purity and Danger: An Analysis of the Concepts of Pollution and Taboo*. London: Routledge.

Døving, R. (2002). *Mat som totalt sosialt fenomen. Noen eksempler med utgangspunkt i Torsvik*. Dissertation. University of Bergen.

Goody, J. (1982). *Cooking, Cuisine and Class*. Cambridge: Cambridge University Press.

Hockey, J. & James, A. (2003). *Social Identities Across the Life Course*. Basingstoke: Palgrave.

James, A. & James, A. L. (2004). *Constructing Childhood. Theory, Policy and Social Practice*. Houndmills: Palgrave Macmillan.

James, A. L. & James, A. (2008). 'Changing childhood in the UK: Reconstructing discourses of risk and protection', in James, A. & A. L. James (eds), *European Childhoods*. Basingstoke: Palgrave Macmillan.

James, A. & Prout, A. (eds) (1990). *Constructing and Reconstructing Childhood*. Basingstoke: Falmer.

Jenkins, R. (1996). *Social Identity.* London: Routledge.

Kjørholt, A. T. (2005). 'Beyond listening. Future prospects', in Clark, A., Kjørholt, A. T. & Moss, P. (eds), *Beyond Listening. Children's Perspectives on Early Childhood Services.* Policy Press: University of Bristol.

Kjørholt, A. T., Tingstad, V. & Brembeck, H. (2005). 'Children, food consumption and culture in the Nordic countries'. *Barn* (23)1: 9–20.

Korsvold, T. (1998). *For alle barn! Barnehagens framvekst i velferdsstaten.* Oslo: Abstrakt forlag, Utdanningsvitenskapelig serie.

Levi-Strauss, C. (1983). *The Raw and the Cooked.* Chicago: Chicago University Press.

Lupton, D. (1998). *Food, the Body and the Self.* London: Sage.

Lyngø, I. J. (2001). 'The national nutrition exhibition: A new nutritional narrative in Norway in the 1930s', in Scholliers, P. (ed.), *Food, Drink and Identity. Cooking, Eating and Drinking in Europe Since the Middle Ages.* Oxford: Berg.

Murcott, A. (1982). 'On the social significance of the "cooked dinner" in South Wales'. *Social Science Information* 21: 677–696.

Murcott, A. (2000). 'Is it still a pleasure to cook for him? Social changes in the household and family'. *Journal of Consumer Studies and Home Economics* 24(2): 78–84.

Scholliers, P. (ed.) (2001). *Food, Drink and Identity. Cooking. Eating and Drinking in Europe Since the Middle Ages.* Oxford: Berg.

Taylor, C. (1991). *The Ethics of Authenticity.* Cambridge, MA: Harvard University Press.

Tingstad, V. (1996). Skolefritidsordninger for 6-åringer og barn i 1.-3. klasse. (Leisure time clubs for 6 year-old children and children from 1st to 3rd grade). *Ministries for Children and Family Affairs and Church, Education and Research. Report* F-4028.

Van Esterik, P. (1997). 'The politics of breastfeeding. An advocacy perspective', in Counihan, C. & Van Esterik, P. (eds), *Food and Culture. A Reader.* London: Routledge.

Warde, A. (1997). *Consumption, Food and Taste. Culinary Antinomies and Commodity Culture.* London: Sage.

Warde, A. & Martens, L. (2000). *Eating Out. Social Differentiation, Consumption and Pleasure.* Cambridge: Cambridge University Press.

1

'It Depends What You Mean by Feeding "on Demand" ': Mothers' Accounts of Babies' Agency in Infant-Feeding Relationships

Julia Keenan, Helen Stapleton

Introduction

This chapter focuses on how mothers construct, understand, and accommodate, their babies' agency within feeding relationships. In particular, it explores mothers' responses to feeding cues in early infancy and the implications of babies' agency in everyday consumption routines. To this end, we discuss findings from our analysis of interviews conducted during 2006–2008 with 60 mothers from a variety of social and family backgrounds living in a large city in the north of England, some of whom were also managing diabetes or were 'obese'. Half of our participants were established mothers,[1] whilst the remainder, who were recruited in late pregnancy and followed through the first year of motherhood, were expecting their first baby.

Childrearing in general, and infant feeding in particular, do not take place in a sociocultural vacuum. Discourses and practices around infant feeding vary across both time and space (Van Esterik 1989; Maher 1992) and are, in complex ways, socially constructed and closely linked to childrearing practices and mothering cultures. Yet, at the same time, they are also intimately intertwined with the evolving emotional relationships between the infant and its mother/carer.[2] The ways in which different mothers perceived and responded to their infants' active communicative signals related to feeding routines, and how these helped construct their own and their babies' identities, is the specific focus of this chapter.

Cultural contexts of mothering and infant feeding

Largely because of their childbearing capacity (Gordon 1982), women have long been positioned as nurturers and carers, and as the primary carers of children. Within family settings, it is widely accepted that women-as-mothers will efface their own needs in order to meet the demands of others, particularly children. However, academic debate has challenged, and gradually eroded, the biological privileging of many social identities and subjectivities, asserting that categories such as motherhood (Everingham 1994; Apple 1995; Hays 1996; Lawler 2000) and childhood (Prout & James 1990; Christiansen & James 2000; Mayall 2002; Corsaro 2005) are not objective, essential or natural states, but must be considered as social constructs located in discourses that reflect specific sociocultural milieus which vary across time and place (Jenks 1996; Holloway & Valentine 2000; Miller 2005). Similarly, constructs and ideologies of motherhood (and parenting) are highly relational and are either closely entwined with, or actually formed on the basis of, prior social constructions of childhood and assumed, biologically determined, needs (Urwin 1985; Valentine 1997; Lawler 1999; Ribbens McCarthy et al. 2000; Murphy 2007).

Thus, just as understandings of the 'state' of a child as s/he enters the world have differed over time (Ariès 1962; Stone 1977; Cunningham 1991, 1995), so have understandings of children's needs and appropriate maternal responses also changed. Within contemporary discourses, for example, infants are frequently portrayed in terms of their 'neediness', and 'vulnerability' (Everingham 1994; Murphy 2007) with mothers positioned as best placed to meet their every demand. Indeed, current debates about generational change and choice, autonomy and self-determinacy in the context of motherhood (Thompson et al. 2008) suggest that the unitary traditional ideal of, self-sacrificial motherhood has been superseded, and that 'choice' is the dominant discourse amongst the current generation of mothers. Yet we would caution that the 'choices' available are culturally circumscribed and the 'freedom' to choose strongly regulated (Rose & Miller 1992) with some 'choices' (particularly breast-feeding) found to be strongly associated with the moral discourse of the 'good', 'self-sacrificial' mother (Carter 1995; Murphy et al. 1998; Wall 2001; Marshall et al. 2007) – privileging particular (educated middle-class) women and having a normalising effect on all mothers. The expectation that mothers will sacrifice their personal needs to meet those of the baby and the stress of new parenthood is compounded by a trend – at least in western societies – for parents to seek less hierarchical and more emotionally rewarding relationships with their children than parents in previous generations (Beck & Beck-Gernsheim 2002; Wade 2005). Moreover, ongoing research in this area confirms that women retain exclusive responsibility for the feeding (DeVault 1991) and healthy development of infants (Murcott 1993) and indeed, as Ann Oakley (1979) indicated almost three decades ago, women's accountability for infant well-being – as evidenced by 'appropriate' infant weight gain and behaviour – is invested with strong moral significance that impacts upon women's identities as mothers:

> A baby that is feeding and growing 'well' is a prize for the mother's efforts, a tangible token of her love and work. Conversely, a baby who gains more weight than it 'should', and who perhaps cries a lot and seems unsatisfied, is a thorn in the mother's flesh, a sign of maternal failure. (Oakley 1979:165)

Oakley's reference to excessive infant weight gain, and by inference to a mother who overfeeds her baby, is particularly apposite in view of current public debates and policy initiatives concerned with rising levels of obesity (DoH 2006; NICE 2006), and diabetes[3] (Wild et al. 2004) in industrialised, and industrialising, nations. Also significant in the context of infant-feeding relations is Oakley's reference to a baby who 'cries a lot and seems unsatisfied' because this draws attention to the baby's agency and to aspects of consumption which are not wholly concerned with hunger but with the more sensuous aspects of food and eating.

Nonetheless, an ever-increasing range of 'expert' opinions on infant feeding has generated a diverse range of information about 'appropriate' infant-feeding regimes which reflects, amongst other things, the socio-economic constraints of industrial and post-industrial societies and the changing role of women (Arnup 1990; Palmer 1993; Blum 2000). That said, a wealth of medical evidence amassed over the last two decades demonstrates significant short- and long-term health and nutritional benefits associated with breast-feeding, both for children and women (Howie et al. 1990; Wilson et al. 1998; Labbok 2001; Fewtrell 2004). Accordingly, national and international public health policies strongly promote and protect breast-feeding and current policy guidelines reiterate the importance of exclusive breast-feeding (i.e., breast milk only, with no additional water, other fluids, or solids) for at least the first six months of infant life, and with supplemented breast-feeding continuing for two years and beyond (WHO & UNICEF 2003; DoH 2007). However, pregnancy and lactation cannot be considered simply as biological events and many childbearing women are burdened with a range of additional stressors throughout their transitions to motherhood.

For example, in relation to our study sample, it is recognised that mothers managing diabetes must exercise a high degree of mindfulness in order to maintain stable, and consistent, physiological control, although this is known to be especially difficult in the context of managing life-course transitions and concomitant identity shifts (Rasmussen et al. 2007), such as motherhood (Poirier-Solomon 2002). Indeed, amongst women managing Type 1 and 2 diabetes, intentions to breastfeed are lower than within the UK population as a whole (CEMACH 2005, 2007), whilst mothers managing Type 1 diabetes who manage to initiate breast-feeding, sustain this activity for a shorter time (Hummel et al. 2007). Similarly, a recent review suggests that for reasons not well understood, overweight and obese women are less likely to breastfeed than normal weight women (Amir & Donath 2007).

Moreover, despite the clearly described advantages for, and the promotion of, breast-feeding, UK Infant-Feeding Surveys have consistently demonstrated that actual rates have remained relatively static over the last 25 years and are persistently below recommended targets. For example, a recent survey indicated that 78% of mothers in England 'initiated' breast-feeding (i.e., attempted to breastfeed once), 66% breastfed exclusively at birth, with this dropping to 46% at one week, 22% at six weeks, whilst by six months the proportion exclusively breast-feeding was negligible (<1%) (Bolling et al. 2007). The introduction of solid food to UK infants also contravenes recommended policy guidance (not before six months) with 51% of UK mothers introducing such foods at, or before, four months[4] (Bolling et al. 2007).[5] Exclusive breast-feeding and delayed introduction of solids are favoured by mothers from managerial and professional occupations (see also Kelly and Watt 2005), those with the highest educational levels, aged 30 or over, first-time mothers, and those able to delay their return to paid employment (see also Hawkins et al. 2007). Ironically, therefore, babies deemed to be in greatest need of the protection afforded by breast milk are least likely to access it and mothers who can least afford to buy formula milk are also least likely to breastfeed (Murphy 1999).

Strong inter and intra-regional variations in infant-feeding data reflect structural influences and localised cultures. For example, breast-feeding initiation rates in Sheffield – where this research was undertaken – vary from 66% to 85%, but overall the second highest rate in the region and relatively high compared to similar districts. Breast-feeding initiation within the city, however, reflects national trends with a substantially

higher uptake (approx 15%) from women living in the more affluent districts (Jones 2007). Research on infant-feeding patterns across
Europe (Yngve & Sjöström 2001) has also highlighted the significance
of favourable maternity leave and generous childcare allowance in
improving breast-feeding rates.

However, Dykes (2005) has also argued that women's mistrust in the
efficacy of their bodies to nurture and satisfy the food-related demands
of their infants is also a significant factor influencing both the initiation
and continuation of breast-feeding. Furthermore, the dominant por-
trayal of contemporary breast-feeding as an innate and intuitive ability
belies the fact that many women experience considerable difficulty in
acquiring the requisite skills and indeed, some authorities suggest that
because such skills are no longer available through intergenerational
transmission, they must be learned (DoH 2006).

But, whilst breast/bottle-feeding debates generate considerable tensions
across academic, lay, and professional groups, whether to feed infants
'on demand' or according to schedule has received rather less attention,
albeit there are a variety of opinions available, with public health imperatives competing with the views of developmental psychologists and an
ever-increasing array of childcare 'experts'. Proponents of feeding 'on
demand' invoke the baby as innocent and agentic, as self-regulating, as
someone who knows instinctively when to feed and eats to satiation,
taking neither more nor less than it requires. This stance is reiterated in
current UK government policy with respect to breast-feeding:

> If you feed as often and for as long as your baby wants, you'll produce
> plenty of milk and give your baby what he or she needs. At first, it
> may seem that you're doing nothing but feeding and changing nap-
> pies. Remember that this stage will not last very long. Young babies
> take longer to feed. As babies get older, the feeding time gets shorter.
> Growth spurts may also affect your baby's feeding patterns.... Your
> baby may feed more frequently at these times, until your milk supply
> increases to meet the bigger demand. (DoH 2006:10–11)

Feeding on 'demand' suggests baby-centred mothering/parenting,
with feeding initiated by the baby communicating hunger cues and
the mother/carer responding to them. Scheduled feeding, on the
other hand, suggests adult-led parenting with feeding initiated at pre-
determined and fixed intervals regardless of infant cues. Our chapter
explores the different approaches to acknowledging babies' agency that
these two practices engender and the tensions they create.

Infant-feeding practices and mother–child relations

Public health policies directed at mothers-to-be tend to portray infant feeding as a series of predominately rational, autonomous choices; as 'decisions' to be made for infants by the adults upon whom they are dependent. Work by sociologists of childhood, however, has emphasised the need to understand children as social actors in their own right, rather than as passive objects to be acted upon (Alanen 1994), or as pre-adult subjects. Research has demonstrated the agency shown by older children when negotiating food choices, particularly within family settings (e.g., Walker et al. 1994 and James et al., Chapter 2 of this volume), yet the agency of young children or infants remains a relatively under-researched area, especially within the sociology of childhood (although see Murphy 2007).

Although significantly dependent upon adults to meet their essential needs, babies are not, without influence in this power relationship as research over the years has shown. While it is not possible to review such an extensive, influential (and not uncontroversial) body of work in the context of this chapter, key texts include: Bowlby's attachment theory (1951), Stern's (1974) work on gazing and the use of head aversion by infants to terminate intrusive maternal behaviour and/or secure attention, and Trevarthen's (1993) research on 'proto-conversation' between carers and infants. All of these suggest that infants' can, and do, exert varying degrees of control over their primary caregiver(s). Attributions of infant 'agency', however, are also embedded within emotionally charged and intimate relationships between mothers and significant others. This wider context emphasises the interdependence of infants, caregivers, and their environments, and highlights the creativity of infants and their role in shaping culture, and maternal and infant identities (Winnicott 1950, 1971; Mahoney and Yngvesson 1992). Thus mothering, although acknowledged as socially and/or culturally constructed, is also – at least to some extent – influenced by biological and emotional ties between mother and infant.

Throughout this chapter we therefore problematise singular notions of infant and maternal agency and question taken-for-granted assumptions linking agency with autonomy, through our focus on mothers' constructions of, and responses to, what they perceived to be their infants' needs or expressions of such agency.

About the study: Design and methods

Our study sample was purposively selected to include women whom we anticipated might have pre-existing concerns about food, health, and/or body weight and shape as a result of managing diabetes[6] or because they self- identified (or had been identified by others) as 'overweight' or 'obese' but also included women of 'average' weight, without diabetes.[7] We were interested to explore whether, and to what extent, women's biographies reflected concerns about appetite/weight regulation, embodied and/or emotional relationships with food including the requirement to maintain blood glucose levels, and how these concerns might influence their infant-feeding relationships. In particular, we wanted to investigate whether, and how, participants' personal experiences influenced how they interpreted and responded to their infant's feeding cues.

In-depth, semi-structured interviews were conducted with 60 women recruited to two cohorts – half were anticipating motherhood for the first time and followed through the transition to motherhood and half were mothers with at least one child aged between nine months and two years.[8] We recruited women from across the social class and age range, all of whom were competent English speakers.

The initial feeding needs of babies and problems with feeding 'on demand'

Most mothers asserted that they were feeding their babies 'on demand' – particularly in the first few days or weeks following birth, a construction that is already suggestive of babies' agency. For a minority of first-time mothers, including those from working-class backgrounds, meeting their babies' feeding needs was described in pragmatic terms, as illustrated by the 'matter of fact' account by Kelly:

> she's a baby. No. Babies eat, that's all babies do, you know? They eat, sleep [...] poo, cry. That's it. (Kelly, aged 18. Unemployed, living with parents)

However, achieving their ideal of feeding 'on demand' provoked considerable anxiety for many other mothers, especially during the early days. This was particularly the case for babies identified as having particular problems. For instance, the babies of women managing diabetes initially required intensive monitoring to ensure blood glucose levels were maintained within normal limits. This often necessitated them being nursed in specialised baby units, separated from their mothers, and being given milk feeds in 'corrective' doses by maternity staff, rather than their mothers offering them milk 'on demand' and in response to perceived hunger needs. Difficulties were magnified when babies with poor sucking reflexes (sometimes due to prematurity) were 'force' fed via a pipette or a cup,[9] which mothers perceived as requiring less effort. Such babies were constructed as unwilling to do the necessary 'work' that feeding from the breast or a bottle involves:

> he didn't really want to do it and they thought that were because he'd been force-fed with a pipette and cup and stuff [...] so he were just used to getting the milk really quickly and then he couldn't be bothered to do any work to get it. (laughs) [...] He just used to sit there. (Anne, aged 29. Window dresser – made redundant, married)

> you're advised to feed on demand, but then you have to feed so much in 24 hours and you must give them this amount of food. So it's not really demand. You're alright if you've got a hungry baby and it keeps demanding, but if you've got a baby that doesn't want to eat it's very difficult. So we swapped to bottles that I was expressing until about 12 weeks, and then I stopped breast-feeding and she went to formula, and then she started to gradually put on her weight. (Dawn, aged 30. Full-time mum, married)

Indeed, some (often premature) newborn babies were described by their mothers as 'too lazy' to suck from the breast – at least in the early days following birth. In order to maintain physiological equilibrium, such infants were therefore subjected to medical interventions in the form of scheduled feeds, irrespective of hunger cues and whilst we exercise caution in taking the attribution of 'laziness' at face-value, some mothers made connections between this overriding of an infant's 'natural' appetite and subsequent feeding-related problems. For example, Anna (who is obese) links the imposition of a strict feeding regime in the early weeks of her child's life with his current food refusal.

> I still feel as if I'm force feeding him a bit [...] and it's ridiculous. It's not rational, but it kinda comes from that, I think, from the original (pause) pipette thing – of having to make sure and then people coming and checking him. 'How much has he had?' and writing it on charts and all that and, 'So he's had 20 mils. Ok.' [...] And when he was putting on weight they were like, 'Well done Mum. Well done.' [...] I think I still have thing now. I get a lot of anxiety around feeding him if he's not eaten. I get panicky [...] And somebody said to me yesterday, 'Don't worry. Babies will always self-regulate.' (Anna, aged 32, Teacher, living with partner)

It is perhaps understandable why the assurance that 'babies will always self-regulate' – given to allay fears that she might inadvertently be overfeeding her son – might, nonetheless, be difficult for Anna to consider.

Although is not known whether lack of maternal confidence may be linked with inappropriate or inadequate feeding regimes which, in turn, may predispose vulnerable infants to overweight/obesity in later life, one (obese) participant made such a direct connection:

> when I was born I was very, I was so thin that, erm, I wasn't feeding I don't think off, off Mum so I was put on bottle and they were that worried about me that my Dad used to double the amount of (pause) mixture so they more or less had to spoon it out and I've got...I put on weight and I never really stopped. (Flora, aged 38. Former florist now unemployed, living with partner)

Hence Flora is concerned that now, as a parent, she may corrupt her infant's self-regulatory potential and agency by encouraging eating environments in which obesity and overweight flourish.

Narratives from mothers of infants suffering from colic also revealed their struggles to identify, and satisfy, their babies' hunger cues. Colic, although not well understood, is characterised by periods of constant crying and mothers attempting to feed 'on demand' reported not knowing whether to offer the breast or a teat (in the form of bottle/pacifier) in response to all infant crying. Accommodating the needs of such infants was reported to be very demanding and frustrating, not least because of the difficulties in distinguishing feeding/hunger needs from comfort needs.

> Er, so the only thing that would calm him from that, er, he, he was not crying when he was in the breast or he was sleeping. But he was crying after the breast so it was not really sure, we were not really thinking that he was hungry. We had, we hadn't a clue of what was going on [...] he had colic so, so he was like doing like this and crying constantly, so it was horrible. (Alejandria, aged 31. Researcher, married)

Similar concerns were expressed on behalf of babies suffering from acid reflux or unexplained vomiting because such behaviour was understood by mothers to interfere with an infant's ability to exercise agency by self-regulating their appetite and food requirements. Mothers worried that inadequate food intake might result in reduced capacity (which some associated with a 'shrunken' stomach) and/or that distress linked with vomiting might lead to diminishing expressions of hunger and hence an inadequate food intake. These mothers reported that infant feeding was hugely demanding; they were especially concerned lest they fail to distinguish cries communicating hunger from other crying and hence inadvertently further jeopardise their infant's health and well-being.

Infantile colic also challenged mothers' ability to meet sociocultural scripts of the 'good' mother. As Amanda describes, this meant responding to her daughter's expressions of agency – her cries – differently in public, compared with private, domestic settings:

> in the house I'll wait until she cries for her bottle or wait until she asks for a bottle and then you know she's hungry. But when I'm out, I tend to warm it up; I think oh I think she might feed in half an hour, I'll do it now and try and feed her because that screeching you know, you don't want people to think that you're hurting her in some way. (Amanda, aged 26. Administrator, married)

Within her home environment Amanda tried to distinguish what she understood to be her daughter's communication 'for her bottle' from other crying. In a public setting however, she was very concerned to avoid projecting an image of herself as a 'bad' mother, hurting a child by not offering food 'on demand' – in response to all cries.

Whereas some mothers were therefore distressed when required to comply with 'force' feeding babies, identified by medical staff as being unable to express 'normal' or adequate needs for sustenance, mothers of 'hungry' babies did not have comparable converse, anxieties, however, about their babies' higher rate of weight gain. Although such mothers often described struggling to meet their infant's demands (which sometimes resulted in the early cessation of breast-feeding) they did not consider them 'greedy' or as displaying excessive, or inappropriate, appetites. Even obese/overweight infants were not seen to require a reduced intake for to deprive a 'hungry baby' of food was perceived as tantamount to 'starving' which, in turn, was perceived as 'cruel'. Indeed, mothers of obese/overweight infants were more likely to express pride because their infant's weight gain was in the upper 'centiles'; the 'innocence' of the infant's hunger, or indeed its agency in respect of feeding, was rarely questioned. Thus, large or 'overweight' babies were not necessarily perceived as problematic but, rather, as embodying family characteristics of 'bigness'. Their (excessive) body size was constructed positively and presented as strong or 'bonny'.[10] Marianne was therefore unusual in speculating that her daughter's persistent vomiting was a consequence of 'greed'; of consuming in excess of her requirements:

> I think she must have problems assessing when she's full, and take more than she needs [...] it might be, erm, greed that causes the sick. (Marianne, aged 32. Former civil servant – now unemployed. Living alone, boyfriend elsewhere)

Whilst newborns could (even jokingly) be construed as 'lazy' and 'force-fed' in their best interests, they were therefore also constructed with the capacity to 'learn' their physical limits.

Finally, although many mothers reported initial difficulties with feeding 'on demand', the majority nonetheless constructed infants in general, and their own in particular, as expressing distinct needs which they interpreted as legitimate and which they felt obliged to satisfy as best they could.

Establishing feeding: Finding routines

By the second or third interview, all first-time mothers referred to finding a feeding routine (in the manner advised by current government policies) by patiently following their baby's cues. However, those mothers who had attempted to introduce a more predictable routine at the point of weaning reported that they had generally failed to achieve their goal and had reverted back to following their baby's agentic cues, even if this was more disruptive to family routines:

> he's not a strict routine baby. You know, I mean when he was younger we tried to sort of say right, we'll sort of like give you this bottle at that time and stuff, but from the breast-feeding you couldn't really do that anyway, like when I was breast-feeding it was always sort of him led. So I think it's just kind of carried on really since then. (Danielle, aged 31. Nurse, living with partner)

However, some breast-feeding mothers who described themselves as feeding 'on demand', nonetheless also described 'front-loading' their babies with milk in anticipation of particular events, a practice that attempted to silence the infant's expression of its own agency in self-regulating its hunger needs. Front-loading infants before leaving home, for example, reduced the risk of mothers being embarrassed or upset by their infant's behaviour in public places; front-loading at bedtime usually resulted in longer sleeping times for both infants and parents.

In the following extract, Betty initially describes her daughter as feeding 'on demand' but hints at her frustration with having to accommodate non-nutritive suckling for comfort, rather than sustenance. She eventually decides to override her baby's agency by 'shaking her awake' in order to feed her; and, after a brief period, once again, her baby was feeding 'on demand' but within the constraints of her mother's routine:

> that's the way she's found her own routine by feeding on demand. The, the only problem is with that five minute feeding was she wasn't feeding on demand she was comforting. Erm, so I'd shake her awake and get her going again and within two or three days, you know, she was back feeding on demand but at, at a more regular […] which, which was more, erm, satisfactory (laugh) shall I say, you know. It suited me better. (Betty, aged 23. Undergraduate, living with partner)

In the following quotation, Elsie blames health professionals for projecting an idealised notion of feeding 'on demand' and of not giving any explanation about what acknowledging a baby's agency means in reality.

> The way they tell you about it in antenatal classes or at the hospital is that when your baby cries, you feed and it doesn't, it really isn't that, it shouldn't be that because otherwise you just become a total slave and your baby will have like five minutes' worth of milk and then think, 'I don't need to feed properly now because I can cry again of in ten minutes and have some more. (Elsie, aged 31. Occupational therapist, living with partner)

The difficulties of accommodating baby-led feeding are also reiterated by Ayan, a teenage mother of two, who decided against breast-feeding her second child.

> Yeah, he were just constantly stuck to me.[…] Okay, when they're babies you have to feed them on demand anyway for the first few weeks, but because I fed him on demand the first few weeks, on demand became literally on demand 24 hours, up until he were 11 months. I'll never do that again. […]It was horrible. (Ayan, aged 23. Full-time mum, single)

And Elsie was one of the few mothers who, in hindsight, questioned the construction of young babies as being entirely innocent, suggesting instead that infants could be wilful and that mothers who automatically offered food in response to crying were vulnerable to being manipulated by the feeding relationship. After consulting an 'expert' guide: What to Expect When You're Breast-feeding, Elsie felt justified to go 'against all the health professionals' advice' and initiate her own feeding routine that necessitated her questioning the practice of comfort feeding:

> I can see why they might do that but I'm not sure whether that's actually helpful for your baby to kind of you know, learn sort of coping skills and ...
> Mmm, to use food as comfort?
> Yeah, yeah, I don't know whether that's particularly helpful. (Elsie, aged 31. Occupational therapist, living with partner)

Mabel was also concerned that always offering the breast in response to distress signals from her infant might discount other needs or mask underlying problems:

> Well it depends what you mean by feeding on demand because I think feeding on demand when he's hungry, not feeding on demand because he's crying. Because he's crying for other reasons. (Mabel, aged 30. Web content developer, married)

Baby-led or 'on demand' feeding was thus portrayed as purposeful feeding which must accommodate maternal schedules. Breastfed babies in particular who failed to 'understand' that access to their mother's breast was primarily for the purpose of sustenance rather than comfort were regarded as problematic and in need of regulating and/or disciplining. Instituting an infant-feeding 'schedule' (which might involve ignoring certain cries/cues, and 'force' feeding, or 'front-loading') whilst simultaneously espousing the mantra of feeding 'on demand' thus helped to reconcile competing agendas. It guaranteed 'the best of both worlds' by reducing infant dependency but without compromising participants' status as 'good' (breast-feeding) mothers. At the second postnatal interview, when babies were about six months old, most mothers thus described a process of identifying, and differentiating, a range of infant behaviour which they interpreted as indicating hunger or satiation. At this stage most participants also reported increasing confidence in their ability to correctly interpret changes in appetite; 'growth spurts' in particular required feeding regimes to be modified to take account of increased food requirements. Infants who were able to effectively communicate their changing needs, and to self-regulate their feeding behaviours, were described as 'intelligent'.

Babies' hunger and developing agency

As babies grew and developed, many mothers reported that their expressed needs for food were influenced not only by hunger and emotive or sensual aspects of carer–infant relations, but also in response to cues from their wider material and social worlds. This greater awareness was taken as a positive sign of development and babies who demonstrated these skills were referred to as 'clever'. Mothers such as Anne credited her baby with the ability to detect, and respond appropriately to, wider environmental (kitchen) sounds connected with family feeding routines:

> I'm sure he can hear the kettle switch on, that's when he starts to cry. (laughs) I'm sure he does. (Anne, aged 29. Window dresser – made redundant, married)

Hayley noticed that her baby demonstrated increasing awareness of sequential cues:

> he takes his cue from us to a certain extent, in that for example, he has his little night time routine [...] he's absolutely happy as larry but the minute you put his babygro on, he's thinking right, it's going to be food next and he starts screaming [...] and it's the same now with his breakfast you know, I put him in his chair and he starts screaming. But if I dance around the kitchen with him he's not bothered because he's taking his cue as I'm going in the chair that means breakfast's on its way. So that's quite good really that you know, we can dictate to him a little bit. (Hayley, aged 37. Countryside officer, married)

Here Hayley questions whether her son's crying for food is really an expression of hunger or recognition of a particular feeding routine, something confirmed in many other narratives. Such crying was interpreted as the anticipation of socio-spatial interactions, rather than hunger, and mothers saw their infants' attempts to assert their agency as opportunities for renegotiating the way they responded to their needs. In Hayley's case, after a prolonged and difficult period of breast-feeding on demand, her son's broader awareness of family feeding routines meant that she was now better placed to negotiate more control in their feeding relationship.

Similar developments of infant agency were described in mothers' weaning accounts and the introduction of solid foods. In her final postnatal interview, Alisha's describes her son's agency in the context of wider social relationships. Her narrative suggests that, by seven months of age, her son can not only recognise his grandmother but also associate her with a sequence of events including the pleasure of receiving chocolate. In the following quotation, Alisha reflects upon her son's developing sense of agency – 'he gets right giddy' – in response to particular stimuli and feeding rituals:

> I think they do get used to habit a lot [...] I think he just knows, because she [son's grandmother] does it [feeds him chocolate] exactly the same way, she'll sit him on her knee and she'll cuddle him and then she'll get the Milky Bar out and she'll open it in front of him and he gets right giddy then because he knows that it's coming. And then yeah, so, because she does it the same way, I think yeah, he does know, definitely. (Alisha, aged 24. Customer care advisor, married)

Many new mothers discussed how they (and their partners) struggled to find the time to prepare food and to eat, especially in the early days of new parenthood. This was initially due to pressures associated with role adjustment, (new) parental identity formation, and the demands of infants, but later narratives suggested that the infant's growing awareness of, and response to, adult mealtimes was also a significant factor:

> as soon as hot food goes on the table she decides that she wants feeding as well. (Amely, aged 38. Teacher, married)

From as early as four months of age, babies were considered capable of holding sophisticated feelings such as jealousy, and of eliciting guilt, although again we should be wary of taking these comments at face-value.

> I think he's just jealous because he's not eating it. I don't know what it is, it's as soon as we've put some food in front of us, he starts kicking off. (Janice, aged 27. Customer service advisor, living with partner)

> I don't eat at the same time, I either eat an hour before or an hour after and it'll tend to be after because she does, she gives you a guilty look when you're eating. (Anne, aged 29. Window dresser – made redundant, married)

Rather than remonstrate with their infants most parents accommodated them, for example, by eating meals in shifts although this often resulted in one or other partner (usually the mother) consuming meals that had gone cold, or deciding against cooking hot meals altogether and resorting to eating 'crap':

> I never get my meal hot so I end up snacking on crap, because I'm scared of cooking a meal 'cause I know I won't get to eat it and then I'll just be really disappointed that I can't eat my meal. (Marianne, aged 32. Former civil servant – now unemployed. Living alone, boyfriend elsewhere)

Finally, mothers managing diabetes described how the need to maintain appropriate blood glucose levels meant that they sometimes had no option but to prioritise their own needs for sustenance over the needs of their infant:

> the only time that I don't put her first is when my blood sugars are low and I need sugar because I can't help anybody then, I have to get my sugar down. (Amanda, aged 26. Administrator, married)

> And the second one, I was breast-feeding fine, she was a hungry baby so she ate properly, and then I had a severe hypo and my husband had to call the ambulance and I went into hospital just to be checked out and released the same day. But it was because she'd had a particularly bad night and fed all the time and I'd not eaten enough, so I just went too low. So though I'd corrected my hypo, because I knew I was hypo, it wasn't enough [...] After that we stopped breast-feeding because it was quite difficult to manage. (Dawn, aged 30. Full-time mum, married)

Different types of diabetes require different management strategies that, in turn, influenced participants' eating habits, activity levels, and medication requirements. Mothers such as Dawn worried about suffering a 'hypo' (hypoglycaemic episode) whilst they were alone in the house with their infants.

Conclusion

Rather than being positioned as a rational project informed by nutritionally driven, autonomous maternal choices (see also Murphy et al. 1998 and Marshall 2007), our research corroborates earlier research suggesting that infant feeding is a highly relational practice embedded within a power relationship, and, as children develop, within wider socio-spatial power relations. Although mothers generally perceived their newborn infants to be 'innocent', and viewed their needs as legitimate, many also acknowledged babies' potential to manipulate the feeding relationship. Narratives confirmed that food and feeding practices were invested with considerable potential for negotiation, particularly at points of transition such as the introduction of solid food. The infants in this study strongly influenced such decisions.

Although the degree of reflexivity in mothers' accounts is variable, particularly in relation to age and social class (see also Thompson et al. 2008), significant maternal thought and feeling are invested in maintaining and supporting evolving mother–infant relationships. Women's caring sensibilities and commitment (love) to the project of mothering develop over time (Mason 1996). However, our data also suggests that conflict is an inherent aspect of the mother–infant relationship and that conflict resolution was seen as a learned skill that participants acquired through constantly (re)negotiating feeding relationships with their babies. Contradictory understandings of feeding 'on demand' and inconsistent advice from health professionals required participants to exercise individual judgment in making decisions.

Our data further suggests that food-related decisions, including changes in feeding routines, are context dependent, embodied, and responsive to affective cues from infants. Current health advice to pregnant women with respect to feeding newborn babies 'on demand' was generally accepted at face-value by study participants, especially those anticipating motherhood for the first time. Most understood this to be a 'common-sense' approach to satisfying a baby whose needs, especially in the early postnatal period, were unpredictable. However, it also caused tensions. Our data show, therefore, that the construction of infants as born innocent and self-regulating, and of idealised and/ or 'good' mothers who are highly attentive to, interpretative of, and responsive to, their baby's cues combined with the significant moral and/or ethical imperatives underpinning infant-feeding directives, fails to problematise baby-led parenting approaches, especially with respect to weaning.

However, as our data also show, focusing on these everyday consumption practices helps to illuminate a range of problems and the ways in which childhood identities are constructed and mediated through food and feeding encounters. We anticipate, therefore, that this work will enable a more measured and insightful understanding of the various and subtle dimensions of the relationship between infants, food and identity than is normally available in the media and within professional and lay discourses.

Notes

1. With at least one child between the ages of 9 months and 2 years old.
2. And also within the wider family and community (see Dykes 2005).
3. We do not wish to imply a simplistic correlation between these phenomena. Whilst obesity is closely associated with the global increase in Type 2 diabetes, other contributory factors have been identified.
4. Reflecting the WHO policy directive (2001) to further delay the introduction of solid foods from 4 months until 6 months, the 2005 Infant-Feeding Survey showed a marked trend towards mothers introducing solid foods later. For example, in 2000 85% of UK mothers had introduced solid foods by four months (Hamlyn et al. 2002), but by 2005 this figure had fallen to 51% (Bolling et al. 2007).
5. The Infant-Feeding Survey was the first to measure exclusive breast-feeding rates.
6. Type 1, Type 2 or gestational diabetes.
7. Determined by a Body Mass Index (BMI) of 35 or above.
8. The findings presented here were generated in the context of a larger study (see: http://www.shef.ac.uk/familiesandfood/projects/changinghabits.html) which contributed to a programme of research (see: http://www.shef.ac.uk/familiesandfood/) which takes food as the lens through which to observe recent changes in family life.
9. This method of feeding babies with an inadequate sucking reflex is widely practised in UK maternity units. As the sucking mechanism required to breastfeed is different from that required to feed from a bottle, offering milk via a pipette, dropper, or cup is thought to reduce the likelihood of 'nipple confusion' and hence the infant subsequently rejecting the breast. Mothers are encouraged to express their own breast milk for this purpose.
10. However, the image of the 'bonny' baby – previously esteemed and cherished for its rounded plumpness – has become imbued with negative meaning. This became apparent when our local NHS 'ethical' reviewers asked us to remove this word from the original title of our research proposal in case participants were offended by contemporary associations with fatness/obesity.

References

Alanen, L. (1994). 'Gender and generation: Feminism and the "child question"', in Qvortrup, J., Bardy, M., Sgritta, G. & Wintersberger, H. (eds), *Childhood Matters: Social Theory, Practice and Politics*. Aldershot: Avebury Press.

Amir, L. H. & Donath, S. (2007). 'A systematic review of maternal obesity and breastfeeding intention, initiation and duration'. *BMC Pregnancy and Childbirth* 7(9).

Apple, R. D. (1995). 'Constructing mothers: Scientific motherhood in the nineteenth and twentieth centuries'. *Social History of Medicine* 8(2): 161–178.

Ariès, P. (1962). *Centuries of Childhood*. New York: Vintage Books.

Arnup, K. (1990). 'Educating mothers: Government advice for women in the inter-war years', in Arnup, K., Levesque, A. & Roach Pierson, R. (eds), *Delivering Motherhood: Maternal Ideologies and Practices in the 19th and 20th Centuries* (pp. 190–210). London: Routledge.

Beck, U. & Beck-Gernsheim, E. (2002). *The Normal Chaos of Love*. London: Sage.

Blum, L. M. (2000). *At the Breast: Ideologies of Breastfeeding and Motherhood in Contemporary United States*. Boston: Beacon Press.

Bolling, K., Grant, C., Hamlyn, B. & Thornton, A. (2007). *Infant-Feeding Survey 2005*. London: The Information Centre.

Bowlby, J. (1951). *Maternal Care and Mental Health*. Geneva: World Health Organisation.

Carter, P. (1995). *Feminism, Breasts and Breastfeeding*. Basingstoke: Macmillan Press.

CEMACH (2005). *Pregnancy in Women with Type 1 and Type 2 Diabetes*. London: CEMACH.

CEMACH (2007). *Diabetes in Pregnancy: Caring for the Baby after Birth*. London: CEMACH.

Christiansen, P. & James, A. (eds) (2000). *Research with Children: Perspectives and Practices*. London: Falmer Press.

Corsaro, W. (2005). *The Sociology of Childhood*. Thousand Oaks, CA: Pine Forge Press.

Cunningham, H. (1991). *The Children of the Poor: Representations of Childhood since the Seventeenth Century*. Oxford: Blackwell.

Cunningham, H. (1995). *Children and Childhood in Western Society since 1500*. Harlow: Longman.

Department of Health (2007). 'Birth to Five'. London: Crown Copyright. Available at: http://www.dh.gov.uk/en/Publicationsandstatistics/Publications/PublicationsPolicyAndGuidance/Browsable/DH_5289328 (accessed 13/10/2008).

DeVault, M. (1991). *Feeding the Family: The Social Organisation of Caring as Gendered Work*. Chicago: University of Chicago Press.

Dykes, F. (2005). '"Supply" and "Demand": Breastfeeding as Labour'. *Social Science & Medicine* 60: 2283–2293.

Everingham, C. (1994). *Motherhood and Modernity*. Buckingham: Open University Press.

Fewtrell, M. S. (2004). 'The long-term benefits of having been breastfed'. *Current Paediatrics* 14(2): 97–103.

Gordon, L. (1982). 'Why nineteenth-century feminists did not support "birth control" and twentieth-century feminists do: Feminism, reproduction and the family', in Thorne, B. & Yalom, M. (eds), *Rethinking the Family: Some Feminist Questions*. London: Longman.

Hamlyn, B., Brooker, S., Oleninikova, K. & Wands, S. (2002). *Infant Feeding Survey 2000*. London: The Stationery Office.

Hawkins, S. S., Griffiths, L. J., Dezateux, C. & Law, C. (2007). 'The impact of maternal employment on breast-feeding duration in the UK Millennium Cohort Study'. *Public Health Nutrition* 10(9): 891–896.

Hays, S. (1996). *The Cultural Contradictions of Motherhood*. New Haven, CT: Yale University Press.

Holloway, S. & Valentine, G. (eds) (2000) *Children's Geographies: Playing, Living, Learning*. London: Routledge.

Howie, P. W., Forsyth, S. J., Ogston, S. A., Clark, A. & du V Florey, C. (1990). 'Protective effect of breastfeeding against infection'. *British Medical Journal* 318: 30–34.

Hummel, S., Winkler, C., Schoen, S., Knopff, A., Marienfeld, S., Bonifacio, E. & Ziegler, A. G. (2007). 'Breastfeeding habits in families with Type 1 diabetes'. *Diabetic Medicine* 24(6): 671–676.

Jenks, C. (1996). *Childhood*. London: Routledge.

Jones, T. (2007). *Breastfeeding in Sheffield: 2006 Statistical Report Public Health Analysis Team*. Available at: http://www.sheffield.nhs.uk/healthdata/resources/breastfeedingmonitoringreport.pdf (accessed 2/6/08).

Kelly, Y. J. & Watt, R. G. (2005). 'Breast-feeding initiation and exclusive duration at 6 months by social class. Results from the Millennium Cohort Study'. *Public Health Nutrition* 8(4): 417–421.

Labbok, M. (2001). 'Effects of breastfeeding on the mother'. *Paediatric Clinics of North America* 48(1): 413–420.

Lawler, S. (1999). 'Children need but mothers only want: The power of "needs talk" in the constitution of childhood', in Seymour, J. & Bagguley, P. (eds), *Relating Intimacies: Power and Resistance* (pp. 64–99). Basingstoke: Macmillan.

Lawler, S. (2000). *Mothering the Self: Mothers, Daughters, Subjects*. London: Routledge.

Maher, V. (1992). *Anthropology of Breastfeeding*. London: Berg.

Mahoney, M. A. & Yngvesson, B. (1992). 'The construction of subjectivity and the paradox of resistance: Reintegrating feminist anthropology and psychology'. *Signs: Journal of Women in Culture and Society* 18(1): 44–73.

Marshall, J. L., Godfrey, M. & Renfrew, M. J. (2007). 'Being a "good mother": Managing breastfeeding and merging identities'. *Social Science and Medicine* 65: 2147–2159.

Mason, J. (1996). 'Gender, care and sensibility in family and kin relationships', in Holland, J. & Adkins, L. (eds), *Sex, Sensibility and the Gendered Body*. London: Macmillan.

Mayall, B. (2002). *Towards a Sociology for Childhood: Thinking from Children's Lives*. Buckingham: Open University Press.

Miller, T. (2005). *Making Sense of Motherhood: A Narrative Approach*. Cambridge: Cambridge University Press.

Murcott, A. (1993). 'Purity and pollution: Body management and the social place of infancy', in Morgan, D. & Scott, S. (eds), *Body Matters: Essays on the Sociology of the Body* (pp. 122–134). London: Falmer Press.

Murphy, E. (1999). '"Breast is best": Infant feeding and maternal deviance'. *Sociology of Health and Illness* 21(2): 187–208.

Murphy, E., Parker, S. & Phipps, C. (1998). 'Competing agendas in infant feeding'. *British Food Journal* 100(3): 128–132.

Murphy, E. A. (2007). 'Images of childhood in mothers' accounts of contemporary childrearing'. *Childhood* 14: 105.

NICE (2006). *Obesity. Guidance on the prevention, identification, assessment and management of overweight and obesity in adults and children*. Clinical Guideline 43. London: National Institute of Clinical Excellence. Available at: http://www.nice.org.uk/nicemedia/pdf/CG43quickrefguide2.pdf (accessed 07/4/08).

Oakley, A. (1979). *Becoming a Mother*. Oxford: Martin Robertson.

Palmer, G. (1993). *The Politics of Breastfeeding*. London: Pandora Press.

Poirier-Solomon, L. (2002). 'A balancing act: Managing motherhood and diabetes'. *Diabetes Forecast* 55(11): 46–47.

Prout, A. & James, A. (1990). 'A new paradigm for the sociology of childhood? Provenance, promise and problems', in James, A. & Prout, A. (eds), *Constructing and Reconstructing Childhood*. London: Falmer Press.

Rasmussen, B., O'Connell, B., Dunning, P. & Cox, H. (2007). 'Young women with type 1 diabetes management of turning points and transitions'. *Qualitative Health Research* 17(3): 300–310.

Ribbens McCarthy, J., Edwards, R. & Gillies, V. (2000). *Parenting and Step-Parenting: Contemporary Moral Tales*, Occasional Paper 4. Oxford: Centre for Family and Household Research, Oxford Brookes University.

Rose, N. & Miller, P. (1992). 'Political power beyond the state: Problematics of government'. *British Journal of Sociology* 43(2): 173–205.

Stern, D. N. (1974). 'Mother and infant at play: The dyadic involving facial, vocal, and gaze behaviors', in Lewis, M. & Rosenblum, L. A. (eds), *The Effect of the Infant on Its Caregiver*. New York: Wiley.

Stone, L. (1977). *The Family, Sex and Marriage in England 1500–1800*. London: Weidenfield and Nicolson.

Trevarthen, C. (1993). 'The functions of emotions in early infant communication and development', in Nadel, J. & Camaori, L. (eds), *New Perspectives on Early Communicative Behaviour*. London: Routledge.

Thompson, R., Kehily, M. J., Hadfield, L. & Sharpe, S. (2008). *The Making of Modern Motherhood: Memories, Representations, Practices*. Project Report, July, 2008. The Open University. Available at: http://www.open.ac.uk/hsc/research/research-projects/making-of-modern-motherhood/making-of-modern-motherhood. php (accessed 1/10/08).

Urwin, C. (1985). 'Constructing motherhood: The persuasion of normal development', in Steedman, C. Unwin, C. & Walkerdine, V. (eds), *Language, Gender and Childhood* (pp. 164–202). London: Routledge and Kegan Paul.

Valentine, G. (1997). ' "My Son's a Bit Dizzy. My Wife's a Bit Soft": Gender, children and cultures of parenting'. *Gender, Place and Culture* 4(1): 37–62.

Van Esterik, P. (1989). *Mother Power and Infant Feeding*. London: Zed Books.

Wade, A. (2005). *Continuity and Change in Parent–Child Relations over Three Generations*. University of Leeds (ESRC Research Grant No: R000239523).

Walker, R., Ashworth, K., Kellard, K., Middlestone, S., Peaker, A. & Thomas, M. (1994). 'Pretty, pretty please – just like a parrot: Persuasion strategies used by children and young people', in Middlestone, S., Ashworth, K. & Walker, R. (eds), *Family Fortunes*. London: Child Poverty Action Group.

Wall, G. (2001). 'Moral constructions of motherhood in breastfeeding discourse'. *Gender & Society* 15(4): 592–610.

Wild, S., Rogli, G., Green, A., Sicree, R. & King, H. (2004). 'Global prevalence of diabetes estimates for the year 2000 and projections for 2030'. *Diabetes Care* 27: 1047–1053.

Wilson, A. C., Forsyth, J. S., Greene, S. A., Irvine, L., Hau, C. & Howie, W. P. (1998). 'Relation of infant diet to childhood health: Seven year follow up of cohort of children in Dundee infant feeding study'. *British Medical Journal* 316: 21–25.

Winnicott, D. W. (1950). *The Family and Individual Development*. London: Tavistock.

Winnicott, D. W. (1971). *Playing and Reality*. London: Tavistock.

WHO (2001). *Infant and Young Child Nutrition*. The Fifty-fourth World Health Assembly, WHA54.2. Available at: http://ftp.who.int/gb/archive/pdf_files/WHA54/ea54r2.pdf. (accessed 3/5/08).

WHO & UNICEF (2003). Global strategy for infant and young child feeding. Geneva. Available at: http://www.who.int/nutrition/publications/gs_infant_feeding_text_eng.pdf.

Yngve, A. & Sjöström, M. (2001). 'Breastfeeding in countries of the European Union and EFTA: Current and proposed recommendations, rationale, prevalence, duration and trends'. *Public Health Nutrition* 4(2B): 631–645.

2

Negotiating Family, Negotiating Food: Children as Family Participants?

Allison James, Penny Curtis, Katie Ellis

There has been a considerable resurgence of interest in families and food within English society, sparked in part by a concern that both family and food have, in some ways, undergone a process of detrimental decline over the last half of the twentieth century. Poised now at the start of the twenty-first century, critical eyes are being cast over rising levels of obesity among children as well as adults, the nutritional deficiencies of school dinners and the propensity for children and young people, as well as their parents, to consume 'junk' food. In respect of the family, observers have noted with alarm the rising levels of divorce, increasingly time-poor family life, the loss of 'traditional' parental authority, and the growing sequestration of children into separate institutionalised leisure spaces in which 'the family' plays a less prominent part (Qvortrup 1994). Taken together these twin trends are, within the popular press, held to account for many of the contemporary ills of English life, sparking waves of government initiatives designed to tackle these new social 'problems'.[1]

It is against the background of these alarmist discourses, therefore, that this chapter is situated as it considers what the mundane and everyday practices that take place within families around about food and eating might tell us, not only about changing dietary habits, but, perhaps more importantly, about English children's identities as family members in the twenty-first century. Our discussion centres on the persistence of the iconic status of the family meal as a symbol of family life where, for the most part, attention has hitherto been focused on women's major role in the provisioning of family meals and, correspondingly, the absence of men's contribution to their preparation. In this chapter, therefore, we revisit these debates but from a rather different perspective – by asking about children's participation in the family meal. And in doing so, we explore the varied range of practices that take place within families in relation to the production and consumption of family meals, practices that reveal different conceptions of childhood identities and of children as family participants.

The study

The project on which this chapter draws was part of a larger research programme exploring food as a vehicle for family practices and interview data was gathered from 120 children of 11–12 years old, attending schools located in different kinds of neighbourhood.[2] These comprised a rural school, a predominantly working-class school, a predominantly middle-class school and a school with high ethnic diversity where 52 languages are spoken. Forty children from these schools were later interviewed again at home, along with their parents. Household composition was chosen as a variable so that our sample included single-parent households, households where there was only one child and households where there were more than three children. In addition, we included a set of households where a family member had a restricted diet of some kind. These categories were, of course, not mutually exclusive so that, for example, our data include households where a single-parent has three or more children and households with large numbers of children where dietary practices are also restricted. Given the qualitative, rather than quantitative, methodology of the project, this cross-over was not especially problematic, however, since we were interested in exploring the range and pattern of family practices, rather than identifying specific determinants for any differences. And, as it turned out, neither family 'type' nor household composition appears to be indicative of the ways in which food and family intersect in everyday family life nor of the ways in which children do – or don't – participate within it. Rather, as we shall go on to explore, more important for the ways in which children participated in family life were the ideas held by parents – and to some extent children themselves – about the nature of childhood and children's identities as *children*.

Theoretical considerations

Morgan (1996) argues that 'the family' is best understood in relation to the practices it adopts, a view that envisages the family as an ongoing and dynamic set of social relationships that are actively 'lived', rather than as a set of roles that are simply inhabited. Within this, the notion of 'doing family' becomes important. This refers to the continual social construction of 'the family' in and through the actions of its members such that the sense and experience of 'family' that emerges is what constitutes 'family' *for* its members. Such a perspective does not reify the family; rather it sees it as a fluid and dynamic set of social encounters between different people that, in everyday life, come to be regarded as 'family life'. Importantly, this also includes people's engagement with rather different 'models' of the family. For example, how individuals take on or reject particular sets of hegemonic ideas about what family is, or should be, can shape how they themselves 'do' family. These ideas may be drawn from a diverse range of sources including for example, public and media discourses as well as personal, intergenerational experiences of 'family' that can involve both the importance of tradition as well as its rejection.

Notwithstanding the 'doing' of family, families are, however, also constituted structurally in terms of the relational identities of parents and children. Indeed as work by Morrow (1998) has shown, from children's own perspectives it is the presence of children that makes a family, a viewpoint that draws our attention to the ways in which children contribute to family practices and hence the making and doing of 'family'. In this respect, Zeiher's (2001) examination of changing patterns of parent–child relations in Germany offers a useful critique of the simplistic assumption that children are simply dependent on their parents. Rather, as she notes, the ways in which children are positioned within families – or indeed position themselves – has to be seen as integral to the ways in which the 'doing' of family tales place. And, as she notes, since the 1960s, rather contradictory trends have developed with respect to the kinds of social identities and subject positions that children are able to take on within the family.

On the one hand, she suggests, children are being increasingly seen as subjects and social actors at earlier ages than ever before, with emphasis given to their autonomy and independence. On the other, children are being placed in positions of social and economic dependency for longer periods through, for example, their extended exclusion from work through the expansion of compulsory schooling (2001:39). Moreover, although the adult–child relationship has begun to be seen in some ways as more equal, 'the structural control imposed on children by educational arrangements [is] greater' (2001:39). These trends, combined with the greater participation by mothers in the labour market, Zeiher argues, have resulted in three rather different patterns of family life and children's participation within it. Moreover, the child identities that emerge through these different patterns of family interaction are also rather different.

According to Zeiher, for some children, parental care has become such an intensive project for furthering children's development and education that this now extends beyond the home and school into children's leisure activities. Although in some ways this has increased children's dependency on their parents, it has, she suggests, also served to mark out distinct adult and child identities. In these families, children have carved out separate children's worlds for themselves that, though legitimated by their parents, provide children with extra-familial contexts to frequent. By contrast, in other families, the care that children receive is 'so overpowering, one-sided and [extending] to all areas of daily life' that children are unable to establish autonomous identities for themselves outside of the family (2001:47). Finally, in some other families, children's independence is enabled and encouraged through their taking on of domestic responsibilities, something that leads to the development of a more egalitarian, interdependent relationship with their parents.

Alanen's (2001) work on children's daily life in Finland parallels these findings in some important respects in her suggestion that different processes of identification are currently taking place in the generational structuring of child–adult relations. She suggests that these need to be understood in respect of the 'possibilities (and limitations) of action' that arise for children across the different social domains in which they participate (2001:131). Thus, in relation to children's identities as actors within families, she is able to differentiate between those children for whom the family predominates as their main identificatory domain (family children) and those others for whom school or friendship with peers provides this role instead. For 'family children', their status and identity as a 'child' is something that is actively fostered for them by their parents, and to some extent also by children themselves, through a variety of what Alanen terms 'childing' practices. For 'family children', such practices centre the child in the family and the home and produce, for the child, 'a self-identification and a (mainly positive) self-image of childness' (2001:138). Non-family children, by contrast, develop strong relationships outside of the family and make greater use of the institutions and services provided in school, clubs and leisure facilities to meet their personal needs, interests and reference points of self-identification. Such children were, correspondingly, often reluctant to identify with popular images of children and childhood.

What both Zeiher and Alanen point to, then, are the rather different ways in which the identity of 'child' is brought into being through the everyday practices of parents and children as they go about the business of 'doing' family. These accounts also suggest that different family practices enable or discourage different degrees of participation by children in the making and doing of ' family', depending on the extent to which 'childness' is understood (by parents and by children) as a key status attribute to be fostered for children within the family.

Drawing on these ideas on the diversities of the status identity of 'child', as it materialises in and through the mundane and everyday relations between adults and children, this chapter now goes on to consider the ways in which the daily food practices of families might be integral to such ongoing processes of generationing (Mayall 2002:27) and social identification (Jenkins 2004) that are constitutive of children's experiences of everyday family life in contemporary English society (see Chapter 3 by Wills et al. this volume). As Jenkins has argued, identity is never a finished business; it is ongoing and processual so that although, as we shall suggest, certain family food practices are revealing of particular kinds of child identities these are single snapshots. Over time, the family dynamics constituted through child–adult relations will change as children and their parents continue to negotiate the patterning of the everyday relationships through which the 'doing' of family takes place.

Proper family dinners, proper families, proper children

Some twenty years ago now Murcott (1982), Charles and Kerr (1988), and DeVault (1991) all demonstrated that the 'proper dinner' constitutes the cement of family life. Cooked by women for their families, the proper dinner not only evidenced women's care and love for their families but also distilled the gendered division of labour that existed within households and evidenced the generational hierarchy between parents and their children. Significantly, our data show that, despite a growing concern about the emergence of grazing and sequential eating patterns within families the proper dinner has retained its iconic status as a symbol for what a proper family does and is something that families continue to aspire to. For example, one boy commented approvingly, 'my mum always makes like a really nice meal at night like a proper meal with everything in it'. And another boy observed that, as a family, they eat all sorts 'as long as you can have vegetables with it 'cause my Mum thinks that you've always got to have a vegetable for your tea'.

Although traditionally such a proper meal might have comprised 'meat and two veg', as the examples above imply, this is now not always the case. Among Asian families in our sample, for instance, a proper dinner comprised curry and rice, for those families on low incomes corned beef hash might fit the bill, and for vegetarian families a vegetarian pie suffices. What still matters, it seems, is that the proper meal is cooked almost exclusively by Mum (see Chapter 5 by Curtis, James and Ellis in this volume), it is a meal that 'has a bit of everything', one that does not make much use of convenience food and, most importantly, it is a meal that parents and children eat together. One mother recalling, somewhat wistfully, her own mother's food provisioning for the family, was both defensive and apologetic about her own ability to ensure that her family has a 'proper meal':

> Meals were always cooked from scratch. She used to cook a main meal, veg and potatoes, meat and potato pie. Whereas me, I do cook from scratch. Now and again but I do use convenience food as well. Tea was always on the table when we came home from school...and it was always lovely.

Other mothers echoed these sentiments. Describing herself as a 'bit of a microwave queen' Jean was keen to point out that, nonetheless, she tried 'to cook a proper meal, cooked from scratch' at least twice a week, while Susan felt the need to apologise:

> when I were a kid, we used to be like meat and two veg everyday...
> ...I know it sounds awful but some days, if I've been working, it's just like a quick pizza put in the oven.

What is clear from these mothers' accounts, therefore, is that the key ingredients of a 'proper dinner' are not simply nutritional ones. As already noted by the early theorists cited above, importantly they include the visible demonstration of the nurturing care that women feel they should ideally provide for their husbands and for their children. That is to say, the making and eating of a proper cooked dinner reproduces the generational and gender orders through which family life is constituted on an everyday basis (see Charles and Kerr 1988). Indeed, as DeVault (1991) argued, the act of making family meals that bring family members together is an integral part of the very 'doing' and making of families.

In our data, the virtues of commensality among family members were often expressed: 'we do try. We've got a dining room, we do try and eat as a family as much as we can.' And even in those families that lacked a dining room or dining table, 'proper dinners' could still be eaten together, sitting on the sofa, as a 'proper family' should. The importance of this togetherness is noted by 11-year-old Zara whose family rearranged their eating arrangements so that the whole family could eat together, while also watching TV:

> we have a big table in the living room. But we used to have it in the kitchen. but we couldn't watch tv so we didn't eat our dinners so my mum and dad decided to have it in the living room so we can watch TV and eat dinner at the same time.

And that the different routines of family members means this ideal of eating a meal together may be difficult to achieve during the week, heightens the importance of Sunday dinner. Thus, as James says:

> Sunday roast ... is ... 'cause it's more like get all family like together sitting round a table with a nice big kind of like beef and stuff like that. Sprouts and parsley and all stuff like that.

Thus, in short, it would seem that proper families still eat proper meals together.

In the light of these findings how then can we understand children's participation in such meals? Is it simply as passive recipients of their mothers' care or is a more nuanced understanding possible? Paul's complaint about a school friend who had come to visit but who had not eaten much of the family evening meal is suggestive. He says:

> I was really angry, I'm like, 'My mum has just spent ... my mum's looking after you for a day. And you won't eat the food she's put on your plate ... that is so unfair'.

In his account, Paul positions himself and his friend not only as the objects of his mother's care – as people who are looked after – but also as active recipients who, in turn, have a duty to acknowledge and respect the work that this care involves. Thus, in the making and eating of the family meal, the generational ordering of this particular family is laid bare, with both child and adult status clearly demarcated in terms of their mutual responsibilities.

In Alanen's terms, then, does the preparation and consumption of a proper dinner work as a key childing practice within families, one that confers a range of different identities upon children? In the following sections, we go on to consider this proposition by exploring in greater detail the ways in which the proper meal does – but also does not – accomplish different kinds of childhood identities within different families.

Family food and child identities

Given the complexities of contemporary modern life when parents may both work, may arrive home at different times and children may have a range of after-school activities, the practical accomplishment of the proper meal/proper family equation can prove problematic. Moreover, cooking a meal that everyone will eat poses additional problems. Meals need to be negotiated within the family so that the different tastes of family members can be accommodated. And this is the more so in families where some members have specific dietary restrictions such as vegetarianism.

However, common though such problems are, among the families in our data set, a range of different solutions have been found, solutions which we suggest reflect rather different understandings of children as family participants. We consider first three families where the solution has been to restrict what the family eats. This practice has, however, different outcomes for the generational order in different families that reflect rather divergent views of children's status identities as children. Moreover, this food practice is accomplished through rather different expectations – and experiences – of the child as a family participant.

First, in Maisey's family, the children's food preferences are taken into account by their parents in acknowledgement of their equal rights as family members. For example, Maisey, whose family is all vegetarian, says that her mother knows what she and her siblings like and her mum agrees: 'I think we know what they like and what they don't'. Therefore, Maisey's mum cooks food that everyone likes to eat – adults and children. However, although both she and her husband are strict vegetarians, Maisey's mum does not wish to dictate what her children eat. She says: 'I mean, they both know that they can eat meat if they decide they want to.' Such egalitarian views are reflected in other of their family practices. Maisey says, for example, that there are no particular rules about who does what in their family: 'My dad or my mum or sometimes my brother cooks stir-fries but like everyone always helps for tea.' Here family food practices appear to collapse the generational order.

By contrast, in Roy's family, familial dietary restrictions are the outcome of childing practices aimed, in Alanen's (2001) terms, at maintaining the generational order by keeping children as children, rather than encouraging their autonomy as family members. Thus, in Roy's family, it is 'children's food' (James 2008) – food such as chips, burgers and pizza – that all the family eat:

> I tend not to give them food that they don't like basically. You know, you learn as they get older, don't you, the things that they do and don't like. We just eat food that everybody likes. Sometimes, if one's away playing somewhere, we'll have something they don't like on that night. (Roy's mum)

Like his brother, Roy's child-status is shored up by his eating of 'children's food' but since all the family also eat this kind of food, what we see here is an indulged and prolonged encouragement of Roy's childness that, as Alanen (2001) and Zeiher (2001) suggest, works to foster his dependency within the family. It is an attitude toward children as family participants that is reflected in other areas of their family life. Here the children are not expected to help at home:

> [T]hat's been a big thing on me 'cause I've always done everything. You know, I've never expected 'em to do anything and I'm the type of person that I like things done in a certain way so it's better to do it my way ... just as I say, I've always brought 'em up to, to not do it really.

Finally, in Gemma's family, the decision to restrict the family's diet has been the outcome of continual arguments and disputes between adults and children. As Gemma admits, food often causes arguments 'between me and my Mum 'cause I'm like, "Oh I don't wanna eat that" '. Restricting what she cooks has therefore been her mum's solution to such arguments:

> usually she asks me if I like it before and I'll just say no. Then she'll say, 'Ok I won't make it.'

In this last example, then, can be seen an instance of the third child identity noted by Zeiher (2001) – a child who has gained a semi-independent status as a child. Gemma's wishes and feelings about food are seen as legitimate by her parents and can therefore often influence the family meals that her mother prepares.

Cooking family food

While the three examples above provide striking instances where family food practices serve to reorder, collapse or preserve the generational order and to foster particular kinds of child identities, for the majority of families in our sample the 'doing' of family through food practices around the family meal is far less clear cut. Instead, what their food practices reveal is a process of muddling through the ongoing and everyday processes of identification involved in family socialisation that is core to the production of social identity (Jenkins 2004).

Thus, for the majority of families, the production of family food that can be eaten together *as a family* involves adapting menus, a process of accommodating children's food preferences, rather than restricting the kind of food that is offered:

> most of the time we try and fit into it so that people will like it. For example, last night there was onion gravy and we know that Billy likes not to have onions so you just scoop the gravy out without the onions. So we try to compromise wherever possible. (mother)
>
> so they just have fish fingers instead of salmon and then eat everything else. (mother)

Here, therefore, children's preferences only partially shape family food practices, since although their wishes are accommodated, they do not determine the ways in which family eating takes place.

This practice is not, however, just a pragmatic solution adopted by busy mothers trying to meet the wide variety of different demands from family members. When Dean's mother makes a curry, for example, she makes three versions – hot, middling and cool – in order to accommodate her children's food preferences and Sarah's mother makes both a pepper free and a regular pasta sauce. Thus, both Dean and Sarah's mothers do more, rather than less, cooking in order that 'family food' can be eaten together *as a family*. Making more, rather than less food, also suggests that the cost of food is not a key issue in the endeavour to eat together *as a family*, although it may, of course, determine what the family eats and from which supermarkets food is purchased. Neither is this practice of adaptation simply a pragmatic response to family size since even in families where there is only one child menus are often also adapted.

It is clear, therefore, that what matters most to these mothers is that everyone should eat the same – as a matter of principle. Indeed, their

mode of expression when talking about cooking family meals sometimes takes on a very principled tone, reflecting the importance they
attach to commensality. For example, in their three-person household,
composed of mother, father and son, the mother said:

> I do ask what people want, but if everybody wants different things
> it's tough and they just have to want one thing.

That this is a food practice that maximises children's identities, not just
as children, but as child participants in the 'doing' of family becomes
explicit in those families where menus are not adapted. Rather, in these
families children are made to participate in family meals through the
'symbolic' sharing of family food:

> I've always given them two carrots on their plate. You know, whether
> they've wanted 'em or not, But I don't really give 'em things they
> don't want 'cause it's a waste. (mother)

> Say we're having mashed potato sausage and peas or something and
> me and my brother'll have mashed potato omelette and peas and
> gravy and they'd all have sausages. But she always gives me a tiny
> bit to try. (girl)

> don't like stew but when she does (it) she just says to eat it. 'Cause
> you should be grateful for what you've been given'. And I say: 'I know
> that but I don't like it'. I just eat and and, I don't like meat. So I just
> left all the meat and everything. (girl)

And in a few families this practice takes on the form of a moral cru-
sade whereby children *should* learn the value of 'family' through the
consumption of family food. Such values may be reflected in the intergenerational nature of family food practices, as mothers try to rep-
licate – or conversely distance themselves from – the ways in which
their own mothers cooked for them (see Curtis, James and Ellis 2009
forthcoming).

Such data suggests, therefore, that, for parents, a child who demonstrates a willingness to eat the same food as other family members
reveals their commitment to and identification with the family more
generally. Indeed, given the symbolic importance of 'family food', not
being a fussy eater becomes a mark, not just of obedience, but of identification; it is a sign of a child's engagement with what 'the family' is and
does. Thus, like a number of other mother's, Martin's mother reflected
back on her son's attitude to food and eating as he was growing up and

commented approvingly: 'He's been very good, he was never fussy and he always tries things'.

The importance of demonstrating family membership through food sharing also explains why some mothers persist in endeavouring to get reluctant children to eat family food:

> It's just don't give up. It's on their plate. If they don't like it they can leave it, but it still gets put on the plate. (mother)

This is clear too in Paula's account when she says that:

> I gotta eat some of it at least and that way I'm having a bit of a meal. But if I just leave it on the plate my Mum'll make me sit there until I eat some of it.

That children's refusal to eat family food constitutes a metaphoric refusal to participate in family life may also explain why children are admonished to eat even a little *'a bit of a meal'* and also why some mothers are so insistent, in the face of constant opposition, that their children *should* eat what they are given.[3]

The absence of family food, the absence of family?

Describing her return home from holiday, 11-year-old Anne recalled that her grandmother had welcomed them all back home by cooking a meal. But this was not any meal. Anne says: 'When we came back from holiday she made us a Sunday dinner, didn't she?'. Given its role as the apogee of a proper dinner in the temporal ordering of meals (Douglas 1975), the specificity of this homecoming meal as a Sunday dinner is significant. Not only does it reveal the importance attached by her grandmother to the idea of family – after all it was she who chose to cook a Sunday dinner not on a Sunday – but it also demonstrates Anne's own understanding of what this meal signified about their extended family's sense of being a family. Anne observed, 'She made us a Sunday dinner, didn't she?', adding, by way of explanation, that she did this 'because she missed us'.

Captured in this example, then, is the powerful hegemonic role that family food plays in processes of identification – family food is core to the doing of family and integral to children's identities as family members. Indeed, so powerful is this mode of thought that Bob and Terry's mum feels the need to justify why, in her family, commensality is rarely practised. And, interestingly, she justifies the apparent lack of family togetherness that this absence might suggest as a function of the *children's* desires, rather than her own, to be doing other things outside of family life:

> The boys tend to eat together and we tend to eat together and that's purely and simply because of the timing, I think. Just for timing. We don't tend to sit at the table, to eat as a family, even if we are eating at the same time. Purely and simply because the boys are always interrupted from whatever they're doing to come and have their tea. So it's a quick thing. Whereas we…we'll come downstairs and have those trays with cushions underneath. On occasions we eat upstairs but as a rule it is a nuisance to try and eat together because they're always in too much of a rush to be off. Back to wherever they've come from.

But in a few families in our sample children's refusal to eat 'family food' is neither seen as problematic nor requiring excuse or explanation. In these families, children can simply choose to make their own food and can decide not to eat what their mothers have cooked if they do not like it:

> If it's something that the dog can eat I'll give it to her and it's alright with my mum as long as I make a sandwich or somemat like that to eat. (boy)

> Yeah, well quite often I'll say, 'Oh well, I'm cooking that for dinner': and then there'll be moans of 'Oh well, I don't like that and I don't want that'. So they'll go and make an egg sandwich or beans on toast. (mother)

In comparison with the majority of other families' food practices, such relaxed attitudes to children's participation in the eating of family food are intriguing for, if as argued above, the creation and eating of 'family food' provides an index of proper family life and of children's identities as family members, what do such practices suggest? Do they indicate a breakdown in the generational order and hierarchy through which the family is constituted?[4] Or is it simply that, for a few families, the doing of family takes place other than through the medium of shared family food?

Returning to Maisey's family allows us to explore in more detail the ways in which other processes of identification might be taking place in those families who do not regularly eat together. While, as noted, restricting menus is one strategy that Maisey's family employs to enable them all to eat together, it is not the only way that the children's identities as family members are expressed. The children are also encouraged to exercise their rights to choose and, although Maisey's mother is inclined to persuade Maisey to eat family food, her father is less insistent. He will say to Maisey: 'Do you want to go and make yourself some toast or something? Get yourself something'. With her strong and shared commitment to Buddhism and to vegetarianism, he sees Maisey as a keen proponent of their family values and, through this, demonstrating in other ways her identity as a family member:

> I think she's certainly more strongly motivated and more strongly principled to be a vegetarian than, than I am certainly, I mean, it kind of comes from her and her own thinking about it. And I think the gelatine more than from me 'cause I mean, for example, I eat gelatine. (dad)

By contrast, Irene's strong and independent views as the only vegetarian in the family means that shared 'family food' can be difficult to prepare and is not often shared. Irene says:

> I don't mind her (mother) making like my lunch or something. But I do mind her making my breakfast. And she has to ask me what I want for tea. I can't sit down and she'd be like 'Oh, we're having pasta or ravioli' or something and I'd be like, 'Well, like it's not the best choice, so why didn't you ask me?' And I'd go hungry or something.

However, although her mother respects her views and accommodates Irene's personal food choices, she insists, nonetheless, on the importance of family rules in other areas of family life. In Irene's family it is in these domains, therefore, that the children's identities as children and as family members are shaped. Irene's mother says: 'I know I'm a bit of a pain at times but I have people's interests at heart' and goes on to describe in some detail the family rules and routines around bedtime:

> I was allowed to fall asleep on the sofa. Whereas to me that's a no way situation. They go to bed. They have reading in bed. Winters more structured than summer obviously. In winter we're upstairs for seven o'clock...Oh, ay. Yeah. Reading. We'll have done homework. We read...in winter. We come home, we do the homework, we

have tea and then it's upstairs. And we'll read. And everybody's in bed by eight o'clock.

Thus, for the few families where the sharing of 'family food' is absent, this does not necessarily mean the absence of a sense of family nor that the children, in Alanen's (2001) terms, necessarily have the status of non-family children. Rather, it may simply be that food does not provide the main medium through which such processes of identification take place.

Conclusion

As this chapter has shown, commensality is an important way in which, for many families, the idea of family is reinforced on an everyday basis, and is an aspect of 'doing family' which many children also feel is important. Commenting somewhat wryly about weekday breakfast in their household which, as in many others, tends to be eaten individually, often alone and always in a rush, Chris's mother said: 'I think he'd (Chris) actually prefer it if we could all get up and have something, even if we just had a cup of tea'. Indeed, that the sharing of food represents a shared sense of family is apparent in the breakfast time routines of another family: although not sitting down at the table to eat breakfast together in the morning, Jessie comments that 'we all are in the same room talking and stuff'. They are still 'doing family' through food and, through eating together with their families, children demonstrate their participation as family members. Indeed, that for most families eating together signals the togetherness of 'the family' is underscored by those occasions when children refuse to eat. As Cathy says, when she is cross with her parents or

if I'm in a bad mood I just grab my food and go upstairs and like shut the door and lock it, But then if I'm in a good mood then we all sit down and eat.

Taken together the family narratives discussed in this chapter display, therefore, what could be said to be a hegemonic model of the ways in which the family meal acts as a mirror for family life. However, as this chapter has also revealed, the food practices that take place around the production and consumption of the family meal are also the medium through which processes of social identification take place on an everyday basis. And in the ongoing 'doingness' of family that these processes unveil can be seen the different generational hierarchies that operate in different families that facilitate rather different kinds of participation by children as family members.

Notes

1. For example, the 5 A Day scheme was launched in 2003 to encourage the general public to increase their consumption of fruit and vegetables. A Food in Schools programme was rolled out in 2003–2004 through a series of pilot schemes in 300 primary schools to support children adopting a healthy approach to food and eating. A Welfare Food Scheme for pregnant women was launched in 2004, now known as Healthy Start and in 2008 a cross-government strategy was launched – Healthy Weight, Healthy Lives – as part of a programme of measures to tackle obesity. In relation to anxieties about the changing nature of family life, the National Family and Parenting Institute's manifesto was revised in 2005 when the government's new family policy was launched – Nine steps to make Britain Family Friendly.
2. The study *Children as Family Participants: negotiating food practices in everyday life* was part of the *Changing Food, Changing Families* programme at the University of Sheffield (2006–2008) sponsored by the Leverhulme Trust.
3. The insistence by parents on children eating particular food may, of course, also reflect the differential power relations that exist within most families. However, this still means that food practices work to shape children's status and position as family participants.
4. While it may be surmised that social class could work as a differentiating factor here there appeared to be no correlation in our data between social class or indeed family type (e.g., single-parent household, large family size) with the absence of regular shared family meals.

References

Alanen, L. (2001). 'Childhood as a generational condition: Children's daily lives in a central Finland town', in Alanen, L. & Mayall, B. (eds), *Conceptualizing Child-Adult Relations*. London: RoutledgeFalmer.

Charles, N. & Kerr, M. (1988). *Women, Food, and Families*. Manchester: Manchester University Press.

Curtis, P., James, A. & Ellis, K. (2009 forthcoming). ' "She's got a really good attitude to healthy food...Nannan's drilled it into her": Intergenerational relations within families', in Jackson, P. (ed.), *Changing Families, Changing Food*. Basingstoke. Palgrave Macmillan.

DeVault, M. L. (1991). *Feeding the Family: The Social Organisation of Caring as Gendered Work*. Chicago: Chicago University Press.

Douglas, M. (1975). 'Deciphering a meal', in Douglas, M. (ed.), *Implicit Meanings: Essays in Anthropology*. London: Routledge and Kegan Paul.

James, A. (2008). *Children's food: An Index of Generational Relations?* Paper presented to the Children and Food Conference, Institute of Education, London.

Jenkins, R. (2004). *Social Identity* (Second edition). London: Routledge.

Mayall, B. (2002). *Towards a Sociology of Childhood*. Buckingham: Open University Press.

Morgan, D. (1996). *Family Connections*. Cambridge: Polity Press.

Morrow, V. (1998). *Understanding Families: Children's Perspectives*. London: National Children's Bureau.

Murcott, A. (1982). 'On the significance of the "cooked dinner" in South Wales'. *Social Science Information* 21(4/5):677–695.

Qvortrup, J. (1994). 'Childhood matters: An introduction', in Qvortrup, J., Bardy, M., Sgritta, G. & Wintersberger, H. (eds), *Childhood Matters: Social Theory, Practice and Politics*. Aldershot: Avebury.

Zeiher, H. (2001). 'Dependent, independent and interdependent relations: Children as members of the family household in West Berlin', in Alanen, L. & Mayall, B. (eds), *Conceptualizing Child-Adult Relations'*. London: RoutledgeFalmer.

3
Consuming Fast Food: The Perceptions and Practices of Middle-Class Young Teenagers

Wendy Wills, Kathryn Backett-Milburn, Julia Lawton, Mei-Li Roberts

Children in the United Kingdom are widely believed to be consuming fast food in vast quantities with little thought for their own health or weight. Enter 'teenagers' and 'fast food' into any internet search engine and you will discover literally millions of web-based stories and sites focusing on addictions to fast food, guides alerting young people to the poor nutritional quality of such food, food scares affecting fast food–eating teenagers and so on. In 2008, the *Daily Mail*, a British tabloid newspaper, reported that the police were using burgers and stuffed crust pizza to bribe teenagers to improve their behaviour (Daily Mail 2008), thus linking the popular obsessions of junk-fuelled diets with problem youth.

Surveys suggest that teenagers and young adults do consume fast food[1] and foods high in fat in greater quantities than older adults (Henderson et al. 2002; Joint Health Surveys Unit et al. 2003). Such work also suggests, however, that those living in socio-economically advantaged households are less likely to consume such foods (Henderson et al. 2002; Joint Health Surveys Unit et al. 2003). Given that not all children appear to be equally consuming fast food, it is pertinent to enquire why some are buying into this aspect of consumer culture whereas others are not. What, from a social and cultural perspective, might some children gain by *not* eating burgers and pizzas? Since, the early teenage years are a time for spending time with friends, away from the parental gaze and asking 'who am I?' (Miles et al. 1998; Denscombe 2001) it might be expected that teenagers have more opportunity and desire to purchase and eat fast food than during earlier parts of the life course. But how such agency interacts with family values about food, and to what extent children draw on what Bourdieu calls the *habitus* (Bourdieu 1984) with regard to deciding what to consume, is unclear.

This chapter aims to explore fast food consumption practices and perceptions of fast food by drawing on the narratives of a group of young teenagers whose everyday lives and voices are largely ignored in contemporary British studies of children: the middle classes. Whilst working-class lives have become demonised as antithetical to policy drives to improve diet and reduce levels of obesity, the middle classes have largely been overlooked, perhaps because their health and related food practices have not been problematised to the same extent as socio-economically disadvantaged groups. By examining middle-class young teenagers' accounts of when, if at all, they eat fast food, where and with whom, we are able to explore whether, and in what ways, fast food practices are integral to middle-class identity-making during this period of the life course. We discuss whether parental values and expectations are evident in children's views about fast food and whether the current prevailing health discourse about avoiding foods high in fat resonates with these teenagers' decisions to eat, or not to eat, fast food.

Consumption: Chances and choices

Consumption practices, usually involving the purchase and display of commodities or 'props', are an important aspect of identity-making work (Warde 1994; Martens et al. 2004). Consuming or not consuming specific food items or products (brands) can act as a badge (Valentine 1999), marking teenagers out as 'fitting in' or 'sticking out' of one social group or another. However, since parents and guardians tend to be the gatekeepers to the majority of food purchased and brought into the home, children rarely have much say about what they eat, or have access to, in this setting (Wills 2005b; Wills et al. 2008). They therefore have little opportunity to put their mark on this family display of 'life-style' or identity through food.

Outside the context of the home, younger children display consumption through the purchase of sweets and confectionery (James 1990; Albon 2005) but older children and teenagers have the opportunity to purchase a wider variety of food on an increasing number of occasions. As they move through their secondary education, for example, children are afforded more freedom during the school day, with many (though not all) schools in the United Kingdom allowing students to leave the school premises at lunchtime once they reach their second year of high school (aged 12–13 years). This, coupled with the opportunity that some children have during adolescence to spend time outside of the parental home in the evening and on weekends, represents a time when young people can begin to make decisions about what food to consume, with less direct involvement of parents or other adults. Their increasing access to money also provides opportunities for autonomous food purchases.

Making the 'wrong' choice about what to eat could have a negative impact on teenagers at a time when they are trying hard to make the 'right' decisions in order to feel their way in a changing social landscape. Just as young people are thought to smoke (Denscombe 2001), or drink alcohol, partly because it is perceived as making them 'look good', choosing to eat, or not to eat, at certain high street fast food restaurants presents a certain 'self' to others and the 'wrong' decision could potentially damage a fragile, shifting identity. Warde has argued that identity destruction through poor consumption choices is more likely for the young as they have a need to belong and to 'follow the rules' and therefore are less likely to want to make individualised, informal choices[2] (Warde 1994).

Habitus and family values

No one, of course, makes truly individualised choices about what to eat. According to Bourdieu, even the everyday, mundane aspects of preparing and eating food are based on the accumulated habits and preferences built up within distinct social groups (Bourdieu 1984, 1990). Habitus is about having a 'feel for the game' (Bourdieu 1990), about unconsciously understanding the unspoken boundaries and rules of acceptable consumption. Social class becomes enacted through the habitus and class is therefore embedded in everyday practice (Williams 1995). Whilst buying, or not buying, food in high street fast food outlets displays teenagers' choices to others, such choices also reflect the social and cultural values that children have been subject to throughout their lives so far. Family practices and family values are powerful drivers of children's choices, since the majority of children in the United Kingdom grow up in a family of one sort or another (but see Chapter 8 by Punch et al. in this volume) and therefore their food and eating practices, as children, are bound by implicit family 'rules' about food. Children's agency may increase in terms of having opportunities to make decisions about food, but few are likely to move completely beyond the boundaries of the known habitus. Changes in eating habits are possible over the life course, but they are never randomly enacted. Habitus represents an entire system of possibilities and the rules are rarely completely rewritten

(Sweetman 2003). In addition, children are perhaps likely, overall, to make friends with others who are 'like them' thereby ensuring complicity in terms of the reproduction of acceptable consumption practices.

A Bourdieuian perspective on class and food would suggest that the middle classes are differentiated from the working classes in terms of valuing aesthetics, form and restraint when they eat (Bourdieu 1984). Assigning high priority to health promoting practices is also thought to be a particularly middle- class concern and therefore choosing food or a dietary regime that is considered as promoting good health or a slimmer body might signify a particularly middle-class outlook on consumption.[3] Not only does choosing practices which promote good health require a certain amount of economic, cultural and social capital but being *recognised* as 'health conscious' (Crawford 2006; Fisher 2008) by one's peers also delivers symbolic capital thereby (re)creating further social distinctiveness at the same time as stigmatising those who 'fail' to achieve 'good health' through the food they eat (Crawford 2006). Indeed, avoiding shame and embarrassment are powerful drivers of normative behaviour within social groups (Sayer 2005). As habitus and family values about food and health are passed on to middle-class children there is presumably a high price to pay when young people 'fail' to succeed (making the 'wrong' food choices), in terms of shaming themselves, their peers and their families. This also means that middle-class parents must feel they have to try hard to instil publicly recognised,[4] 'authentic' dietary practices into and onto their children to avoid their own embarrassment and 'failure' as parents.

The study

This chapter draws on interview data from an ESRC-funded study of middle-class families and their experiences and perceptions of food, weight and health.[5] The decision to focus on middle-class families was taken following the completion of an earlier study involving working-class young teenagers and their parents/guardians.[6] We wished to explore whether class 'matters' in relation to food and eating practices, weight and health. Interviews were conducted with 36 young middle-class teenagers aged 13–15 years. Participants were recruited from four schools located in areas of relatively high socio-economic status in Scotland. The schools chosen had below average numbers of students eligible for free school meals (a proxy indicator of socio-economic status). Three of the participating schools were state schools and one was a private, fee-paying school. Two schools were located in a city, one in a town and one in a relatively rural area. All schools were located within 30 miles of the capital city, Edinburgh.

Consenting teenagers completed a screening questionnaire and had their height and weight measured; we then selected 36 teenagers to interview at home. Selection for interview was based on our criteria for classifying families as being middle class. We used home postcode, family affluence and parental occupation/s[7] to decide whether families were eligible to be interviewed. The teenagers interviewed were predominantly white/Scottish, reflecting the ethnicity of the local population. Half of those selected were girls and half the sample was defined by their body mass index (BMI) as overweight or obese. Selected teenagers were contacted and an interview conducted in private, in the family home. As we were interested in family context and habitus, we also interviewed participant's parents. In total, 33 mothers and 2 fathers were interviewed (one parent declined to be interviewed for personal reasons). Whilst we did not steer teenagers towards nominating their mothers to be interviewed, invariably it was mothers who were suggested by participants (one boy nominated his father as he said he did most of the cooking) or who themselves volunteered as the parent responsible for feeding children and being available for interview (a second father was interviewed because he was the parent at home when the researcher visited the teenager). Most teenagers' mothers were working; two had no employment and two were full-time students. Most fathers worked full time (three were reported as not currently employed). Interviews were tape recorded with participants' consent and transcribed verbatim. In the interviews we asked participants to talk through typical and non-typical days which enabled us to probe, in some detail, all food consumed by the participating teenager and his/her family and the context for this consumption (where, with whom and when consumption took place, for example). Asking about everyday practice also set food and eating into the wider social context as we were able to explore what other activities young people were involved in. A thematic analysis of the transcribed interview data was undertaken, which involved all members of the research team. All names cited are pseudonyms and some place details have been changed to respect anonymity and confidentiality.

'Children's food' and generational identities

There have been few studies which have analysed the consumption of particular food items or focused on specific food 'events' (though see Marten and Warde 1997; Williams 1997). Fast food is interesting because it is available to take-away, ready to eat, but has also been reproduced as a 'convenience food' for the home cooking market (Carrigan 2006) with the likes of frozen or ready-to-cook pizzas and microwaveable burgers and chips. Such reproductions vary in quality and taste in relation to the take-away version and may or may not have greater nutritional value. Whilst few of the middle-class families in our study said they ate burgers or chips at home, pizza was regularly consumed by teenagers in the home setting (but rarely by parents). The pizza on offer was occasionally bought from a take-away outlet but more usually bought ready-to-cook, with some teenagers describing how parents added items to the pizza, like vegetables, before putting the pizza in the oven. Parents offered pizza when time was particularly short or adults were intending to eat separately from their children. This perhaps gave the impression that pizza is not 'proper', but a standby food.

INTERVIEWER: 'So, would your Mum normally cook things from scratch rather than get anything processed in?'

BENJAMIN: 'Yeah, unless it's, like, we've got, I've got to rush to football and she'll get, she'll have a pizza or something warm afterwards, I expect'.

Parents offered pizza as a (fast) food that they perceived children liked and would eat without creating a 'fuss' ('I mean they all like pizza, don't they?' (Leah's mum)). Pizza was perceived as 'children's food', as food that is bland and would not be chosen by parents themselves.

INTERVIEWER: 'Do you think her friends have similar tastes to her or are they different?

JUDITH'S MUM: 'I think...I think most of them would be like her, I think most of them like their bland food or this cheese pizza with nothing on it or...you know, just 'I don't like salad, I don't like vegetables' that sort of thing'.

By offering pizza parents also fostered the idea in children that food is not just about what parents want and that parents are capable of compromise and balance. However, it could be argued that offering pizza also created a hierarchical and generational distinction in consumption and reminded children who was in charge (see Chapter 2 by James, Curtis and Ellis in this volume). Teenagers in the study could not, for example, get pizza on demand at home; the offer of pizza was strictly controlled and regulated by parents, which perhaps simultaneously served to set it up both as 'special' food and a food that parents considered inferior. Many teenagers reported that pizza was routinely offered when they brought friends home to eat with them:

> '[My friends'] parents don't make similar food to what I have made at home but they make similar food to what my parents'll make when I've got a friend coming round 'cause it's kind of … you need to make something that you know that they'll eat. So it's like pasta or pizza – kind of more basic things rather than like really spicy stuff like that'. (Alan)

> 'Some days when I have friends over, because mum doesn't know what they would like to eat so she makes them like pizza or lasagne or something'. (Rachel)

The consumption of pizza at home raises the notion that fast food is for children not adults and that parents 'other' children (their own and other people's) by occasionally offering food not regularly eaten by the family. Offering 'children's food' did not extend to regularly serving burgers or chips, however. There is therefore something 'about' pizza that makes this an acceptable fast food for children, even when children themselves would prefer not to eat it:

> 'I don't like it, it just gets a bit annoying after a wee while,… I do like the carry-outs, it's just you get like pizza or fish and chips like every week [at her Gran's house] so … and you can't exactly say 'no' to it anyway'. (Fiona)

The costs of consumption: Social contexts and 'fitting in'

Young people are known to be savvy consumers, particularly at school, in terms of wanting value for money and not wanting to queue to buy food (Wills et al. 2005; Scottish Consumer Council 2008). All the teenagers interviewed had their own money, either as pocket money, money from parents specifically to buy lunch/food or, occasionally, money earned from part time jobs (like a paper round). None of the teenagers said that high street food outlets and fast food restaurants were inaccessible in terms of being located too far from school or home (though some said the choice of outlets was limited). Indeed, one teenager reported that his friend took a taxi from school to the high street at lunchtime to ensure he could purchase the food he wanted in the time available. Young people reflected on their position as consumers, with some reporting that the perceived 'healthier' options, like ready-made sandwiches and fruit, were expensive and therefore not as attractive as buying chips, or hot pies from the local bakery, for example. Using a discourse of affordability therefore allowed many teenagers to 'authorise' their fast food choices:

> 'it's cheaper to buy rubbish to eat than it is to buy healthy stuff and if you don't have like a lot of money, like at lunch times and stuff it's better to go and get like a chippy or something for £1 than it is to go and buy like a fruit salad or something'. (Judith)

> 'like O'Briens [a chain of sandwich shops] is quite a healthy place for sandwiches and things but it's really expensive to go there but going to the chippy, a bag of chips is like £1 so they [teenagers] want to spend as less as possible'. (Isobel)

Teenagers are often reported as being influenced to perform or undertake specific practices if their close friends are known or perceived to be doing so (Pavis et al. 1998). That is not to say that children are directly influenced (in terms of 'peer pressure') but, often, friends from similar backgrounds are minded to take up a particular behaviour so there is collective complicity once a practice has been initiated. Certainly several teenagers in this study indicated that they had started to shop for fast food during school once their friends had expressed a desire to do so.[8] The pull of spending time with friends and fitting in with peer groups was strong for many teenagers during this unsupervised part of the school day. Many said they had to juggle the need to eat and the desire to spend time with friends into the school lunch break (typically 50–60 minutes long). Drew and his friends, for example, had changed where they bought lunch so that they could play football for longer:

DREW:	'We…we used to always go down to em…the Co-op or…Subway [sandwich chain] or Gregg's [bakery and sandwich chain]'
INTERVIEWER:	'And what changed, why did you start going to [place name] instead?'
DREW:	'Cause it was closer and we had longer time to play football. And everyone else went down town and we had more time to play football on our own before they all come up and start playing'.

Being with friends sometimes created a dilemma or tension, however, if fast food was not something that one or more people in a friendship group wanted to eat.

INTERVIEWER: 'Like when you go down [town] for school lunches do you go with a group of people or is it just...?'

FIONA: 'Yeah. Six or seven...mainly girls...they usually just go down town with me, then we split up, they go to the chippy and pizza shop and all that.'

INTERVIEWER: 'Okay, all right (laughs). So are you the only one that gets stuff in [the bakers] or are there others...?'

FIONA: 'There's a couple of folk but that's about it'.

INTERVIEWER: 'And is there any reason why you prefer that than like the chippy or...?'

FIONA: 'Yeah. Because it's like fatty stuff and it's minging [Scottish word meaning 'disgusting'] (laughs)'.

INTERVIEWER: 'And what about your friends, do they like eating similar food to you or are they quite different?'

BLAIR: '[Laughs] Well, most do but they don't like when I want to go to McDonald's and they're like 'oh no, I can't go there, it's too bad for you'. But er, I'm always willing to go there. And they do like all sorts of foods I like, yeah' [...]

INTERVIEWER: 'And what do you think about that when they're kind of saying that...?'

BLAIR: 'I – I don't really mind 'cause I know it's not very good for you but I just think it tastes better. So I'll just go with whatever they want, really.'

The ways in which teenagers negotiated with their friends, whether to eat or not eat fast food, illustrates the importance of 'belonging', of finding a way to remain connected to the group whilst not compromising or pushing the boundaries of the habitus too far beyond an individual's comfort zone. Most teenagers presented this negotiation as something with which they were fairly comfortable; there were no instances when participants expressed great distress about having to 'give in' or persuade others that their consumption practices were somehow better or preferable. This is in contrast with working-class teenagers who often reported being very uncomfortable with the choices of others or feeling excluded from a friendship group and eating alone (see Wills et al. 2005).

Teenagers, particularly working-class teenagers, are often reported as spending time in the local neighbourhood in the evening, this being a time when many try out practices and behaviours with peers, away from the parental gaze (MacDonald et al. 2005). This is a period when 'lifestyles' develop and friendships are forged (or fought over) over a drink (Wills 2005a), a cigarette (Pavis et al. 1998) or a bag of chips (Wills et al. 2008). Social class is embedded in these lifestyle practices just as being middle class underpinned the social contexts in which these teenagers described themselves as participating. It was the rare middle-class teenager who said he/she went out completely unsupervised in the evening and few reported spending any unstructured time with friends after school. This period was devoted, mainly, to extracurricular activities, particularly sporting or physical activities. If fast food was eaten, this was explained as being because it was practical or convenient and was intended to replace an evening meal that had been missed.

> I used to have chips a lot more when I did hockey 'cause we would get chips at, 'cause it finished late and we'd just go down and get chips most of the time but er sometimes, er, but I joined rugby now so it's changed. (Stephen)

EMILY: 'Tuesday I have 3 dance classes on so I am there for most of the night actually I get back at, not 'til like 10, which isn't too good, but erm, then Friday I get my own private ballet lesson for an hour'.

INTERVIEWER: 'So on those days when you are going to dance, when would you normally eat your tea?'

EMILY: 'Erm, I have, well I have a snack on the train up, just like an apple and something like that and then on the way back, er coming back in the car, we stop off somewhere and get something, take... sometimes we go to Marks and Spencer's on the way and pick up a sandwich, or other times if we didn't have time to do that we'd have to have MacDonald's, which isn't too good'.

Whilst these teenagers reported less autonomy throughout the week than was described by those from working class families (Wills et al. 2008), it seems that there was a shift towards less structured activities at the weekend. Weekends were a time when teenagers were (sometimes) able to plan their own time, to sleep in on a Saturday, for example, prepare their own lunch at home or spend time with friends. It was not always clear what parents or siblings were doing during this time or how these more autonomous practices had evolved or been negotiated within families. However, at this stage of the life course greater reflexivity and democratisation (Solomon et al. 2002; Williams and Williams 2005) would be expected within families to acknowledge the dynamic identity-making work that teenagers undertake at this time. When teenagers were consuming fast food at the weekend it was usually with their friends. Few, however, talked about enjoying this food and, indeed, many were critical of the food on offer to them and their friends. We turn now to explore discourses relating to taste, ethics and nutrition and the particular distinctions of being a middle-class child.

Discerning consumption and nutritional discourses

The recent turn towards asking children about their own lives means we know relatively little about the nuanced aspects of children's preferences and attitudes to everyday food and eating practices. We found, however, that teenagers were often happy to express their opinions about fast food and were reflective about the taste, perceived poor quality and nutritional status of some fast food.

> If you've got more money you can afford to like go somewhere nicer and it's usually better for you. Like because I like to go to Starbucks but it's quite expensive because like what they sell is quite good but like McDonalds is quite cheap just because it's like not very good quality. (Anna)

These perceptions very often reflected parents' attitudes to fast food or were indicative of the social and cultural capital of the family. Rather than indicating that children are merely cultural (or familial) dupes, however, we take this to indicate that middle-class teenagers' practices and perceptions are firmly embedded according to the family habitus. Children's consumption practices, even when outside the home, are relational to those of the family. Isobel, for example, was typical of several teenagers who had their own thoughts about why they did not like eating at some fast food restaurants but these opinions were integrated with the knowledge that parents did not approve of the consumption of 'unhealthy' food (see Chapter 4 by Dryden et al. in this volume). There was, therefore, a 'fit' between children's own moral discourse and that of their parents:

> INTERVIEWER: 'Okay and you know with your friends, do you
>   ever eat together with them?'

ISOBEL:	'We go sometimes for meals, like maybe up town somewhere to a restaurant but yeah we do eat quite a lot together....We go to Jimmy Chung's, the Chinese food restaurant and they tend to go to McDonalds quite a lot but I really don't like McDonalds (laughs)'
INTERVIEWER:	'Okay and what is it that you don't like about McDonalds?'
ISOBEL:	'Well you hear a lot of stories about like mistreatment of animals and things and I just...my mum tells me it's really unhealthy...and the film "Supersize Me" as well, it really just put me off it (laughs)'.
INTERVIEWER:	'So is your mum not keen on you going to eat there then?'
ISOBEL:	'No, no, not at all'.

Some teenagers did, however, have strategies to resist the predominant, nutritional discourse, finding ways to 'sneak' (see extract from Natasha, below) fast food into their diet. Many, though, said they felt guilty about this practice, or anxious that they were not eating healthily. Natasha went on to say that eating at McDonald's made her feel 'yucky':

INTERVIEWER:	'Okay and do you ever have like McDonald's or KFC or chippies?'
NATASHA:	'I'm not allowed McDonald's.'
INTERVIEWER:	'Okay so you're not allowed that at all?'
NATASHA:	'No but I sometimes sneak it, like Monday I had one but I've not had it in years.'
INTERVIEWER:	'So when you sneak it, where do you go and get it?'
NATASHA:	'When I'm in Edinburgh with my friends and they do go there for lunch'.
INTERVIEWER:	'Okay so would you ever tell your mum that you'd had a McDonald's?'
NATASHA:	'Not really, just say I've had a sandwich or something'.

Many teenagers, however, seemed to value being able to spend this time with friends at the weekend, more than the simply the opportunity to 'eat out'. Thus, the consumption of readily available fast food did not, in itself, seem to contribute as much to these middle-class teenagers' identities as did this unsupervised time with peers. Nonetheless, by visiting Starbucks, or other coffee shops and cafés, some teenagers were able to spend time with friends whilst being somewhere that was perceived as selling better quality food (though this often came at a higher price), thereby not contravening their own or their parent's values about 'healthy' food:

> INTERVIEWER: 'So what kind of things do you like to do together with your friends?'
>
> JESSICA: 'Well we just go into town and go shopping, sometimes we do like alternative stuff, like go to the cinema or erm like Dynamic Earth or Edinburgh Dungeons, but it tends just to be into town and meet and just sit in Starbucks'.
>
> 'Erm, well, like the [restaurant] would probably be like £6 for like erm, a drink and like a baguette with chips, but erm, [the café] would be like just a couple of pounds for like a panini or something'. (Penny)

Conclusion

Whilst it has been suggested that self-identity is increasingly based and built upon individualised choices rather than restricted by class boundaries or a classed habitus, these middle-class teenagers' accounts suggest that this is not the case in relation to the perceptions and consumption of fast food. Many teenagers were not making purely personal choices to eat or not eat fast food. Their decisions and the restrictions that they placed on their own consumption of fast food were underpinned by values and discourses that reflected (middle-class) parental expectations about food and eating and these were different to the discourses and expectations of working-class parents and teenagers (Backett-Milburn et al. 2006; Wills et al. 2008). We found limited evidence that middle-class teenagers had fragmented self-identities, (what Denscombe refers to as 'multiple mes' (Denscombe 2001:160) in terms of expressing desires or exhibiting practices which differed greatly in one setting compared with another (being at home versus being with peers, for example). There was, overall, a fairly close 'fit' between teenagers' own desired eating habits, including when outside the home and when consumption was under the more direct surveillance of parents. Indeed, it was interesting to note that parents offered, and children accepted (or even asked for), pizza at home, despite many teenagers not appearing to enjoy eating such food.

It seems, therefore, that *avoiding* rather than consuming fast food was a central aspect of middle-class young teenagers' identity-making work. In addition, many teenagers wanted to avoid particular fast food establishments because they were perceived as offering poor quality or ethically questionable food. Teenagers were able to assert their identity by making a stand but were also able to fit in with peer groups by negotiating where food was eaten and giving in to friends' preferences on some occasions. Young people's social ease and confidence at expressing opinions is perhaps connected with the importance that middle-class parents place on improving children's life chances through enhanced social and educational opportunities (Sullivan 2007; Vincent and Ball 2007). Such opportunities that working-class parents are less able to access and less likely to prioritise because of the need to cope with the more pressing and challenging realities presented by working-class lifestyles (Backett-Milburn et al. 2006).

Teenagers' avoidance of fast food is also aided by the 'busyness' of being a middle-class child. All participants were taking part in regular, structured activities after school (and sometimes at weekends too) which meant there was less time available for 'hanging out' with friends after school, a time when working-class teenagers regularly consumed fast food (Wills et al. 2008). By promoting and nurturing improvements in social and cultural capital middle-class parents are therefore, albeit inadvertently, aiding the consumption of a diet low in quantities of fast food. This complements the overt direction that parents gave to their teenagers about the need to eat healthily and to restrict their consumption of fast food. Most teenagers expressed awareness of, and said they wanted to implement, the nutritional discourse put forward by parents. Indeed, many young people, when asked what they wanted to change about their diets stated reducing the amount of 'fatty' fast food that they ate, even though such consumption was infrequent. This desire to avoid fast food seems partly driven by shame and guilt; whether such emotions are conducive to middle-class teenagers' well-being, beyond (sometimes) achieving dietary perfection, is thus worthy of exploration. A preoccupation with achieving a 'good diet' reflects a middle-class disposition for being 'health conscious' and for taking on board 'authentic' health and dietary messages, that is, those sanctioned by (government) experts. By wishing to avoid fast food teenagers are also therefore maintaining the distinction of being 'other', that is, different from those who more frequently eat in fast food restaurants (i.e., the working classes).

Notes

1. We are defining fast food here as food that is usually high in fat and/or salt, for example, burgers, pizza and chips. We are also defining, except where we state otherwise, that fast food is purchased – cooked and ready to eat – either to be taken away and eaten elsewhere or to be eaten on-site, for example, in McDonalds restaurants. We are using the term 'fast food' rather than 'junk food' as we are not including in our discussion consumption of 'snack' foods like crisps or chocolate.
2. Warde does however state that the young are also among the least likely to make 'mistakes', not being highly exposed to opportunities for stepping outside the 'boundaries' of acceptable consumption (Warde 1994).
3. See Backett-Milburn et al. (2006) for a discussion of working-class families and their priorities for themselves and their children and the role that health/diet plays in their lives.
4. By 'publicly recognised' we mean the kind of dietary regime favoured by 'experts'. 'Health conscious' individuals are more likely to favour such validated practices (Fisher 2008).
5. The study was funded by the Economic and Social Research Council (Ref: RES000231504) in 2006–2008.
6. (Wills 2005b; Wills et al. 2005; Backett-Milburn et al. 2006; Wills et al. 2006, 2008).
7. We chose teenagers where at least one parent's occupation was reported to be in class 1 or 2 of the NS-SEC (Office of National Statistics, 2004). Family affluence was ascertained from positive responses to two items adapted from the Family Affluence Scale (Currie 1997) – whether the teenager had their own bedroom and whether the family had at least one holiday in the past year. Deprivation was assessed using the 2001 Carstairs scores for Scottish postcode sectors (McClone 2004) with households falling into the least deprived quintile being eligible for interview. As an additional check, we also looked at the Scottish Index of Deprivation (see http://www.scotland.gov.uk/News/Releases/2006/10/17104536).
8. We asked young people to tell us about their friends and whether they had similar habits and lifestyles to them; we found little evidence that the participating teenagers were mixing with peers from very different backgrounds.

References

Albon, D. J. (2005). 'Approaches to the study of children, food and sweet eating: A review of the literature'. *Early Child Development and Care* 175(5):407–417.
Backett-Milburn, K., Wills, W. J., Gregory, S. & Lawton, J. (2006). 'Making sense of eating, weight and risk in the early teenage years: Views and concerns of

parents in poorer socio-economic circumstances'. *Social Science & Medicine* 63(3):624–635.

Bourdieu, P. (1984). *Distinction: A Social Critique of the Judgement of Taste*. London: Routledge and Kegan Paul.

Bourdieu, P. (1990). *The Logic of Practice*. Cambridge: Polity Press.

Carrigan, M. (2006). 'Managing routine food choices in UK families: The role of convenience consumption'. *Appetite* 47:372–383.

Crawford, R. (2006). 'Health as a meaningful social practice'. *Health: An Interdisciplinary Journal for the Social Study of Health, Illness and Medicine* 10(4):401–420.

Currie, C., Elton, R., Todd, J. & Platt, S. (1997). 'Indicators of socioeconomic status for adolescents: The WHO health behaviour in school-aged children survey'. *Health Education Research* 12:385–397.

Daily Mail (2008). 'Police offer teenagers junk food for good behaviour'. http://www.dailymail.co.uk/news/article-1038454/Police-bribe-teenagers-junk-food-good-behaviour.html.

Denscombe, M. (2001). 'Uncertain identities and health-risking behaviour: The case of young people and smoking in late modernity'. *British Journal of Sociology* 52(1):157–177.

Fisher, F. (2008). 'Wellbeing and empowerment: The importance of recognition'. *Sociology of Health & Illness* 30(4):583–598.

Henderson, L., Gregory, J. & Swann, G. (2002). *The National Diet and Nutrition Survey: Adults aged 19 to 64 years*. London: Office for National Statistics.

James, A. (1990). 'The good, the bad and the delicious: The role of confectionery in British society'. *Sociological Review* 38(4):666–688.

James, A., Jenks, C. & Prout, A. (1998).*Theorizing Childhood*. Cambridge: Polity Press.

Joint Health Surveys Unit, National Centre for Social Research & University College London (2003). *Health Survey for England: Key Findings*. London: Department of Health.

MacDonald, R., Shildrick, T., Webster, C. & Simpson, D. (2005). 'Growing up in poor neighbourhoods: The significance of class and place in the extended transitions of "socially excluded" young adults'. *Sociology* 39(5):873–891.

Marten, L. & Warde, A. (1997). 'Urban pleasure? On the meaning of eating out in a northern city', in Caplan, P. (ed.), *Food Health and Identity*. London: Routledge.

Martens, L., Southerton, D. & Scott, S. (2004). 'Bringing children (and parents) into the sociology of consumption: Towards a theoretical and empirical agenda'. *Journal of Consumer Culture* 4(2):155–182.

McClone, P. (2004). *Carstairs Scores for Scottish Postcode Sectors from the 2001 Census*. Glasgow: MRC Social and Public Health Sciences Unit.

Miles, S., Cliff, D. & Burr, V. (1998). ' "Fitting in and sticking out": Consumption, consumer meanings and the construction of young people's identities'. *Journal of Youth Studies* 1(1):81–96.

Pavis, S., Cunningham-Burley, S. & Amos, A. (1998). 'Health related behavioural change in context: young people in transition'. *Social Science and Medicine* 47(10):1407–1418.

Sayer, A. (2005). 'Class, moral worth and recognition'. *Sociology* 39(5):947–963.

Scottish Consumer Council (2008). *Out to Lunch?* Glasgow: Scottish Consumer Council.

Solomon, Y., Warin, J., Lewis, C. & Langford, W. (2002). 'Intimate talk between parents and their teenage children: Democratic openness or covert control?' *Sociology* 36(4):965–983.

Sullivan, A. (2007). 'Cultural capital, cultural knowledge and ability' *Sociological Research Online* 12(6).

Sweetman, P. (2003). 'Twenty-first century dis-ease? Habitual reflexivity or the reflexive habitus'. *The Sociological Review* 51(4):528–549.

Valentine, G. (1999). 'Eating in home, consumption and identity'. *The Sociological Review* 47(3): 491–524.

Vincent, C. & Ball, S. J. (2007). ' "Making up" the middle-class child: Families, activities and class dispositions'. *Sociology* 41(6):1061–1077.

Warde, A. (1994). 'Consumption, identity formation and uncertainty'. *Sociology* 28(4):877–898.

Williams, J. (1997). ' "We never eat like this at home" Food on Holiday', in Caplan, P. (ed.), *Food Health and Identity*. London: Routledge.

Williams, S. (1995). 'Theorising class, health and lifestyles: Can Bourdieu help us?'. *Sociology of Health and Illness* 17(5):577–604.

Williams, S. & Williams, L. (2005). 'Space invaders: The negotiation of teenage boundaries through the mobile phone'. *The Sociological Review* 53(2):314–331.

Wills, W. J. (2005a). 'Food and eating practices during the transition from secondary school to new social contexts'. *Journal of Youth Studies* 8(1):97–110.

Wills, W. J. (2005b). *Food, Eating, Health and Fatness: the Perceptions and Experiences of Young Teenagers from disadvantaged Families*. Edinburgh: RUHBC, University of Edinburgh.

Wills, W. J., Backett-Milburn, K., Gregory, S. & Lawton, J. (2005). 'The influence of the secondary school setting on the food practices of young teenagers from disadvantaged backgrounds in Scotland'. *Health Education Research* 20(4):458–465.

Wills, W. J., Backett-Milburn, K., Gregory, S. & Lawton, J. (2006). 'Young teenagers' perceptions of their own and others' bodies: a qualitative study of obese, overweight and "normal" weight young people in Scotland'. *Social Science & Medicine* 62(2):396–406.

Wills, W. J., Backett-Milburn, K., Gregory, S. & Lawton, J. (2008). 'If the food looks dodgy I dinnae eat it': Teenagers' accounts of food and eating practices in socio-economically disadvantaged families'. *Sociological Research Online* 13(1).

4
Picturing the Lunchbox: Children Drawing and Talking about 'Dream' and 'Nightmare' Lunchboxes in the Primary School Setting

Caroline Dryden, Alan Metcalfe, Jenny Owen, Geraldine Shipton

Introduction

The question of what children eat at school, and how they eat, has attracted increasing attention in the United Kingdom in recent years, and this interest has intensified recently with evidence of rising levels of childhood obesity. In this chapter, we want to contribute to the debate about children and food (and we should emphasise here that we are defining food in its broadest terms from chocolate to sandwiches), reporting on some of the findings from an ethnographic research initiative related to food practices in the school setting. As part of a wider study concerning fatherhood, food and family life, we spent some time talking with children during school dinnertimes, and inviting them to draw and comment on 'dream' and 'nightmare' lunchboxes, during classroom-based arts activities, in order to explore their own ideas about food and eating.[1] These children were aged between nine and eleven: old enough to exercise a degree of autonomy in terms of what they ate, where and how – even if only by discarding or exchanging their lunchbox or dinner tray contents – and yet still firmly held within the gaze of teachers, parents and other caregivers. Envisaging 'dream' and 'nightmare' lunchboxes thus represented a rare opportunity for the children to freely express their ideas.

We begin by outlining our starting points as members of an interdisciplinary research team with common interests in researching children's perspectives on food and family practices. We then go on to discuss two particular aspects of our analysis of children's pictures and accompanying commentaries. First, we explore the ways in which children actively play with and incorporate 'brand' images into their constructions and representations of identity. Second, in explaining their food choices, we show how children mobilise contrasting discourses: some reflecting notions of individual consumer choice and others ascribing strong moral connotations to particular foods. In conclusion, we raise some questions for future consideration arising from these findings.

Starting points

As a team, we draw on backgrounds in sociology, social psychology, psychoanalysis and geography. We share a view of children as social beings who are experts in their own lives, with the capacity to engage actively and critically in research processes, as in other forms of social interaction. At the same time, our perspective draws on psychoanalytic and critical-discursive ideas about the psyche and human interaction. For us, the individual is 'always already social' (Henriques et al. 1984) and identity needs to be understood as thoroughly social in nature. Identities, in this perspective, are viewed as produced *through* situated social interaction (e.g., see Wetherell 1998; Frosh et al. 2003; Dryden et al. forthcoming). Work in ethnomethodology and in discursive psychology has highlighted ways in which identities can be shaped and re-shaped through interaction. From this perspective, therefore, school food practices – of which those associated with the lunchbox and its contents are our particular focus here – offer a route through which to interrogate processes of identity formation and management, and the ways in which these interact with specific contexts in children's lives.

The school lunchbox in children's lives: Themes in recent research

Julian Baggini recently suggested that the English conception of 'the good life' places a heavy emphasis on convenience, and underlined the ubiquity of the 'packed lunch' in this context:

> The national dish of England is often said to be chicken tikka masala, but, in fact, the meal most people eat almost every day is the packed lunch. No Soviet-style central state government could impose uniformity more effectively. The core of this meal is a sandwich, preferably filled with some form of cheese or ham, and a packet of crisps…the health-conscious go for wholemeal bread and may swap

crisps or chocolate for yoghurt and an extra piece of fruit. But the basic formula is the same all over the country. (Baggini 2007:118–119)

In relation to children in the United Kingdom, both packed lunches and cooked dinners provided by schools have become the object of increasing public scrutiny – and formal regulation, in some respects – in recent years (see Chapter 9 by Tingstad in this volume for a discussion of the Norwegian context). The proportion of children up to age 11 who eat packed lunches rather than school dinners varies between schools. For example, a recent survey of 151 primary schools found that, on average, 42% of children took a school meal, with most others bringing a packed lunch rather than returning home to eat (Nelson et al. 2005). The food industry clearly engages with children as active consumers in this context, for example through the marketing of specific commodities and spaces as 'for children' (see Cook 2003 and Chapter 6 in this volume). 'Playful' items such as cheese strings, 'easy peeler' fruit, sweetened drinks and brightly packaged yoghurts are marketed as snack and lunch items for children, along with a range of specifically branded and designed containers (of which more later). Some recent research suggests, however, that children still perceive their food choices to be heavily dominated by adults, in general (Robinson 2000). Nonetheless, with specific reference to packed lunches, almost a quarter of the children interviewed for another study felt that they had considerable control over the selection of contents (Douglas 1999). However, these research findings predate the current generation of UK government policies on healthy eating guidelines, within schools and more generally.

Turning to more recent research about food consumption in the school setting, we find a somewhat polarised picture. On the one hand, there is an increasing body of work that makes concerns with health its starting point, often drawing on public health or other applied policy perspectives, and taking many aspects of the distinction between 'healthy' and 'unhealthy' food for granted. Rogers et al. (2007), for example, compared school dinners and packed lunches in nutritional terms. They found that both types of meals commonly failed to match up to current UK healthy eating guidelines, for instance in terms of recommended levels of fruit and vegetables, but that packed lunches were distinctly lower in nutritional range and quality. Warren et al. (2008) examined primary school students' own views about food choices, finding a general preference for 'unhealthy' items such as crisps and pizza. Children in that study attached a strong premium to being able to make personal choices, felt that they did have a substantial degree of choice, and were well aware of current distinctions between 'healthy' and 'unhealthy' foods. In some cases, for example, they described themselves as balancing an 'unhealthy' food choice with a compensatory strategy, such as taking more exercise or eating extra fruit. In studies of this kind, therefore, food (and some aspects of food practices) are sharply in focus, but the wider context – including the changing social meanings attached to specific food practices – have receded somewhat into the distance.

At the other end of the spectrum are studies that note the rather belated recognition of children and childhood within the sociology of consumption, and argue for their inclusion in examinations of aspects of material culture – 'the relationship between people and things' (Martens et al. 2004:171) – including food practices. Valentine (2000), for example, carried out a study in a secondary school and mapped a change in the 'narratives of identity' through which children are positioned in relation to adults, via food practices in the school setting. The provision of school meals in England originated in the 1906 Education Act, as part of a range of policies designed to combat poverty, with the emphasis on a 'civilising' approach to table manners, as well as on the provision of physically nourishing, cooked meals. In this context, children were positioned as vulnerable, dependent and in need of both control and protection. By 1980, a new Education Act had loosened controls over schools, removing the requirement to offer a cooked midday meal and paving the way for cafeteria-style options, often provided by commercial contractors. In the context of pressures to limit public spending and introduce 'quasi-market' structures and values, children were addressed as individual agents: knowledgeable consumers entitled to choose from the menu (however limited or shaped this might be, by forces external to the school). Valentine finds the school's food practices to be an arena in which personal choice and flexibility are emphasised, embodying 'principles that owe more to equality and dissolving divisions between adults and children, than hierarchy or deference' (Valentine 2000:259). This perspective helps us to develop a more critical understanding of schools and food practices, but still leaves us needing to know more about children's own perceptions of food practices, particularly about the experiences of those younger than Valentine's teenage participants.

Earlier ethnographic studies by Mauthner et al. (1993) and Burgess and Morrison (1998) do offer some insights into the experiences of younger children. Findings from children's diaries, sorting and drawing activities and researcher observations included examples of primary school children exchanging snack and packed lunch items as part of establishing or maintaining friendships – showing, among other things, how tenuous any direct adult influence over food intake may become in the school setting. Both studies also noted the ways in which dinnertime has become 'part of a pupil-processing system' in some schools (Burgess and Morrison 1998), with pressures to 'eat up' before the next sitting. Some studies have also indicated that lunchboxes may attract unwanted attention, not only from dining-hall supervisors but also more importantly from peers, including actual or anticipated ridicule. Murcott (1997), for instance, found instances of children whose lunchboxes contained only bread and margarine, and who felt unable to open them in front of peers with more generous provision. More recent developments in school policy concerning packed lunches, at a local level, have included attempts to ban items such as chocolate, sweets and fizzy drinks. Occasionally this has resulted in a child being excluded from the dinner hall: for example, in 2006, the BBC reported an instance in which a school in Kent obliged a child to eat his dinner away from other children because 'a lunch was brought in which was not in keeping with our new guidelines…the pupil was given the chance to have his dinner outside the hall with supervision.' (BBC News, 13/10/06: 'pupil banished over "snack quota"').

About the study

As noted at the outset, the research upon which this chapter draws focuses on children's drawings and, as Malchiodi (1998) suggests, drawing can provide a window into a child's preoccupations and passions. It is an activity in which children readily engage and is generally experienced as enjoyable (Hill 2006). Other researchers (e.g., see James 1990) have also used this method to good effect, and have argued that children's drawings can be linked to, for example, cultural roots (Kline 1993), and to social practices and media preferences (La Ville 2004) in our 'media rich' UK society (Buckingham 2002). More generally, in sociology and critical psychology, there is a growing trend towards incorporating the visual as part of research endeavour – given the growing realisation that, with adults as well as children, transcribed talk can only ever give a partial understanding of complex social processes (Henwood et al. 2008).

Our aim, therefore, was to invite children to draw pictures of lunchboxes in class, and to comment on their drawings as they produced them. More specifically, we invited children to draw either a 'dream' or a 'nightmare' lunchbox image. By doing this, we aimed to give children a lot of flexibility in the way they interpreted the task, and to make it fun. We also wanted to use the task as a focus for eliciting children's verbal as well as pictorial sense-making about food, without imposing too rigid a framework. However, in choosing the wording for this task, we were also aware that use of the terms 'dream' and 'nightmare' could be seen to conjure up undertones of the contemporary, adult-defined, debate around morality and food (e.g., see Lupton 1996). We needed, therefore, to recognise that our research was itself, in an important sense, part of the social context we were trying to understand when we came to analyse our data.

A total of 156 primary school children, ages nine to eleven, took part, from four schools in three contrasting neighbourhoods. Christopher Street Primary is an inner-city school in a large Yorkshire city; its intake is very diverse in terms of ethnicity, religion, parental education levels and incomes. Vale Primary, in a former mining village in Yorkshire, has a more homogenous intake: most local families are white, either Christian or non-religious, and are living on lower than average incomes. Finally, in rural Lancashire, Netherhope and Upperhope are two small schools situated in villages ten miles apart. These serve a largely professional and highly educated population, which is almost exclusively white. A small number of families in both areas are still employed in agriculture. The researcher was a white male who also talked to the children about what they were drawing and (where parental permission was given) recorded their conversations. We obtained 203 pictures in all: at least one drawing from each child who participated and, in some cases, two. (Although children were asked to draw either a dream or a nightmare box, some drew both).

Children's approach to the task

Children entered into the 'dream and nightmare' activity with considerable energy and imagination, indicating that they did enjoy taking part. Their interpretations were diverse: for example, some drew pictures that represented the decorations on the outside of a lunchbox; some invented imaginative lunchbox designs; some depicted the contents of a lunchbox in detail (food items, but sometimes also other items such as people, cars, animals and monsters). However, whichever way children interpreted and approached the task, it quickly became obvious that this food-related task *in itself* presented them with an excellent opportunity for exploring versions of social identities for themselves through their interaction with the researcher and each other. As we argue below, children are by no means simply passive recipients of advertising and branding. Rather, they actively mobilise, play with or subvert such images in the process of doing identity work. Secondly, however, although children's active engagement with the commercial dimensions of food marketing and consumption can be viewed with some relief, our data do, nonetheless, give clear evidence of more subtle ways in which ideas about choice, individualism and morality pervade talk about food, even amongst nine to eleven year olds (see Chapter 9 by Tingstad and Chapter 6 by Cook in this volume). We expand on these points below.

Lunchbox pictures and social identity work

Analysis of children's discussions about their drawings quickly revealed that the dominant forms of identity work elicited by the exercise revolved around gender and age. So, for example, in the following extract the researcher is asking one child, Sukira, to describe her lunchbox picture (reproduced in Figure 4.1). Sukira provides a 'girly' construction of her self through the explanation of her picture, and is further identified in these gendered terms through her friend Elly's interjection:

INTERVIEWER: Tell me about the cover
SUKIRA: [laughs]
INTERVIEWER: 'On your way to 5 a day' and 'Sukira's lunchbox'.
SUKIRA: Yeah
INTERVIEWER: Ok
SUKIRA: And that's me with my crown on
INTERVIEWER: Ah, so you're a princess?
SUKIRA: Yeah.
ELLY: You're like Barbie.

As can be seen here, children often invoked brands, logos or characters from popular culture when fashioning identities for themselves. Others have pointed to the role of brands as badges or placeholders for identity building (e.g., see Thorne 2005, discussed in Nukaga 2008; Chaplin & John 2005). In her lunchbox drawing, Sukira has picked up on the public health slogan '5 a day';[2] she has also selected specific brands of chocolate – 'Snickers' and M & Ms' – as she goes on to explain to the interviewer. In amongst these branded items is a clear focus of identification for Sukira, as the 'princess' wearing a crown. Her friend Elly rounds off the conversation by likening Sukira to Barbie.

In another extract, however, we can see how characters from popular culture can also be used as an object for identification through

Figure 4.1 'Girl with crown' lunch-box picture

distancing oneself, rather than asserting similarity. Here, a boy clearly locates the 'girly' Barbie figure as 'other':

DAVID: And in my nightmare, I done like a Barbie girl ont'
                   front and it says Barbie.
INTERVIEWER: And it says 'boo' again.
DAVID: Yeah. And I don't like it being written inside, or
                   I don't want Barbie milk or worm sandwich or

Barbie bar, or I don't want a Barbie doll or I don't want it to say Barbie really.

Barbie, being read as a symbol of femininity here, is something that this boy can have fun describing but something that he can simultaneously make clear is nothing like the way he wants to be! For David, a discourse of hegemonic masculinity clearly provides an unconscious system of accountability here: he is socially 'accountable' for distancing himself from identification with this girlie image, or else risking the threat of loss of face (Goffman 1972; Dryden et al. forthcoming). Reciprocally, in distancing, he can fashion a masculine identity for himself through placing Barbie in his nightmare box, along with a worm sandwich. In the same way, other boys also used 'girly' icons and images, such as Barbie and Bratz, to signify what would be a girl's box and therefore a nightmare for a boy to possess.

Lunchbox manufacturers commonly use cartoon characters and well-known toy images to adorn the real thing, and so it is not surprising to find images such as 'Barbie' alongside a '5-a-day' slogan on an imagined lunchbox. Nor is it surprising that little boys might want to distance themselves from such a 'hyper-girly' image. However, our analysis also highlighted clearly the way in which children's use of brands was anything but passive and – from a commercial point of view – it is also easy to see how the status of a brand could be very fragile or changeable. So, for example, some girls wanted to make clear that they did not view Barbie as something to identify with at all (or expressed ambivalence), as can be seen in the following discussion about another 'nightmare' lunchbox:

INTERVIEWER: You don't like Barbie
APRIL: No
INTERVIEWER: reading from April's picture] 'I am a Barbie girl in a Barbie world.'
APRIL: That's the song
INTERVIEWER: So are these nightmare lunchboxes then?
APRIL: Yeah. [inaudible] and there's like Coke, bubble gum and Mars bar.
INTERVIEWER: You don't like them then?
APRIL: I like coke but it gets me hyper.
INTERVIEWER: And do you never eat Mars bars? So what do you like then?
APRIL: Galaxy
INTERVIEWER: So who's this then, is that you?

APRIL:	That's Barbie girl
INTERVIEWER:	And what's this?
APRIL:	a lipstick and a bag.
INTERVIEWER:	So what's so bad about Barbie?
APRIL:	It's too babyish
INTERVIEWER:	Ah I see. And have you got some Barbie at home?
APRIL:	No

Clearly, in amongst the discussion of food brands such as Coke and Mars Bars, age is a factor shaping the identity work going on here. Barbie is becoming problematic for April, who does not want to identify as 'childish'. For her, Barbie obviously has childish connotations; her distancing comments are used as a mechanism for teenage rather than child identification – or to put it another way, for 'doing growing up'.

In a related way, *failing to distance* could, in this context, be conceived as a failure to 'do growing up' and therefore, to remain 'childish'. Ambivalence concerning the meaning of icons such as Barbie – and the pleasure that can be gained from such toys – could also be seen to fuel some of this interaction. For example, the above dialogue continues with a second child entering into the conversation as follows:-

INTERVIEWER:	Ah I see. And have you got some Barbies at home?
APRIL:	No
FLEUR:	I have
INTERVIEWER:	So go on Fleur, you tell me about yours then. You've got Barbies at home?
FLEUR:	Yes because I want to get money for them.
INTERVIEWER:	Because you want to get money for them?
FLEUR:	Yeah, I'm waiting for them to peak.

In this extract with Fleur, we see a fascinating demonstration of the mobilisation of entrepreneurial discourse to handle probable ambivalence about Barbie – since she's still got some Barbies at home – whilst simultaneously managing to 'do growing up' and avoid the label 'childish'.

In another example of the complex connections between 'doing gender' and 'doing growing up', four girls in one particular class selected the Playboy icon to decorate their lunchboxes (Figure 4.2). Again, the choice of logo is not particularly surprising to anyone who has frequented high street shops such as Claire's Accessories with female children. It is already possible to buy items such as teenagers' duffle bags with this logo on them. What is interesting here, however, is the way a

Figure 4.2 'Playboy' lunch-box picture

group of children interactively handle an explanation for our researcher about one girl's choice of logo.

JANE:	Well this is my dream one.
INTERVIEWER:	So tell me Jane, why have you got Playboy on your lunchbox?
JANE:	[inaudible]
INTERVIEWER:	Yeah alright, why have you got Playboy on your....?
(SECOND CHILD):	Because they like Playboy
JANE:	Because you can get it, erm
INTERVIEWER:	So what's Playboy then?
(SECOND CHILD):	By the way Jane, he's recording you
(THIRD CHILD):	You really don't want to know
(SECOND CHILD):	Strippers
INTERVIEWER:	Strippers?
(SECOND CHILD):	*Women strippers* [our italics]
JANE:	It's a make

Two key points emerge from this extract, indicated in italics above. First, one child points out to Jane during the discussion that she is being recorded and another tells our researcher he 'really doesn't want to know'. This implies that there is something needing to be hidden here. Second, the term 'women' is used towards the end of the extract – indicating that the children are talking about something quite grown-up here. Shortly after this exchange, the following dialogue occurs in the same classroom:

MICHAEL:	[to researcher] aren't you a woman and a man when you're 18?
INTERVIEWER:	[at first not understanding the question] Sorry, say again.
MICHAEL:	Aren't you a woman and a man when you're 18?
INTERVIEWER:	Er yeah.
MICHAEL:	Thank you

The Playboy brand possibly gains its appeal from the opportunities it presents to connect a childhood world of pink rabbits and soft fluffy ears to an adult world. However, this adult world is suffused with connotations of sex that need to be handled carefully, an undercurrent evident in the warning to Jane, in the earlier extract, that she is being recorded. It also seems to be driving the following dialogue a bit later, with another girl and her friend in the same class:

INTERVIEWER:	Hello Ruth. Now what's this?
RUTH:	Playboy
INTERVIEWER:	Playboy, why do you like Playboy?
RUTH:	Because of its [inaudible] picture
INTERVIEWER:	Right, do you know what it means?
RUTH:	No.
INTERVIEWER:	Oh right OK then.
SUSIE:	I do
INTERVIEWER:	What does it mean Susie?
SUSIE:	Not telling you
INTERVIEWER:	You're not telling me? Alright well what's in your lunchbox then?

In this extract, Susie claims to know the meaning of the icon, although she is not prepared to reveal it to the researcher.

We could argue, then, that in all these extracts 'doing growing up' is claimed through prior knowledge of the 'adult' world whilst simultaneously the girls act as moral guardians of these identities by refusing to tell the researcher what the Playboy icon means. Arguably, Susie, for example, both protects herself from having to address the issue with an adult and/or wins back some privacy for a girl who might want to play with the idea of 'girlyness' and sexuality in fantasy.[3]

In sum, so far we have illustrated some of the ways in which concerns with age and gender, in identity work, could be seen at work within children's explanations and creations of food-related artwork. However, in examining their use of Barbie and Playboy icons on their lunchbox drawings it is important to emphasise the interactive aspects of our data collection: children imitated, copied and developed ideas and understandings from each other, creating waves of shared imagery drawn from the differing social and cultural contexts of their lives, including Barbie, Bratz, Superman and Playboy. In the socially and ethnically diverse inner-city school in our sample, for example, westernised brands such as Barbie were less common than in the other schools, whereas characters and symbols from X-rated action/horror movies and games were more frequent – particularly amongst boys. Nevertheless, gender and age were obvious organising principles, shaping how children across our whole sample related to this food-related task. Analysis of children's dialogue underlined that they were highly active in shaping identities, through the mobilization of brands and other cultural images; they were by no means the passive victims or objects of an externally imposed consumer culture (see Chapter 9 by Tingstad in this volume).

In the next section, we move on to explore the relationship between identity work and food more closely through an examination of children's explanations for the presence or absence of particular food items in their lunchbox pictures.

Chocolate, lemons, pizza: Accounting for specific food items

As reflected in the three drawings (Figures 4.3, 4.4 and 4.5), a content analyst would struggle to find consistent differences between the items children placed in 'dream' versus 'nightmare' lunchboxes. Fruit and vegetable items could be found in either type of box, as could sweets, chocolate, cake or fizzy drinks. This is not surprising; the same pattern would probably be true for adults undertaking this task, because of the variable and conflicting meanings of food in general, as well as specific foods, in western societies, including connotations of good and evil, strength and weakness, health-promoting or health-damaging and so on (see Coveney 2006; Williams 1998). In the rest of this chapter, therefore, we want to focus, not on *what* children put in their boxes, but *how they accounted for*

Figure 4.3   'Chocolate dream' lunch-box picture

Figure 4.4   'Healthy-eating' lunch-box picture

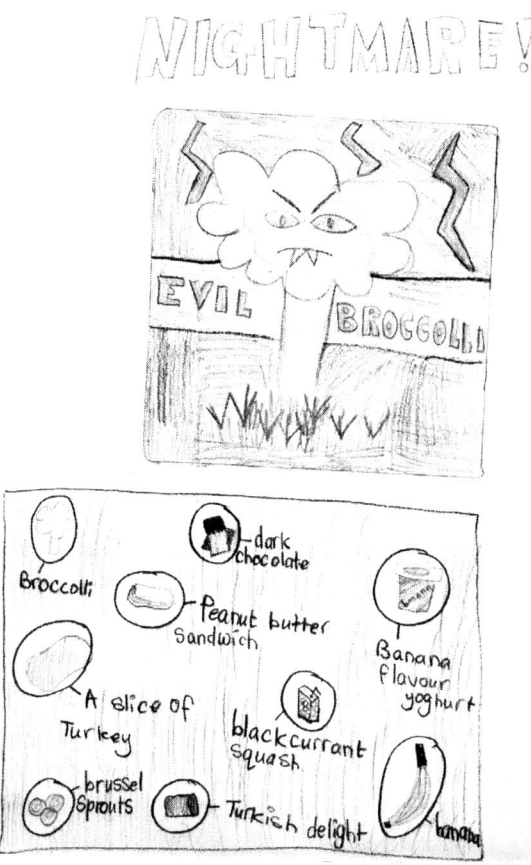

Figure 4.5 'Mixed nightmare' lunch-box picture

their choices to our researcher. We found three main types of explanation: personal preference; notions of 'healthy eating'; and the demonstration of 'informed choice-making'. We will discuss each in turn.

Selection based on personal preference

ANITA: Well I've got [inaudible] lunchbox full of fruit because I like fruit.

INTERVIEWER: You like fruit?

ANITA: Yeah. And I've got apples and oranges and bananas and lemons and grapes, they're one of my favourite fruits.

The most common type of explanation for the appearance of a particular item in a lunchbox involved personal preference. In the above extract, Anita is using this explanation to justify the presence of fruit in a dream lunchbox. With recourse to personal preference, children would frequently justify all sorts of items as appearing in dream boxes (whether 'healthy' or 'unhealthy' by current standards) and, likewise, all sorts of items appearing in a nightmare box (again, whether 'healthy' or 'unhealthy'). We suggest that this reflects the emphasis in late modernity on a philosophy of individualism, which stresses an individual's right to make independent choices without any outside interference (see Chapter 9 by Tingstad in this volume). As indicated above in relation to Valentine's work (Valentine 2000), late modern 'identity narratives' position children as entitled to some choice and control in their lives, in particular settings. Indeed, children in our study often went to some lengths to articulate choices that were based on very subtle preferences between apparently similar foodstuffs. Other researchers, including Cook (Chapter 6 in this volume), have also emphasised how children's apparent 'fads' about food can drive parents to distraction.

Selection based on specific references to 'healthy eating'

However, nestled within such an individualistic framework of personal rights and autonomy, there also resides another set of dominant current assumptions about food practices, essentially involving the notion of personal *responsibility* to eat things that are *good for you*, where 'good for you' is invariably defined with reference to scientific analysis of nutritional content (see Coveney 2006; Williams 1998). Reality TV programmes focused on obesity, the interventions of Jamie Oliver and other celebrity chefs (Hollows 2003) and government policy initiatives have all tended to characterise personal food preferences as questionable if they do not prioritise the nutritional value of food when making choices.

In our study, we found that the second most common explanation for food choices given by the children was, indeed, couched in the language of nutrition, science and government 'healthy eating' agendas. So, for example, the dialogue quoted above with Anita continues:

INTERVIEWER: And you've got a banana sandwich and you've got grapes and you've got a lemon – you like to eat lemon, do you?

ANITA: Yeah.

INTERVIEWER:	You actually like to eat lemon?
ANITA:	Yeah.
INTERVIEWER:	How do you eat lemon?
ANITA:	[inaudible]
INTERVIEWER:	Do you slice it up and like eat some, like oranges?
ANITA:	Yeah.
INTERVIEWER:	No! Really? Gosh. So what about other types of food, do you like other types of food?
ANITA:	I like chocolate
INTERVIEWER:	But you don't want those in your lunchbox?
ANITA:	No.
INTERVIEWER:	Why not?
ANITA:	Because it's unhealthy.

We are not suggesting here, however, that what children told the researcher in these discussions simply mirrored their actual eating practices. As the above extract shows, the researcher is gently challenging Anita in her choice of lemon as a favourite food – suspecting that this choice may be more to do with trying to produce a drawing that was perceived by the child to be 'acceptable' or 'required' by the adults in this classroom-based exercise. As mentioned in our introduction, the very terms of the exercise – 'draw your dream or nightmare lunchbox' – keys into current moral debates around food, at some level. It would be understandable, therefore, to pick up quite a lot of 'what children thought we wanted to hear'. Indeed, a potential disjuncture between 'actual' preference and 'presented' preference in the exercise was sometime alluded to humorously, in interactions between children, as in the following:

INTERVIEWER:	Is this your dream or your nightmare one?
MATTHEW:	Dream.
CAMERON:	Matthew, you never eat fruit.
MATHEW:	Yeah I do, I love it, I always eat it at home. Scoff it down.

The potentially yawning gap between what we say and what we do is apparent in the next picture (Figure 4.6) as compared to the artist's explanation of contents to our interviewer:

| INTERVIEWER: | Ah, so you like crisp sandwiches, but going mouldy they're nightmarish. And what's that? |

GAVIN: Chewing gum
INTERVIEWER: So you don't like chewing gum? Have you not got chewing gum now? So if you've got chewing gum now, why don't you like it?
GAVIN: Erm, I just do it for a laugh.
INTERVIEWER: Do it for a laugh? OK.
GAVIN: Erm, Joe next door said everybody's put chewing gum so, it's like me and Joe work together.

However, the point we want to make here is that, regardless of whether children's accounts reflected actual preferences, affirmed friendship links as in the case above, or were mainly for the benefit of the researcher, the ease with which many children deployed the language of nutrition and healthy eating, when accounting for their drawings, was notable. In the next section, we examine ways in which children's use of the language of nutrition and healthy eating often connected to moral categorisation of food in interaction with the researcher and each other. In our conclusion, we raise some questions concerning the possible implications of this.

Figure 4.6   'Chewing-gum and chocolate' lunch-box picture

Selection based on informed choice-making

Explanations of choice given by the children in relation to 'healthy eating' often went hand in hand with a categorization of food items as either 'good' or 'bad', with reference to their nutritional status. This can be seen in a continuation of the conversation with Gavin, quoted above, about his 'nightmare' lunchbox:

INTERVIEWER: You and Joe work together? You play football together as well? So what's ...?
GAVIN: I don't like chocolate
INTERVIEWER: You don't like chocolate, really?
GAVIN: Yep
INTERVIEWER: So if I gave you ten chocolate bars you'd turn me away? So why don't you like chocolate?
GAVIN: I dunt
INTERVIEWER: You just don't?
GAVIN: Mmm
INTERVIEWER: OK.
GAVIN: fizzy pop
INTERVIEWER: You don't like fizzy pop either?
GAVIN: No, not really
INTERVIEWER: So what do you prefer to drink then?
GAVIN: I prefer dilute or water
INTERVIEWER: Oh really, so do you drink fizzy pop a lot then? No? So do you drink dilute pop a lot? And you've got cake and jelly babies. Tell me about your cake
GAVIN: Cake is bad for you
INTERVIEWER: Aha, why is it bad for you?
GAVIN: Because it's made out of sugar, and stuff like that, that can rot your teeth, and jelly babies are sweet and they've got all different kinds of ingredients that can rot your teeth.

In this interaction, a moral categorization of cake as 'bad' may perhaps reflect current local and national 'healthy eating' campaigns and policies, designed to educate children in schools about the detrimental effects of eating sweet things; these moves include new school policies and levels of surveillance relating specifically to packed lunches. In fact, Gavin's explanation continues with a justification based in a discourse that is familiar from government documents and advertising

Figure 4.7   'Rubbed-out chocolate' lunch-box picture

campaigns about diet and health. However, what are the identity impli-cations of labelling foodstuffs as variously 'good' or 'bad', in a society underpinned by notions of individualism and personal choice?

In our final extract, relating to Figure 4.7 above, we can see what hap-pens when discourses of choice based on personal preference, and choice based on nutritional value, are drawn on in the same interaction:

INTERVIEWER:	Is this your dream one or your nightmare?
RUTH:	Dream.
INTERVIEWER:	...So you've got a lot of fruit there. And brown bread. And that's just brown bread, there's no sandwich – or is that a sandwich?
RUTH:	Sandwich.
INTERVIEWER:	What's on it?
RUTH:	Supposed to be ham.
INTERVIEWER:	Supposed to be ham is it? That looks like ham to me. So, oh that looks like you've put something there and then took it out, what was there?
RUTH:	It's supposed to be chocolate.
INTERVIEWER:	And why did you rub it out?
RUTH:	Because I didn't want it in
INTERVIEWER:	You didn't want it in, why not?
RUTH:	Because I don't like chocolate
INTERVIEWER:	You don't like chocolate?

BILLY: She does really.
RUTH: (laughs) Not as much.
INTERVIEWER: As what? So you prefer to have a drink of lemon
                than some chocolate?
RUTH: Yeah.

As the dialogue proceeds, Ruth admits that she had drawn a picture of chocolate, but rubbed it out. Pressed by the researcher as to why, she asserts that she doesn't like chocolate. Despite her classmate's interjection that 'she does really', we would argue that what Ruth is doing here is attempting to demonstrate *informed* or *responsible* or *good* personal choices to the interviewer. Chocolate is bad for you, therefore she doesn't like it (or 'not as much' as a drink of lemon juice). The implication is that if she doesn't eat chocolate, she is being virtuous, and if she does eat chocolate – well, maybe the opposite is true?

Of course, we cannot know whether children in the study, when depicting certain foods as 'bad' or 'good' , are necessarily 'buying into' a moral discourse of food. This is only one reading and there may be other 'less visible' meanings that children are attaching to these labels. However, as McSeveny (2009) have pointed out in their recent study of an online commercial weight management organisation, religious references permeate weight loss discourse and choosing 'bad' food is frequently linked to notions of a 'morally weak' consumer (see also Lupton 1996). We will explore these points a little further below.

Conclusion

In presenting and discussing the drawings and the extracts from children's conversations included above, we have suggested first that children responded to an arts activity about food by engaging in complex social identity work, notably relating to gender and to age. This identity work frequently involved the deployment of 'brand' images, logos and well-known, mass-produced food items. However, our analysis has highlighted that children were not passively internalizing consumer images and pressures here. Instead, they were very active in making meanings with these images and manipulating them, within their interactions with peers and with adults (not least, with the researcher). The 'Barbie' figure decorating a lunchbox, for example, could be deployed both to stand for femininity (whether one wanted to lay claim to this, or to distance oneself from it), and to highlight a boundary related to age and maturity ('it's too babyish ...').

Second, we found that in explaining their lunchbox food selections, children tended to mobilise a number of underlying concepts or discourses which were to some extent in tension with each other, and that this tension is an important one to examine in future research with children about food practices. In some very familiar and understandable ways, children's talk and their drawings were rooted in philosophical concepts of individualism – an entitlement to articulate individual preferences was taken for granted. Any food item selected could be justified based on personal preference and this was invariably part of the way in which children explained the presence of 'non-healthy' items such as chocolate and crisps. At the same time, however, a second important way in which children often justified food choices involved invoking ideas and concepts from nutritional discourses and science. Explanations based in nutritional discourse often provided the basis for children going on to make moral distinctions between different food stuffs (see Coveney 2006). When food was positioned as good or bad by reference to its nutritional value, children implied that their related choices could be evaluated in the same way. As discussed above, Ruth, for example, rubbed out her earlier picture of chocolate. Thus, although there was also often evidence of a certain disjuncture between healthy eating claims made and, for example, peer observations about actual choices, nevertheless, these primary school children aged between 9 and 11 were clearly able to rehearse explanations of food choices linked to this kind of moral evaluation.

As discussed earlier, other researchers such as Warren et al. (2008) have shown that children are well aware of current healthy eating agendas and that, like adults, they also know that sometimes they express choices and desires that diverge from these. In conducting a discursive analysis of children's explanations of choice here, however, we want to draw attention to the possibility that the deployment of a system of moral discrimination, based on nutritional discourse and science, could end up functioning in identity terms as a personal *accounting system* (Buttny 1993). McSeveny (2009) found in her recent analysis of online weight watchers' discourse that choosing 'good' food tends to reflect a notion of individual responsibility and self-control, whereas, choosing 'bad' food needs to be explained away in order to avoid being depicted as 'morally weak'. Yet, as this author has also pointed out, 'bad foods are simultaneously signalled as desirable in western culture (naughty but nice)'. We could argue, therefore, that there are latent identity tensions embedded in nutritional moralising that could shape future ideas of self-worth. We do not think that it is a big step to imagine some of the children in our study beginning to position their own choices in relation to food as morally charged. Whether this means that *young* children will increasingly experience levels of anxiety about food, body shape and health similar to those experienced by many teenagers and adults remains to be seen. At the very least, future initiatives in research and policy about childhood and food need to be sensitive to the potential implications of current 'moralising' associations around the nutritional value of particular foodstuffs and food practices. It hardly needs saying that this is all the more important, given the financial hardships that many people are currently facing in the United Kingdom, and the lack of personal power most people have in influencing the current mechanisms of global food production.

Notes

1. The *Men, Children and Food'* project was part of the *Changing Families, Changing Food* research programme, based at the University of Sheffield and Royal Holloway, University of London. It was funded by the Leverhulme Trust from 2006–2008.
2. That is, the current UK government public health campaign to encourage people to eat at least five portions of fruit and vegetables per day. This campaign has included posters, guidelines for health professionals and other health promotion activities.
3. The otherization of girls and their sexuality has been discussed at some length, for example, by Walkerdine (1997), who suggests we try to avoid over-simplification when considering their use of popular culture and its symbols, especially as little girls have their own fantasies, including sexual ones.

References

Baggini, J. (2007). *Welcome to Everytown: a Journey into the English Mind.* London: Granta Books.
Buckingham, D. (2002). *Children and Media.* UNESCO, http:/www.media-online. de (accessed 24/03/08).
Burgess, R. & Morrison, M. (1998). Chapatis and chips: Encountering food use in primary school settings. *British Food Journal* 3:141–146.
Buttny, R. (1993). *Social Accountability in Communication.* London: Sage.
Chaplin, L. N. & John, R. D. (2005). The development of self-brand connections in children and adolescents. *Journal of Consumer Research* 32, June: 119–129.
Cook, D. (2003). Spatial biographies of children's consumption. *Journal of Consumer Culture* 3(2):147–169.
Coveney, J. (2006). *Food, Morals and Meaning: The Pleasure and Anxiety of Eating.* New York: Routledge.
Douglas, L. (1999). Contribution of 'packed lunches' to the dietary intake of 11–12 year old children. *Nutrition and Food Science* 4:181–186.

Dryden, C., Doherty, K. D. and Nicolson, P. (forthcoming). Accounting for the hero: A critical psycho-discursive approach to children's experience of domestic violence and the construction of masculinities. *British Journal of Social Psychology.*

Frosh, S., Phoenix, A. and Pattman, R. (2003). Taking a stand: Using psychoanalysis to explore the positioning of subjects in discourse. *British Journal of Social Psychology* 42:39–53.

Goffman, E. (1972). *Interaction Ritual: Essays on Face-To-Face Behaviour.* London: Allen Lane.

Henriques, J., Hollway, W., Urwin, C., Venn, C. & Walkerdine, V. (1984). *Changing the Subject: Psychology, Social Regulation, Subjectivity.* London: Methuen.

Henwood, K., Finn, M. & Shirani, F. (2008). Use of visual methods to explore paternal identities in historical time and social change: Reflections from the 'men as fathers' project. *Qualitative Researcher* 9, Sept.:2–5.

Hill, M. (2006). Children's voices on ways of having a voice: Children's and young peoples' perspectives on methods used in research and consultation. *Childhood* 13(1):69–89.

Hollows, J. (2003). Oliver's twist: Leisure, labour and domestic masculinity in the Naked Chef. *International Journal of Cultural Studies* 6: 229–248.

James, A. (1990). *Childhood Identities.* Edinburgh: Edinburgh University Press.

Kline, S. (1993). *Out of the Garden. Toys, TV and Children's Culture in the Age of Marketing.* New York: Verso.

La Ville, V. I. (2004). L'activitè de consommation enfantine: les prèmices d'un dialogue transdisciplinaire? in Diasio, N. (ed.), *Au Palais de Dame Tartine. Regards europèens sur la consommation enfantine* (pp. 27–41). Paris: L'Harmattan.

Lupton, D. (1996). *Food, the Body and the Self,* London: Sage.

Malchiodi, C. A. (1998) .*Understanding Children's Drawings.* New York: The Guilford Press.

Mauthner, M., Mayall, L. B. & Turner, S. (1993). *Children and Food at Primary School.* London: Social Science Research Unit, Institute of Education University of London.

Martens, L., Southerton, D. & Scott, S. (2004). Bringing children (and parents) into the sociology of consumption: Towards a theoretical and empirical agenda. *Journal of Consumer Culture* 4: 155–182.

McSeveny, K. (2009). 'The management of identity and accountability in Online Weight Loss Discourse'. Unpublished PhD thesis, Sheffield Hallam University.

Murcott, A. (1997). 'The nation's diet': An overview of early results. *British Food Journal* 99(3):89–96.

Nelson, M., Nicholas, J., Suleiman, S., Davies, O., Prior, G., Hall, L., Wreford, S. & Poulter, J. (2005). *School Meals in Primary Schools in England.* Research Report no 753. London: King's College.

Nukaga, M. (2008). The underlife of kids' school lunchtime: Negotiating ethnic boundaries and identity in food exchange. *Journal of Contemporary Ethnography* 37:342–380.

Robinson, S. (2000). Children's perceptions of who controls their food. *Journal of Human Nutrition and Dietetics* 13:163–171.

Rogers, I. S., Ness, A. R., Hebditch, K., Jones, L. R. & Emmett, P. M. (2007). Quality of food eaten in English primary schools: School dinners vs packed lunches. *European Journal of Clinical Nutrition* 61:856–864.

Thorne, B. (2005). Unpacking school lunchtime: Structure, practice and the negotiation of differences, in Cooper, C.R., Coll, C. G. T., Bartko, W. T., Davis, H .M., & Chatman, C. (eds), *Developmental Pathways Through Middle Childhood* (pp. 63–87). Chicago: University of Chicago Press.

Valentine, G. (2000) .Exploring children and young people's narratives of identity. *Geoforum* 31:257–267.

Walkerdine, V. (1997). *Daddy's Girl: Young Girls and Popular Culture.* Basingstoke: Macmillan.

Warren, E., Parry, O., Lynch, R. & Murphy, S. (2008). ' "If I don't like it then I can choose what I want": Welsh school children's accounts of preference for and control over good choice. *Health Promotion International* 23(2):144–151.

Wetherell, M. (1998). Positioning and interpretive repertoires: Conversation analysis and poststructuralism in dialogue. *Discourse and Society* 9(3):387–412.

Williams, S. J. (1998). Health as moral performance: Ritual, transgression and taboo. *Health* 2(4): 435–457.

5
Fathering through Food: Children's Perceptions of Fathers' Contributions to Family Food Practices

Penny Curtis, Allison James, Katie Ellis

A few years ago, the BBC hosted a national competition for amateur chefs. The 2006 Masterchef title went to a man named Peter Bayless who charted his own experience of learning to cook in a book entitled *My Father Could Only Boil Cornflakes* – a sardonic title which serves to reaffirm Morgan's observation that the 'alleged incompetence of men in the kitchen is frequently the subject of considerable humour and right comment' (1996:159). *My Father Could Only Boil Cornflakes* both emphasises Bayless's expertise *and* implies incompetence in other men, particularly those of a different generation.

In relation to children's experience of family life in England, in this chapter we ask whether Bayless is a harbinger of change, symbolising a broader cultural transformation. The father of a previous generation may not have been able to cook, but can – and do – fathers cook within families now? If so, how do children understand their fathers' role as chef and what meanings do they attribute to this? To what extent do gendered and generational food practices shape children's perceptions and experiences of their own engagement with cooking and other food-related practices? And, finally, what might all this tell us about children's understandings of their own and other familial identities in contemporary English society?

In tackling these questions this chapter follows the lead of Morgan (1996) who, in his now seminal work *Family Connections*, helped to spearhead a shift from seeing families as institutions to which individuals belong, to a more relational, processual understanding of family as an aspect of social life that is expressed through the activities of its members. Here, family is to be understood as creatively constituted through the practices of individuals (Finch 2007) and 'those relationships and activities that are constructed as being to do with family matters' (Morgan 1996:192). Thus, by cooking dinner for his children, a father is 'doing family' – he is undertaking activities that are imbued with meanings that are associated with family. But, as Morgan points out, such practices are fluid and open-ended and, significantly, they may be described in more than one way. Thus, just as fathers' food-related activities may be imbued with meanings that are associated with family, so they may also be imbued with meanings that are associated with gender and, importantly, with generation. Indeed, the very term 'father' conveys such relational, gendered positioning: to be a father there must also be a differently positioned actor occupying the social position of child, a child–adult relationship that is often seen in hierarchical terms (Alanen & Mayall 2001; Mayall 2001).

Food-related practices as 'family practices' are therefore also 'gendered practices' and 'generational practices', conferring particular kinds of identities through the subject positions they make manifest. In this chapter, however, we tease out the shifting sands on which some of these identities and relationships are built since, as we shall show, in some families, with respect to food provisioning, children and fathers can come to occupy similar subject positions, thereby collapsing the hierarchical and generational order upon which father–child relations are normally premised. In sum, if food can be seen as a powerful 'marker of identity and difference', as Caplan (1997:1) has suggested, we demonstrate that, in relation to food practices, generation turns out to be a variable rather than fixed marker of familial identity.

Changing fathers, changing families in the European context?

Since the optimistic days of the 1970s, there has been a widespread assumption in Europe that the economic and structural changes associated with women's increasing participation in the paid labour market, would be reflected in an increase in men's participation in domestic labour and parenting work. Freed from sole economic responsibility for the family and household, men would, it was assumed, take on a more equal share of work within the home (Jump & Haas 1987; Windebank 2001). At least in dual-career families, men were seen to be in a state of transition 'moving from the traditional perspective of fatherhood toward a more egalitarian model' (Jump & Haas 1987:111). Their different relationship to the domestic arena would enable men to explore new aspects of masculinity: the haven of the home would provide a space in which they could safely experience their caring and expressive qualities. The transition was exemplified in the stereotype of the 'New Man' (Morgan 1992), who participates in the taken-for-granted activities of family, in the cooking and cleaning, and someone who is happy to be actively involved in fathering.

There have, however, been highly critical responses to the notion of transitional man and scepticism about the emergence of the 'new man' and the 'new father'. Stimulated by feminist critiques, the dominant focus upon men's experiences of fatherhood has been criticised as being 'too uncritical and positive' (Brandth & Kvande 1998:295) and the earlier optimism that predicted an increased democratisation of heterosexual relationships (Giddens 1992) has since been revealed as illusionary (Backett 1987; Segal 2007). While attitudes towards and expectations of fatherhood are undoubtedly changing, nonetheless, it is clear that men still continue to undertake relatively little domestic and childcare work (Segal 2007, Matheson & Summerfield 2001). Women, by contrast, increasingly participate in paid work outside the home and undertake a 'Second Shift' (Hochschild 1989) within the home and indeed, a 'triple shift' of paid work, domestic work and emotional labour (Duncombe & Marsden 1995).

Gender differences within the family are further highlighted through the distinction between helping with and taking responsibility for, household labour and childcare (Coleman 1993). Fathers, in general, are often able to select which tasks they are willing to do (Segal 2007), leaving mothers to pick up what is left. This has led some to suggest that men are 'playing' at parenthood (McKee & O'Brien 1982; Lewis & O'Brien 1987): their ability to extricate themselves from tasks that they do not wish to undertake enables fathers to distance themselves from mothers as they negotiate their understanding of their masculine identity, as fathers, within the home (Brandth & Kvande 1998).

Such negotiations around domestic work and childcare are therefore an important element of the gendering processes of everyday family life through which both mothers and fathers simultaneously 'do' family and 'do' gender. These are also processes that children observe and experience and, arguably therefore, they constitute some of the interactional processes through which children come to learn about their own gendered and generational identities:

> By using an interactional perspective we understand both gender-differences and similarities as something mothers and fathers 'do' in interaction primarily with each other. Thus masculinity (and

femininity) are formed and maintained in everyday negotiations about child-care, house work and employment. (Brandth & Kvande 1998:296)

However, within the broader literature, as Brandth and Kvande (2003) point out, limited attention has been paid to exploring how interactions with children influence fathering practices or, indeed, to understanding what children themselves make of those interactions. For example, while in their study of Norwegian fathers, Brandth and Kvande (1998) sought to examine how very young children could influence their fathers' care practices, their discussion of the dynamic, relational process through which gendered identities are negotiated between adults suggests only a limited space for children's agency. In our discussion, therefore, we foreground the experiences of children, those 'astute and canny parental observers, commentators, confidants and consultants on family outcomes' (Jensen & McKee 2003:3), to explore the ways in which children influence, and are influenced by, the gendered and generational processes of 'doing' family through food practices. In doing so, we examine the negotiation of gendered and generational identities within the family.

Finch suggests that narratives are important tools through which individuals 'display' family, and convey 'to each other and to relevant audiences that certain of their actions do constitute 'doing family things' and thereby confirm that these relationships are 'family' relationships' (Finch 2007:67). This suggests that the ways in which children talk about their fathers – in relation to the practical (activities such as those associated with food purchasing and preparation) and moral (the meanings that are conveyed and the judgments that are made about the value of social relationships and social positioning within the family) dimensions of food practices – constitute an important resource: they are tools of display (Finch 2007) which serve to confirm their relationship with their fathers as a specific kinds of gendered and generational family relationship.

Children's participation in family life

The *Children as Family Participants* study,[1] on which this chapter draws, explored children's participation in family life by asking children and their parents about their everyday decision making. The initial phase of data collection took place in four schools[2]: a deprived inner-city school, a multi-ethnic inner-city school, an affluent suburban school and a rural school. One group of approximately 30 children, aged 11–12, was recruited from each site, and these children took part in one-hour long interviews in small, friendship groups of (usually) two children. Children also completed a questionnaire about family structure and eating practices: 108 children consented to take part in the first stage of the study (54 girls and 54 boys). Although a range of ethnicities were represented in the study, the majority of children labelled themselves as 'white British'. During the school-based phase of the research, participant observation was also carried out in eating and leisure spaces within each school site and in the immediate environs.

In the second phase of data collection, children were selectively invited to participate in a further interview in the home. At this stage, we sought to represent children from a variety of family forms: children from single-parent families (all 10 children in this category lived with their mothers[3]); families with only one child; families with two or more children; and families following a restricted diet for health, religious or social reasons. Thirty children (18 girls and 12 boys) subsequently participated in interviews in their own home. A parallel but separate interview was also carried out with one parent from each of the 30 families. The majority of children (77%) lived with both their mother and father, although there were occasions when children referred to their stepfather as their father. In such cases, we have respected and maintained the labels applied by children. The majority of parents were in paid employment: the highest number of dual-income families was recorded in the 'deprived inner-city school'. The lowest number of parents in employment was in the multi-ethnic school.

Fathering and food provision

In the majority of families, children's narratives reflect what Mennell and colleagues (1992:95) describe as the 'pervasive assumption' that cooking at home is generally women's work. Though in our data we note some temporal nuances – fathers, for example, are sometimes described as contributing to the preparation of children's breakfasts and packed lunches for school – we focus here on father's involvement in cooking the main meal of the day that involves families eating together. Variably described in our data as 'tea' or 'dinner', it is this meal that has long been regarded as the key symbolic family meal (Murcott 1983; Charles & Kerr; and see Chapter 2 by James, Curtis and Ellis, this volume) and is therefore the one in which gendered and generational identities are likely to be writ large. As Caplan notes, 'food is never 'just food'…it is intimately bound up with social relations' (1997:3) and thus it is against the backdrop of the gendered assumption that it is mum who normally does the cooking that the children in our study made sense of their fathers' rather different engagement with food preparation practices. They did so through reference to three identity types, which we have termed the 'useless and unwilling chef', the 'supply chef' and the 'expert chef'.

Father as useless and unwilling chef

When a mother was absent and unable to exercise her cooking responsibility the father, whom we term the useless and unwilling chef, either avoided the need to cook the family meal altogether, or provided his children with food that required minimal time and skill in its preparation. For example, buying take-away food or eating out enabled fathers to avoid cooking for their children: Holly, for example suggested that if her mother was out or away 'we like might go out'. In some families this might mean a visit to the 'chippy', while in other families the father might seek more exotic alternatives – Peter's father, for example, would 'go out for something like sushi'. From the children's perspectives, therefore, the gendered nature of the division of labour in relation to food preparation was maintained through their fathers' actions and, indeed, was arguably strengthened by their father's avoidance, even in a temporary manner, of any responsibility for food preparation.

In other families, when fathers did occasionally take on the role of cook, they limited the amount of effort that they put in by providing what might be characterised as 'it'll do' food for their children. From the children's perspectives, however, the resultant, often poor, food quality was not an issue since this was regarded by them as but a temporary dislocation of domestic arrangements: it was seen by the children as a necessary alternative to, rather than a substitute for, their mother's provisioning. Normal service would be resumed shortly – when their mother returned:

'He's really good at pasta.... But he can't really be bothered' (Abdul)

'if she's like out or away.... My dad either makes like a toasty or he might do pasta. But sometimes we like might go out.... When she went away for like a week with work.... I don't know how many nights we went to a pub and had a meal.' (Holly)

Such food-related practices therefore distance fathers, as gendered actors, from this aspect of household responsibility and convey implicit generational meaning within families. In the practical activity of preparing and presenting 'quick' food, children perceive a moral message: fathers demonstrate their care for their children to a lesser extent through food than their mothers do – as Abdul notes dad 'can't be bothered'. However, more pragmatically, the children are also aware that taking the easy option of a take-away or toastie also reflected their fathers' limited cooking skills:

'he can cook but not good cook.... He gave me food poisoning.' (Brogan)

'Dad's cooking's dreadful!' (Esther)

That this was a common and shared experience for many children can be seen in the following exchange between two boys:

INTERVIEWER: Yeah. And what would your Dad make you do you think?
NICK: He'd probably just get us a tin of spaghetti or something
HARRY: Yeah that
NICK: and he'd go, 'Do you want some beans on toast and stuff like that.'
HARRY: My Dad'd probably
NICK: And then he'd make it us.
HARRY: make me spaghetti he can't make, make much. Dun't know what he's doing.

In their interviews, mothers also described these fathers as not willing or not skilled enough to shoulder the responsibility for cooking in their place 'I wouldn't let anybody else do it [...] I don't think they'll do it properly and I think they'll shove that in, shove that in' (Kerry's mum). Only one mother (Amanda's mother) suggested that she did all the cooking 'because I quite like doing it'. This reluctance to allow men to cook and/or men's own reluctance to do it meant that mothers had to plan for their absence and prepare food in advance. Tim's mother, for example, described cooking the night before or in the morning before work and leaving instructions about when to turn the oven on. Wayne's mother also ensured that she fulfilled her responsibility as cook even when she was not present in the family home at mealtime:

'And they just wait till I get home[...]. I occasionally make Thursdays dinner on Wednesday. You know like lasagne or a shepherd's pie[...].When I come home at lunchtime I set the cooker for like four hours.'

Following Lamb et al. (1987), the actions of Wayne's mother might evidence her concern to maintain power within the family by refusing to cede responsibility for cooking to Wayne's father, even when she is out at work. Segal (2007:40), however, offers a more nuanced interpretation, arguing that 'it is women's comparative *powerlessness*, both inside and outside the home, which induces this desire to feel uniquely needed, in some way – if only to scrub the toilet basin' – or, within Wayne's family, by making a shepherd's pie the night before. Nonetheless, whatever explanation might be given of Wayne's mother's actions, the gendered power relationships within that family around cooking are observed and experienced by the children: cooking is women's work. And indeed, this was the case for many families in our sample.

Father as supply chef

The 'supply chef' role characterises those families where fathers accept limited delegated responsibility for food preparation and cooking for their children. However, although the supply chef father accepts responsibility for the provision of some food, and will undertake cooking when this fits in with his availability, this is always contingent and is readily relinquished when the mother is present. Children recognise this gendered and delegated responsibility. Rachel, for example, recalls that 'when mum was in 'Europe' dad cooked the tea and we had like really burnt chips and really burnt', and Susie notes that 'my mum is probably better than my dad (at cooking), like my dad only does it when my mum is not in'. It is also clear where the ultimate responsibility lies – as Rachel says 'mum tells dad what to do'.

Moreover, as some children acutely observed, these supply chef fathers convey particular meanings about their identities *as chefs* through the kinds of food that they choose to prepare; it is food that requires limited skill and fathers may have only a limited repertoire. Thus, Mary says: 'my dad usually makes sausage and mash and stuff. My mom just makes everything'. In such families, rather than conveying care, in the manner that their mothers demonstrate through their careful choosing of a wide range of family menus (see Chapter 2 by James, Curtis and Ellis, this volume), their fathers' cooking of the main meal of the day is perceived, by children, more as a service activity of 'feeding'.

Thus, in the transitory and irregular nature in which these fathers engage with cooking, particular gendered and generational meanings are conveyed such that fathers might be said to be 'playing at' cooking in the same way that others have argued that fathers play at parenting. As Lewis and O'Brien (1987), for example, have argued, real responsibility continues to reside with the mother and, therefore, despite fathers' occasional participation, there may be no fundamental redefinition of the gendered division of labour. In these families, children's experiences of and interaction with these fathering practices remain embedded within the security of their mothers as the main and ongoing providers of food.

Children interact differently, for example, with the cooking practices of their mother and their father. Fathers' cooking may be confined to particular situations or specific days rather than generalised throughout the week: 'Sundays, it's mainly the day when my dad makes something'. These meals cooked by Dad are therefore marked as different from the routine everyday practices of the mother. As Mohammed says:

'On the weekend sometimes my dad kind of like makes up some sort of thing what we try and like see if it's good or not.'

And since the cooking activities of the supply chef are not core to family eating practices, children feel more able to criticise the food quality through explicit comparison with their mothers' – much better – cooking:

'my dad. ... When he makes me things my mum makes, that (laughs) didn't taste as nice' (Susie)
    'If I don't like what my dad has cooked and if it has made me ill then I won't eat it.' (Jamie)

Indeed, there is no compulsion for the food to be good since this is an extraordinary practice, rather than an intrinsic part of day-to-day cooking. With his cooking constructed as different to that of the mother, the supply chef father is able to negotiate – and therefore limit – the extent to which his responsibility for food preparation and cooking becomes integrated into his role as family member, a fathering practice that may – or may not – reflect his participation in the family across other domains. Moreover, that this limited role of cook is accepted and legitimised by mothers as well as by children serves once more to reinforce the gendering of family food. Mary's mother, for example, commented that:

'Recently he's done things like jacket potatoes and bacon but he's trying very hard.'

Thus, as these gendered identities are continually constructed through the interactions that take place between their mothers and fathers around cooking activities, so children's understandings of these practices are influenced by what Hochschild (1989) has termed an economy of gratitude.

While this gives an illusion of equality and moral order within the family, at the same time, it nonetheless assigns rather different values to mothers' and fathers' cooking activities within the family context.

Father as expert chef

The third typology characterises the cooking practices of those five fathers in our sample who claim to have become, or who are recognised by other family members to be, skilled cooks. However, their adoption of this role is seen by some children simply to be a practical solution to a practical problem, rather than revealing a significant shift in the gendered balance of domestic work in their family. Thus, for example, in some dual-income families where fathers are expert cooks, children's narratives reveal an understanding of the influence that working patterns have on the division of domestic labour (an influence that is widely recognised in the broader literature, for example, Moen & Han 2002) and specifically, on the division of parental food-work. Martin, for example, suggests that, during the working week, 'My mum'd cook about three times and my dad two. 'Cause we get home earlier than my dad.' Similarly, Graham, recognising that his mother cooks more frequently that his father, attributes this to their different working hours, 'Because she's back earlier'. According to both Martin and Graham, whose fathers are considered to be competent cooks, the gendered division of labour in their families is a rational response to adults' different patterns of engagement with the labour market. In this sense, their mother's cooking is not understood by the children as an active choice to cook; it is more a matter of necessity.

However, in these families, where the father was regarded as an expert cook, his skills were compared favourably with, or considered better than, those of the mother. As Kurt's mum notes:

'He'll just...chuck a load of veg together and make something out of it (laughs). Whereas I think: 'Oh, I can't be bothered to do that. But he is a lot more adventurous than me.'

Similarly, Beth's mum says of her husband's cooking:

'He's more, he can concoct things out of what's in the fridge and if I try it it dun't really work.... I'll try my best but. But I, I mean, I can cook but I would say [he's] a better cook, a bit more adventurous.'

However, expert as they are, such fathers' food practices are still judged in relational terms – in relation to those of the mother. Thus, as adventurous and extraordinary food practices they are not a routinised part of everyday family life, like those of the mother. Indeed, Graham makes this explicit when he refers to his father's cooking as 'a bit of an occasion so it'll be something a bit more special'. And as Kurt's mother clarifies, though a skilled and adventurous cook, Kurt's father still retains discretion over whether or not he will choose to exercise his skills.

> INTERVIEWER: And how do you decide who's going to cook? [...]
> KURT'S MUM: Usually on a weekday, if he's working I'll cook. But at weekends he likes to do it. You know, if he's in.

Findings from our study therefore support those in the broader literature that attest to men's ability to determine the extent to which they contribute to such family practices as cooking and the continuation of marked gender differences in relation to domestic work.

And that it is in the narratives of children that such perceptions of fathering in relation to food provision are to be found indicates not only the deep-seated nature of the gendered division of labour within family food practices but also raises questions about how children understand their own responsibility, as boys and as girls, for food preparation and cooking? To what extent are these gender differences being replicated in the next generation and, if they are not, what implications does this have for family practices? In order to explore these issues, in the next section, we look first at children's narratives about the responsibility for food-related decisions within the family and then consider children's discussion of their own contributions to domestic work in relation to food.

Gendered and generational responsibilities for food practices

As with cooking, other forms of food-related activity within the family also show clearly gendered and, indeed generational, characteristics, though there were some differences and variations between families. Just as Charles and Kerr (1988) described, in a few families fathers exerted considerable control over eating practices, and indeed, some children described their fathers' influence in terms of overt rules. Cory says, for example, that her father, 'always tells us what we're having for tea', while Steph's dentist father forbade his daughter from eating chocolate in the mornings and thereby prevented her from eating cereals like Coco Pops. Graham too felt that his father dominated food-related decisions at times:

> 'Well I hate Indian but love Chinese which explains why we always have Indian really [...]. My life is a bit like that[...]. Parents! [...] Well

my dad really. My dad says we're gonna have this and my mom kind of nods'.

In most other families, however, even where such rules existed, they were not always applied consistently. For example, Harry's father had 'made this rule, you can't get like get supper after eight or either half eight, but it don't apply all the time though'. And in Kurt's, James's and Damien's families, their fathers had made food-related decisions in relation to their own food preferences, but these did not impact on other family members. Kurt's father was described by his wife as 'a right health freak', 'whereas the kids are[...] "I'm not having that"'. Similarly, James' father was a vegetarian and so his mother substituted the meat in whatever she was preparing for the rest of the family in order to cater for her husband's preferences. His vegetarianism was not seen as having influenced her own or her children's diet.

However, in contrast to these examples, in the majority of families, children's narratives confirm that it is their mothers, rather than fathers, who exercise principal responsibility for food-related decisions within the family (but see Chapter 2 by James, Curtis and Ellis, this volume for how these are made) and for family food purchasing practices. Thus, both fathers and their children are understood to be working to mothers' directions, as Chris describes when talking about shopping: 'cause she says like, "you eat the food as well", so sometimes I have to come and my dad has to come with us sometimes as well.' Similarly, Hannah and Jayne make it clear who holds the responsibility for food shopping in their family, for although their father, who is the only car driver in the family, usually does the 'big shop', 'he needs to get the list from mum'.

Mothers' responsibilities also extend to monitoring financial management and to concern about food quality. Rachel, for example, describes her mother as 'always worried about the price' while Wayne compares the different approaches to shopping taken by his mother and his father:

'My dad just goes, to like, 'Waitrose' which is really expensive and just buys whatever he can see that is really expensive and gets good brand stuff and then my mum, she gets all the cheap and nasty stuff and they go, well my mum really just writes someat on the shopping list and she sticks to that list and she forgets everything but she looks at the list.'

Wayne's discussion of his father's laissez-faire attitude hints at moral approbation – his father is less responsible about shopping – although his mother's management of this element of the family budget does lead her to buy the 'nasty stuff'! Susie also compares the practices of her mother and father, though here, it is food quality rather than price that is the issue:

> 'when I go shopping with my mum she's like, "That's far too like unhealthy" and stuff like that, but then with my dad he's just, "Put it in the trolley". You're allowed to get like three or four items that, what aren't like too bad but then he won't let like a whole trolley full of (pause) junk.'

Thus, in children's narratives, fathers are characterised as being less responsible than mothers in the food purchasing decisions that they make. As with cooking, fathers' responsibility is both delegated and partial and this may mean that there is greater fluidity in decisions about what is, and what is not, purchased. Indeed, while discussing shopping in an interview in which his wife was present, Beth's father admitted to his wife: 'Certainly you're much more kind of, erm, (pause) what's the word, sort of, assertive about not buying unhealthy things than I am...I'm much more relaxed about it aren't I!' However, it is this very fluidity – the more 'relaxed' attitude to food purchasing decisions – that provides children with opportunities to exert their own influence: fathers can be seen by children as something of a pushover! Susie makes it clear that she prefers to go shopping with her dad as 'I just put them in the trolley and he always says 'Okay' and mum says, Oh no! – she reads the label and stuff and you think, No! Don't do that!'

While Ahmed, believes that his influence derives from being an only child – his father 'will get me anything...'cause I'm the only child' – children in families with more than one child also suggest that their fathers can be more easily swayed than mothers. Brogan, for example, has two siblings. Her strategy for persuading her father involves emotional manipulation:

> 'I just go, 'But daddy' and like make him feel bad and then he lets me buy it. Yeah, if I go shopping with my mum she doesn't.' (Brogan)

And other strategies for negotiation are also evident:

> 'I go, "Oh, can we have that?" Or, "That looks nice", hint, hint. [INTERVIEWER: And do they fall for the hint?] Well, my dad sometimes does but my mum is just like, "Well, you, you don't want" it's like, "You've had something already"'. (Nora)

'When I go shopping with my mum she's like, "That's far too like unhealthy" and stuff like that but then with my dad, he's just, "Put it in the trolley"'. (Beth)

This gendered distinction between 'helping with' and being 'responsible for' a range of food-related practices within the family thus forms the backdrop to children's own food-related interactions with their parents and, as we now go on to explore, has significant implications for the ways in which generational identities shift and change within the family.

Family hierarchies and generational identities

Just like their fathers, very few children, whether boys or girls, report any significant cooking activity. Only infrequently do they help their mother with food preparation and the cooking of family meals and those children who do occasionally cook, prepare 'treat' foods such as cakes or biscuits or snack foods.[4] Like the unwilling or supply chef cooking practiced by fathers, these are one-off, rather than routine cooking events. The types of quickly prepared foodstuffs that children reported included 'noodles out of the packet', pasta, tinned soup, cheese on toast and bacon and eggs. Just like the foods prepared by many fathers, such food items do not carry high symbolic value; they may appease immediate hunger but they do not convey the caring practices that are associated with their mothers' preparation of a shared family meal (DeVault 1991; Chapter 2 by James, Curtis and Ellis this volume). As Chantelle explained, 'I'd use like noodles out of the packet and stuff, so it's kinda lazy' or as Mary described: 'I make cheese on toast with beans on toast. And eggs'. For most children therefore, cooking is just an occasional activity akin to, though less frequent than, the activity of the father as supply chef.

But even when children do prepare hot food for themselves, they do not necessarily recognise or accept responsibility for clearing up afterwards and for maintaining order within the household. Mary, for example, is not unusual in leaving the clearing up to a parent – in her case it is Dad. The most commonly cited chore that children are made responsible for is taking the eating utensils from the dining room (or other eating site) into the kitchen, though their responsibility does not usually extend to washing these.

'I sometimes take the plates out and then my dad or my mum washes them or put them in the dishwasher. But I usually take them out.' (Amanda)

'Well me and my sister usually take the plates and then my mum'll or dad'll like wipe the table.' (Steph)

'Well, my mum tidies up the pans and stuff but I just tidy up my plates and the cutlery. Mum gets the hard bit.' (James)

And, although some children are expected to keep their own bedrooms tidy, domestic work is not generally seen to be children's responsibility. Rather, like their fathers, children help their mothers on whom the majority of domestic work falls and, although they may see this as unfair, they are still often reluctant to do more themselves.

'My dad usually washes up and my mum, like my mum cooks and my dad is like washes up [...] 'cause if my mum cooks then it's not fair on her to wash up'. (Amanda)

While Kerry suggests that she does not need to be asked to participate in domestic work ('I offer to') the majority of children help out around the house only when they are 'not busy' or when their mother imposes specific requirements upon them. Beth acknowledges that

'we don't have set jobs. Mum just asks me to do like put the washing out or put the dishwasher or the other washer on or something. And I do it. I think my parents do more work than us. Than me and my brother'.

Thus, parents, but particularly mothers, are recognised as being primarily responsible for the day-to-day well-being and management of the household and there is little routine delegation to children.

Like their fathers' gendered identity in relation to cooking, then, children appeared to be positioned within intergenerational relations as 'supply workers'. They occupy a position at the bottom of the hierarchy of familial responsibility, where their participation in work is contingent and inconsistent and usually only done when instructed by the mother. Indeed, that responsibility for domestic work is not routinely vested in the identity of 'the child' is reflected in the use of rewards and punishment in many families. Children may be encouraged to help out by the reward of, for example, mobile phone credits, financial inducements or other treats. Similarly, housework can be given as a punishment for misbehaviour. Such rewards and punishments highlight the extraordinary, rather than ordinary, participation of children in food-related and other forms of domestic work and indeed only one child, Sarah, suggested that it would be inappropriate for her to be paid for undertaking household chores 'cause it's my own house'.

Conclusion

Through its exploration of cooking and other food-related practices within the everyday lives of families this chapter has shown the ways in which particular gendered and generational identities are enacted. In particular, it has argued that despite suggestions that there has been a more general shift towards greater gender equality in relation to domestic work in families, mothers still assume principle responsibility in relation to food practices. Both fathers and children take on subservient roles, acting only as helpers or assistants when mothers are absent. While fathers are seen by children to do more domestic work than they themselves do (for example, in relation to washing up or tidying away after the meal), nonetheless, in many respects, fathers' generational position within the child–adult relationships that characterise everyday family life in relation to food and domestic work, is in many respects akin to their own. Both fathers and children are serviced by mothers and/or do what mothers tell them.

This partial collapse of the generational order of the family in one very significant domain of family life – food and eating – is instructive. First, it reveals that as Jenkins has argued, the process of identification is ongoing and recursive, 'never a final or settled matter' (1996:4), for as we have seen, gender and generational identities shift and change in relation to food practices. Second, the vertical relations that normally characterise father–child relations are flattened in relation to food practices, so that fathers and children occupy similar positions in relation to mothers. And, significantly, in our data, there was little variation in this patterning of activity that could be clearly attributed to differences in social class or ethnicity (but see note 4). While, as we have shown, this means that both boys and girls, along with fathers, in practice, do very little in relation to food preparation and cooking, or indeed other household chores, ironically, this may not signal a sea change in gender and generational identities in the next generation. Rather, what children are seeing and experiencing, is that mothers continue to exercise power in the domestic sphere, from which fathers remain more or less excluded, thus replicating, rather than reconstructing, traditional generational roles. Moreover, through this, what we may also be seeing is the entrenchment of some dimensions of gendered order. Children do not 'do' women's work: they do not undertake food practices or share responsibility for

the household *while* they are children. In this sense there is no explicit gender socialisation taking place. However, as boy and girl children,
they are clearly observant of their own futures, as adults – indeed, as we
have seen, they are very knowledgeable about the different gender roles
that adults assume within the family. Thus, the 11- to 12-year-old children in this study have the potential to develop a 'common consciousness' of both a gendered and generational identity that may persist into
their own experience of being mothers and fathers when, as apparently
unique individuals, they will be 'in fact taking forward part of the past'
in their own future fathering and mothering (Smart 2007:45).

Notes

1. The *Children as Family Participants* research study focused upon food and eating practices as a lens through which to examine family life and formed part
   of an interdisciplinary programme of research, *'Changing Families, Changing
   Food'*. (http://www.sheffield.ac.uk/familiesandfood/)
2. This chapter draws upon data collected with children (school year 7) and
   their parents, living in the North midlands and South Yorkshire regions of
   the United Kingdom.
3. Only one of the 108 children who participated in the study reported that
   they lived only with their father, 24 children reported that they lived only
   with their mother.
4. On occasions, children reported that their parents were concerned about
   them cooking, believing that hot doors and sharp knives posed unnecessary
   dangers. Those children most likely to independently prepare cooked snacks
   for themselves – and occasionally for their siblings – were the white and
   mixed heritage children attending the multi-ethnic inner-city school, suggesting that such activity patterns may be class rather than gender related.

References

Alanen, L. & Mayall, B. (2001). *Conceptualizing Child-Adult Relations.* London:
   Routledge Falmer.
Backett, K. (1987). 'The negotiation of fatherhood', in Lewis, C. & O'Brien, M.
   (eds), *Reassessing Fatherhood.* London: Sage.
Brandth, B. & Kvande, E. (1998). 'Masculinity and childcare: The reconstruction
   of fathering'. *The Sociological Review* 46(2):293–313.
Brandth, B. & Kvande, E. (2003). 'Father presence in childcare', in Jensen, A. &
   McKee, L. (eds), *Children and the Changing Family. Between Transformation and
   Negotiation.* London: Routledge Falmer.
Caplan, P. (ed.) (1997). *Food, Health and Identity.* London: Routledge.
Charles, N. & Kerr, M. (1988). *Women, Food and Families.* Manchester: Manchester
   University Press.
Coleman, M. T. (1993). 'The division of household labour: Suggestions for future
   empirical consideration and theoretical development'. *Journal of Family Issues*
   9:132–148.

DeVault, M. L. (1991) *Feeding the Family: The Social Organization of Care as Domestic Work*. Chicago: University of Chicago Press.

Duncombe, J. & Marsden, D. (1995). ' "Workaholics" and "whining women": theorising intimacy and emotion work – the last frontier of gender inequality?' *Sociological Review* 43:150–169.

Finch, J. (2007). Displaying Families. *Sociology* 41(1):65–81.

Giddens, A. (1992). *The Transformation of Intimacy*. Cambridge: Polity.

Hochschild, A. (1989). *The Second Shift*. New York: Avon.

Jenkins, R. (1996). *Social Identity*. London: Routledge.

Jensen, A-M. & McKee, L. (2003). 'Theorising childhood and family change', in Jensen, A. and McKee, L. (eds), *Children and the Changing Family. Between Transformation and Negotiation*. London: Routledge Falmer.

Jump, T. & Haas, L. (1987). 'Fathers in transition. Dual-career fathers participating in childcare', in Kimmel, M. (ed.), *Changing Men*. London: Sage.

Lamb, M., Pleck, J. & Levine, J. (1987). 'Effects of increased paternal involvement on fathers and mothers', in McKee, L. & O'Brien, M. (eds), *The Father Figure*. London: Tavistock.

Lewis, C. & O'Brien, M. (eds) (1987). *Reassessing Fatherhood*. London: Sage.

Matheson, J. & Summerfield, C. (eds) (2001). *Social Focus on Men*. London: HMSO.

Mayall, B. (2001). 'Introduction', in L. Alanen, L. & Mayall, B. (eds), *Conceptualising Child – Adults Relations*. London: Routledge Falmer.

McKee, L. & O'Brien, M. (1982). 'The father figure: Some current orientations and historical perspectives', in McKee, L. & O'Brien, M. (eds), *The Father Figure*. London: Tavistock.

Mennell, S., Murcott, A. & Van Orrerloo, A. H. (1992). *The Sociology of Food*. London: Sage.

Moen, P. & Han, S-K. (2002). 'Gendered careers: A life-course perspective', in R. Hertz, R. & Marshall, N. (eds), *Working Families. The Transformation of the American Home. Berkeley:* University of California Press.

Morgan D. (1992). *Discovering Men. Critical Studies on Men and Masculinities*. London: Routledge.

Morgan, D. (1996). *Family Connections*. Cambridge: Polity Press.

Murcott, A. (1983). 'Cooking and the cooked: A note on the domestic preparation of meals', in Murcott, A. (ed.), *The Sociology of Food and Eating*. Aldershot: Gower.

Segal, L. (2007). *Slow motion: Changing Masculinities, Changing Men* (Third edition). Basingstoke: Palgrave Macmillan.

Smart, C. (2007). *Personal Life*. Cambridge: Polity Press.

Windebank, J. (2001). 'Dual-earner couples in Britain and France: Gender divisions of domestic labour and parenting work in different welfare states'. *Work, Employment and Society* 15(2):269–290.

6
Children's Subjectivities and Commercial Meaning: The Delicate Battle Mothers Wage When Feeding Their Children*

Daniel Thomas Cook

This chapter seeks to challenge a generally held and widely voiced conviction that posits that marketing and advertising 'invade' family life. It is a view based on an assumption that commerce originates outside the sphere of the household, subsequently enters it and, in so doing, introduces the taint of pecuniary value into family relations (see, for instance, Hochschild 2003, 2005; Zelizer 2005). Markets, in this way of thinking, stand as discrete from and foreign to the household, contaminate authentic expressions of sentiment and exert an inordinate (and often unwelcome) effect on children who lack adequate defences against incessant and daily commercial incursions. Family members – both parents and children – in this configuration are thought to be fooled more often than not by the commercial sleight-of-hand of marketing and advertising into making decisions counter to their own interests. This way of approaching consumer culture leaves little room for comprehending how family members and relationships confer social meaning onto, with and through commercial goods, as a good deal of research argues and demonstrates (Douglas & Isherwood 1979; DeVault 1991; Miller 1998; Chin 2001; Casey & Martens 2007; Phillips 2008).

As will be detailed below, mothers in particular wage battles with the brands and media characters associated with foods in their attempts to provide what they consider a healthful alimentary life for their children. These battles cannot be divorced from daily practice, constituting as they do significant aspects of parenting efforts and of relationships between mothers and their children. Expressions of care regularly arise through negotiations over food and meals in the home. The commercial meanings of foodstuffs are often central to the terms of these negotiations. To decry outright anything commercial as *de facto* alien to the expression of sentiment and care ignores significant scholarly work (cited above) and the practices of everyday life, thereby obscuring how they can be and often are mutually constitutive.

My approach to examining 'children's food' positions children, childhood, food and economic activity as culturally informed and mutually intertwined categories of social life from the outset. Instead of conceptualising children as beings initially untouched by the commercial world of goods who are then subsequently overrun by commodities as they move through the early life course, I understand children as coming to realise forms of social personhood through commercial involvement, not in spite of it (Cook 2004; see also Clarke 2004). In this view childhood obesity, for instance, arises from children's (and adults') meaningful involvement *with* consumer culture, in the making and remaking of selves with and through goods (Douglas & Isherwood 1979; Slater 1997; Miller 1998). It is not something merely brought to and imposed on them from the 'outside'.

In order to break through this epistemological impasse, it is important to examine children's food not simply as one commodity among many to be seen as equal with all others in the eyes of capital – as a Marxian perspective might construe the matter. Rather, the preferable point of departure inquires about the peculiarity of food as a cultural object and the particularity of children as social subjects. When food and children come together a unique dynamic ensues – one that implicates the push and pull of commercial meaning, the efforts and practices of care giving and the play of social identity.

To give outline and dimension to these considerations, I offer an examination of how some American mothers craft strategies for feeding young children in light of their understandings of their children's subjectivities– that is, preferences and expressions of desire – with an eye on received understandings of the commercial meanings of foodstuffs (see Chapter 4 by Dryden et al. in this volume). At issue is how these women understand and handle the interplay of children's subjectivities, commercial meaning and nutrition imperatives in the context of a consumer culture that – in ways obvious and explicit as well as subtle and hardly detectable – inform everyday actions. Through their narratives, I illustrate how mothers resist, deploy and transform commercial meanings attached to foodstuffs in the attempt to produce order in the alimentary lives of their children. In the process, these women enact beliefs about children and childhood, the power of commercial life and their own place in this nexus as they seek to help shape favourable identities for their children.

In order to provide context for the interview material, I first lay bare some of the conceptual underpinnings informing my approach to the interconnections between food, children, identity and care. After a brief note on methodological considerations, I move on to examine mothers' narratives taken from interviews about how they wage a delicate battle with their children's pleasures and desires by making use of tactics like food rules, compromises and downright deception so as to fashion something of an alimentary order of everyday life. The concluding section addresses some of the larger implications of understanding children, food, identity and commerce.

Linking children and food, commerce and care

To feed a child requires the action and immediate cooperation of others since young children are at pains to acquire food and to feed themselves and will perish without assistance. Feeding children is thus a moral (and legal) imperative of parenting, and food a key material in enacting an ethic of care (DeVault 1991; Kaplan 2000). Unsurprisingly, mothers remain the primary caregivers of children and caretakers of the household. That responsibility often, perhaps inevitably, extends well beyond the basic provisioning of raw sustenance and into providing for the emotional content and context of life. Indeed it is women, as DeVault (1991) details, who produce the household and the family through their efforts (see also Charles & Kerr 1988; Philips 2008).

Food in this way serves as a primary, and most intimate, material vehicle for the expression and creation of love and social bonds (DeVault 1991; Kaplan 2000). The market sphere, particularly in the form of grocery shopping, as DeVault (1991) demonstrates, unavoidably accompanies and intermixes with the provisioning a mother or caretaker undertakes with regard to procuring and preparing food. DeVault did not, however, address to any significant degree the commercial meanings attaching to food and how these may inform women's notions of meals, family and, consequently, their feeding practices. It is as if once the food entered the sphere of the home, consumer culture was left at the door.

In contemporary contexts, as in the United States, where consumer-media culture approaches near ubiquity in everyday life, mothers deal with the meanings of goods and the feelings of their children as a matter of course in daily life. Children – as economic dependents – are required to petition (and sometimes nag) their parents about the kinds of things they wish to have acquired for them from the marketplace, producing a sometimes combative relationship that can occupy a significant part of family life and interaction. Goods, brands and associated commercial meanings thereby figure directly into the shape of the emotional lives of children and, significantly, the mother–child relationship (Clarke 2004; Pugh 2009).

Children thus become part of the culture of consumption in large part through others who are acting as caring loved ones, tied to them not through a commodity logic but by threads of intimacy. Yet, the influence and aura of commodity relations remain active in interactions and expressions of sentiment to various degrees and in various intensities. Food, in this way, never escapes the semantic reach of commerce. Commercial meanings, including the meaning-making work incessantly pursued by brand managers and advertising firms, cannot be divorced from the cultural place of edibles in social life. Mothers and caretakers must contend with the social, including commercial, meanings of foodstuffs – what I elsewhere have defined as 'semantic provisioning' (Cook 2009) – alongside considerations of flavour, appropriateness and nutrition. Feeding the children, in other words, requires a level of semantic labour.

It is at these nodes of intersection between marketing, consumption and provision where personal control, choice and decision come into play. Many mothers and caretakers struggle on a daily, even hourly basis, with the tension between what they believe are good and appropriate food practices and the often countervailing flow of a child's wishes. Taste, pleasure and hunger – when encountered at the level of the palette – position children's subjectivities as authoritative. Pleasure, like pain (Scarry 1985), cannot readily be adjudicated or contested by another; it can only be believed or disbelieved, accepted or rejected. In the end, no one has direct access to another's pleasure – to another's subjectivity or experience – as philosopher Max Scheler (1992) discusses in relation to the nature of sympathy.

Food items are things over which children gain a subjective sense of propriety early in life. Consuming food – here in the sense of eating, but extending to experiencing and purchasing – thus centres the child's perspective, thereby crowding out, even at times displacing, that of the adult. In pushing away the spoonful of mashed peas, a child exhibits not just a preference but effectively asserts a right to pleasure, to seek pleasure – a pleasure only oneself can adjudicate and assess. Concerns about nutrition and nourishment, as will be illustrated below, may very well impel a mother to try to override her child's desires on the moral grounds of health and long-term benefit, but that type of caring moral authority has been met with another, quite powerful, moral force – the sanctity of the choosing self, enshrined as the hallmark of contemporary consumer culture (Slater 1997).

A note on methodological considerations

Between 2004 and 2006, I interviewed 23 mothers with at least one child aged 2 through 8. Some were employed outside the home, some employed at home and others laboured exclusively as 'stay-at-home moms.' Many lived in the Champaign-Urbana, Illinois area and in Chicago; most were of white, European descent; and most would be considered middle-class or professionals. I found some interviewees through an online mothering group, others through snowball sampling and others through personal contacts. My purpose centred on gaining insight about how mothers of young children thought about and felt about the everyday practices of feeding their children.

In the semi-structured, open-ended interviews (McCracken 1988; Rubin & Rubin 2005), I inquired specifically about daily routines and the thinking behind the choices and practices described by the mothers. In the course of these discussions about foods and meals, issues arose regarding such things as commercialism, media, the influence of grandparents and peers, as well as mothers' beliefs about who children are and how they should be handled.

As a middle-aged male, my identity set an interactional context where a different kind of relationship emerged than what may be the case with a female interviewer who shares the world and responsibilities of motherhood. During requests for interviews and in the interviews themselves, I positioned myself as an outsider, as someone who wanted to learn about their routines and thoughts. Being an Other, in this sense, allowed me to ask questions about practices, feelings and situations perhaps taken for granted as part of a woman's/mother's experience; it also disallowed me from sharing in and empathizing with the pressures, responsibilities and the subtly understood expectations which comprise contemporary motherhood.

My sense is that my outsider status permitted a particular kind of rapport to develop during the brief encounter of the interview. As a non-mother, non-woman, I did not represent the same kind of judgmental threat that a peer might and often does when children and childrearing are at issue. There was no explicit or implied competitiveness between us as to the proper way to raise or feed a child.

The result is by no means some clear pathway to some pre-existent 'truth', however. It is simply a particular kind of relationship surrounding the activity of eliciting narratives – a relationship that can never be totally separated from the material gathered. This is not to say that there was no anxiety on the part of interviewees about how they appeared to me as a mother. Indeed, the underlying tone, the subtext, of all the interviews revolved around the interviewee demonstrating to me in one way or another that she was indeed a 'good mother.' The 'good mother' narrative, the normative practices thereby entailed and the implied surveillance of a woman's actions suffused the research context. There is no escaping the ideological weight of intensive mothering (Hayes 1996) and the manifestations of the 'mommy myth' (Douglas & Michaels 2006). These do not disappear but rearrange themselves and change shape contingent upon circumstances, including the interview context.

Given the admittedly limited sample and scope of the original research, I intend the following to be illustrative of a conceptual approach to children, food and commercial culture rather than an empirically definitive statement. The idea is to suggest some ways of apprehending the relationship between children, food and identity that remains attentive to how economic and gustatory consumption inform each other at the level of practice.

Forging an alimentary order

Concerns about nutrition, unsurprisingly, rest squarely in the centre of mothers' worries and preoccupations about their children's food intake, informing their practice and animating their sentiments. Any mention of children's food, or of feeding their children, prompted them to discuss nutrition and the difficulties faced in trying to provide nutritious foods on a consistent basis. Significantly, mothers' concerns about nutrition rarely focused on a single food item or single type of food. Interview materials indicate, rather, that mothers' interventions and practices aimed at creating some sort of order in the everyday activities surrounding eating and food. Part of the order sought after involved negotiations around defining the categories into which certain foods would be classified.

These negotiations with children are made in (oft-times frustrating) conversation with media and promotional practices. The mothers interviewed reported some level of concern or exasperation related to their child's attraction to brands and media-generated characters used to promote foodstuffs. Mary, a 37-year-old mother of two daughters, relates her experience with the confounding effect that media characters have on her children's ability to learn proper distinctions between foodstuffs:

> My kids are into these Gogurts [yogurt].... They're all the same flavors, no matter what's on the front of the package. I mean, if you buy the one that says it's cotton candy and raspberry, whatever, that's what's in the package, regardless of the character. They came out with Shrek ones...
>   Go ahead (DC)
>   Well, they [her daughters] only wanted the Shrek ones. And eventually the store starts running out of Shrek after a certain time and I'd say 'This is the same flavor. It's the same blue Gogurt, it just doesn't have the donkey on the front of it anymore' and they don't want it. They want the ones that.... And there's nothing I can do about that, I mean, if they're taking them off the shelves, they're taking them off the shelves.

Mary's aggravation here is understandable. Her attempt to define for her children what characters and labels mean is trumped, in this case, by the meaning-making power of commerce and media. Her position and role as mother has been made secondary to a corporate construction.

The annoyance Mary feels with the yogurt is part of a larger displeasure with what she sees as the power of the commercial world to define foods and other goods and imbue them with meanings that she sees as essentially irrelevant to the product. Her children 'know the difference' among the different grocery stores in the Champaign-Urbana area and which stores have which kinds of foods and toys. Their consumer knowledge makes for sometimes highly emotionally charged confrontations with them as she has difficulty asserting her authority over their desires, because these are reinforced by corporate strategy. Food packaging is Mary's nemesis. It represents how 'they [food companies] will do just about anything' to sell 'junk'.

Many mothers, especially those whose children have yet to attend school or pre-school, exhibit a similar kind of aggravation that they cannot go about their business of parenting without having to stave off incessant marketing. Thirty-three-year-old Elizabeth takes snacks, like crackers, out of the original packaging and puts them in clear plastic baggies precisely so that her three-year-old daughter does not associate these foods with particular characters or brands. A number of others do not allow their children to watch television directly. They either show videotapes of approved films or record programs like *Blues Clues* and *Dora the Explorer* digitally and then cut out the commercials before the children view them. Most admit however, that their efforts in this regard may be in vain as it is impossible to control all exposure to media and 'unhealthy' foods due to the influences of other children, practices at day care and school and the ever-ubiquitous doting grandparents who visit and sometimes sit with the children for a time.

Defining categories: 'That's the rule here'

One oft-employed tactic to produce a household, alimentary order was to institute various kinds of rules meant to help distinguish kinds of foods from each other and define occasions of eating. Missy, a 34-year-old mother of two, gives a sense of the family morning routine:

> The kids get up and have cereal usually.... Reilly [age six and a half] goes for Cheerios, Annie [age three and a half] goes for Cocoa Puffs.... Or they go for Pop Tarts, although I had to put an ixnay on that once Reilly started school full-time.
>
> How come? (DC)
>
> Because a Pop Tart is not enough to get him from 6:30 in the morning until 11:30 lunch. So I told my husband 'he can have a Pop Tart after he has Cheerios.' So that's the rule here. Annie, I don't worry about so much because she has pre-school. She can have some fruit or something before she goes to pre-school and then they have some sort of healthy snack at pre-school. I'm not worried about her being hungry.

With Reilly going to school and thus out of Missy's surveillance, she worries about his nutritional intake away from home. To attenuate her anxiety and ease her unease about his morning food intake, she formulated a summary 'rule' of the household that Reilly gets 'no Pop Tarts until after Cheerios' when he is going to school and communicated it to her husband to ensure their mutual enforcement. Working with the categories and brands of commercial foodstuffs, these acts serve to relieve some of her uncertainty about the child who will be out of her purview for a time.

Food and eating are, for mothers of young children, ongoing concerns. Encouraging and enforcing the hoped-for alimentary order is an iterative process. These middle-class mothers evaluate each meal and snack in relation what was ingested previously and what the next food consumption opportunity might bring. Commercialised, child-targeted – and therefore often seen as unhealthy – foodstuffs pose something of a continuous threat to any kind of regimen mothers attempt to impose. These thus are key sources of concern and the object of interdictions by food rules:

> Oh, I try. I try. Like, of course, they wake up and ask for candy. 'Can I have candy? Can I have candy?' 'No, you can't have candy. It's too early.' We've gotta have breakfast and lunch. You know, if they're good they get candy. It's the rule. (Debbie, age 42)

Candy here becomes a 'treat' or a 'reward' for eating proper foods at proper times and thus serves as a semantic marker delineating 'proper' from 'improper' as well as 'adult' from 'child.' A 'treat' becomes something special or apart from the everyday only when placed in an overall sequence of eating occasions. Mother's labour, here, concentrates on the provisioning of meaning as much as the preparing of foodstuffs.

In this and in Missy's case, it is not simply the edibles that are at issue. Through such food rules, children acquire and reacquire an identity as 'children' – i.e., as family members who are subject to categorical strictures. The making and enforcing food rules by mothers thereby recognises the play and force of children's desires – particularly when exceptions or compromises are allowed (see below). Rules furthermore help mothers codify and distance their super-ordinate position vis-à-vis their children by instituting an abstract standard.

Rules serve as a counter-balance to children's desires for 'junk', an oft-used term to indicate food that is disruptive of the sought after regimen. 'Junk' refers to that which emanates from outside the home and family circle, that is, not prepared at home and is deemed by mothers and caretaking adults as 'unhealthy' (cf. James 1982). Junk food is often fast food, but more properly, reminiscent of Mary Douglas (1966), it is food out of place.

Here, Staci, 34, tries to articulate her thinking about different kinds of foods her five-year-old son can have and when he can have it:

> if he has a sandwich and chips [crisps] then he needs like a cheese or something. Or some fruit. If he has a sandwich and fruit he could maybe have a cookie.
>
>   And what's the thinking behind that? (DC)
>
>   I guess usually I let him have his, what I call food that's not really nutritious. Like he'll get his Pop Tart or his cookie [biscuit]. I'd rather him have something at school, I mean, he doesn't need chips [crisps] and a cookie. [LAUGHTER]...And he doesn't get chips a lot. If he has crackers or something I don't mind if he has a cookie. Cause I

usually buy the big Goldfish or the big cheese its or whatever those kinds of crackers are. I just tend to not want to give him a lot of what I call junk.

Note the conditional if-then structure of Staci's reasoning. A good deal of her efforts are put forward to counter her son's desires for what she defines as junk. As gatekeeper, she takes it upon herself not to banish the Pop Tarts outright simply because they are commercialised, but to put them in relation to other foods – either those not strictly branded like fruit, or highly branded, but obviously allowable foods like Goldfish crackers.

Junk can represent a source of disorder, and disordering influences are not easily identifiable as arising directly from the world of advertising or branding. Debbie, a 42-year-old mother of three who works as a nurse, complains about the amount and type of foods her father brings the children when he visits or baby-sits:

> God, they're always eating...like Lauren will constantly eat all day. They want chips. They want candy. They want cookies. They want everything, you know, all day long. So, I don't...I try not to give it to them so much, whereas, I know when my mom and dad are here, they eat like crazy...I mean they eat...my dad brings stuff for them too. He brings them junk – doughnuts and cakes and cookies.

Others interviewed expressed similar concerns about the sources of disorder to the regimen and pattern they have tried to impose which include grandmothers, parties, day care and when the husband or partner is in charge of feeding the children (see Chapter 5 by Curtis, James and Ellis in this volume). Here, the concern with nutrition and commercial foods revolves around the mothers' control or lack thereof regarding the timing and introduction of junk. Yet, it is many of these same kinds of items and brands that provide fodder for children's constructions of their own identities, often through a sense of propriety, of cultural ownership, of certain kinds of edibles.

Compromise: 'I'm not a Nazi about it'

The fundamental struggle in which mothers engage involves their children's desires – desires that are often counter to her better judgment regarding health and nutrition. Whereas, much of the thrust of marketing foods to children – from advertising to character licensing to television programming to advergaming (CSPI 2003) – privileges and seeks to evoke children's desires. Marketing positions itself on the side of children, addressing them in their visual, verbal and narrative 'languages' and encouraging their active participation and expressions of want (Cook 2003; Coffey et al. 2006; Banet-Wiser 2007). Hence, many mothers find themselves waging a delicate battle at the level of their child's subjectivity – seeking to please her children, to acknowledge their preferences and include them in the family in this way, but not please or appease them unconditionally.

Many mothers, in essence, fear what the world of commercial influence will do to their children if they are left to their own devices without intervention or instruction (see Chapter 9 by Tingstad in this volume). Knowing that 'exposure' – an oft-used term – to this world is inevitable anytime the child leaves the home to attend a party, go to day care or visit relatives, a number of mothers attempt to limit and regulate this exposure, even as they recognise its ultimate inevitability. Interestingly, the underlying view of their child in this context is that of a relatively weak, vulnerable being who is susceptible to influence (see Murphy 2007).

Addressing her concerns about sugar, Cindy, age 33, notes a similarity between the family dog and her three-year-old daughter and five-year-old son:

> I have to compromise, yeah. Things like Cheerios or Life cereal or...
> Of course, now they don't want plain Cheerios, it needs to be the
> Honey Nut Cheerios. But those are fine.... You know...it's kind of
> like our puppy. Once she got a taste for a Honey Nut Cheerio she
> didn't want to go back to her dog food. It's the same way with the
> kids. Once they got hooked on cereal that had a little bit of sugar, if I
> already gave them just plain Cheerios they would just totally revolt.
> It would not be...a good thing.

Cindy has learned from experience what to keep from her children to avoid conflict.

Other mothers preemptively attempt to limit what their children eat and watch on television so as to introduce these things in the ways they chose. Elizabeth, a 37-year-old artist who lives with her female partner in Chicago, speaks about her feelings and approach to their three-year-old daughter:

> I buy organic for Anna but not for us. Like I want to...maybe protect
> her or at least kind of ease her into the world of food or the world of
> processing and chemicals and stuff. Slowly, it's not like I never want
> her to eat McDonald's. I just didn't want to throw it at her early. I

guess I feel the same way about TV exposure and kind of all those things in the world. Like I don't want to prevent her from trying it, like she can eat Oreos, she can eat some cookies, I just wouldn't give them to her all the time or very soon, and just kind of let her accommodate slowly. Does that make sense?

Tracey, who seemed at pains to demonstrate to me how 'healthy' her daughters were eating, made sure to justify the occasional forays to McDonald's:

> it's kind of, like, 'Let's go do something fun'.... It normally is when Mike [husband] is out of town and I'm looking for something to do. And so we'll go over there at, like, 3 in the afternoon and then they can play for a while and then we can get our food.... Elizabeth is more into the salads, because that's what I eat. And so, I'll get her a Happy Meal but she'll sit there and pick my salad. The thing with my kids is, I haven't exposed them to all the junk, so they don't know to ask for it, you know what I mean?

For Tracey, 'fun' here represents the acknowledgement of the legitimacy of her children's desires yet their preferences emanate directly from her parenting practices.

The commercial world of junk, processed foods and television is ever present and handling it in relation to children's social existence figures intimately into the practices of parenting. The case of 36-year-year old Sandy, who schools her two children ages five and seven at home, illustrates the intricate dance many mothers perform in the way that the parent–child relationship becomes enfolded into the enactment of practices surrounding food:

> They almost always try to get me to get the Trix yogurt or...I try not to get stuff with a lot of artificial color in it too.
>   So you read the labels a lot? (DC)
>   I do. I mean I'm not a Nazi about it, but I try to at least be aware of what's in there.

Not wanting to be a 'Nazi' about food, she finds it necessary and useful to allow her children to pick a 'junk cereal' every once in awhile, to offer a 'token,' as she put it.

Sandy's expressed ambivalence here arises out of way she structures her home life. Making the effort to school her children at home and expressly enjoying the 'flexibility' of a schedule where they 'study what they want when they want,' the idea of having to enforce prohibitions on her children's diets and activities is quite unappealing. The tensions are unavoidable when shopping where she tries to educate them about price differences and film-character-brand tie-ins: 'This box of Rice Krispies costs $5, but the store brand costs $2. So even though the Chicken Little bobblehead is in the Rice Krispies, we're going to buy these.'

Sandy established her parenting strategy in part as a way of dealing with the media-consumer culture of childhood generally and in a way that does not make herself the enemy or obstacle to her children's enjoyment. She again exhibits some ambivalence when discussing her decision to allow her daughter to watch television shows of which she doesn't completely approve:

> I'm not very crazy about what's on the Disney Channel at all. Like I said, I allow it in small doses 'cause I don't want it to become so taboo that, I don't know. I'm torn about that, I can definitely say that. I think I would be less... the commercials definitely bother me. And some of the themes on some of those shows are inappropriate.

She continues on to discuss mild sexual innuendo in stories and personality traits of some characters that concern her and the fact that she can't control what her children watch when they are at other children's houses. 'I try to make other parents in the neighbourhood aware that I'm not super keen on that stuff. But I'm not going to be the TV Nazi either'.

Caught between her own preferences, those of her children and her own preferred authoritative posture toward them, this mother vacillates between uncomfortable permissiveness and uncomfortable invocations of her authority. Sandy's dilemma encapsulates a general tension with regard to children's consumer culture whereby children's desires and subjectivities often conflict with parental wishes (see Seiter 1993). Commercial images and creations provide fodder and content that fuel these ongoing tensions and inform the parent–child relation.

Stealthy mothering: The peas are 'for mom'

Mothers' struggles are not always with specific items or brands or characters but with consumer culture generally. It is a culture often working counter to their efforts to provide structure and nutrition and, at times, putting mothers at odds with their children's desires. The battles waged, as we have seen, were never against commercial goods or commercial culture *in toto*. Many, in fact, either selectively appropriated desired foodstuffs for their children or sought to introduce to their children the more undesirable aspects of commercial foods in a deliberate and gradual manner.

The women interviewed also took up and made use of commercial meanings of foodstuffs to counter some of the more subtle ways that the world of commercialised food provides structures against which practices emerge. A recurrent theme in the mothers' narratives centred on their concern and felt duty to introduce variety into their children's diet. Variety may be lacking due to a number of factors including a child's 'natural inclination' to eat the some foods, a 'phase' the child is going through or the influence of commercial media in promoting a narrow range of foods – i.e., sweet, fatty, 'junk' foods. To the extent that mothers actively seek to increase the variety in their children's diet, they work counter to the 'omnivore's paradox' by encouraging a limited form of risk taking in the tasting of new foods.

Mothers report a number of tactics toward this end, many of which are deceptive. Julie actively tricks their children into eating healthy foods that they otherwise would not. She admits to calling soy hotdogs by the brand name of meat product, Ballpark Franks, and for a time had her son believing that a granola bar was a candy bar, calling it a 'mommy candy bar.' Tracey, who above was proud of her daughters' 'choice' of salad at McDonald's, adds things she finds desirable to some dishes:

> And then I have my little bag of flaxseeds, they usually kind of sprinkle on top. And that's just sort of to make me feel better, you know. Sort of...
> And they eat them? (DC)
> I have been known to say...they'll say 'Well, what is that?' and I'll say 'Oh, this is what makes it taste good'.
> So, what do you do for lunch, then? (DC)
> Lunch is typically a...the peanut butter sandwich. Katherine likes it with honey. Elizabeth likes it with jelly.... And yogurt and then some type of fruit. That's one lunch. A lot of times it's also macaroni and cheese, they're kids...and then you throw in the peas and mix it up.
> And the peas are for...? (DC)
> ...for Mom.

Trickery and lies, apparently quite commonplace – Elizabeth sneaks cauliflower into pizza and Staci mixes cranberry juice in 7Up – serve as a mother's prerogative in these cases in order to secure ultimate benefits (i.e., nutritional) for her children.

Not all mothers resorted to benevolent treachery. After describing the absolutely exhausting fights she has with her daughters to eat something other than 'junk', Cindy relates how she attempted the 'fun' approach often advocated in parenting magazines:

> You know, I've tried doing a lot of things with vegetables and food and it doesn't…. It doesn't matter. We can call raw broccoli 'a little tree' and dip, you know, 'snow' or whatever and it's still…. Same way with green eggs and ham. I try to get them to eat eggs by putting green food coloring in and doing like the Seuss book, *Green Eggs and Ham*. And they wouldn't try it.
>
> Here my husband and I had to eat the green eggs then for supper, so…

Related with a humorous attitude, Cindy's exhaustion and frustration were manifest in her attempt to use pop culture as a vehicle for the introduction of new and, to her mind, beneficial foods.

Conclusion

In the context of the household and related through mothers' narratives, it is evident that children's subjectivities reside at the crux of contemporary anxieties about food and commercialism. Those interviewed exuded a preoccupation with creating order surrounding eating and meals, the main obstacle to which is their children's exercise of agency as expressed through their gustatory desires and willingness (or not) to co-operate. In response the facticity of their children's agentive presence, mothers developed abstract standards to codify foods and meal (i.e., food rules), made compromises with their children and some engaged in purposeful deception.

Commercial meanings figure integrally in the tussles around food and eating. None thought to ban commercialised food altogether, acknowledging the impossibility of doing so. The struggle, rather, centred on how to *selectively engage* with consumer culture and the evident attraction it has to their children. In their interdictions, mothers participated in the process of delineating that which is properly seen as belonging to 'children' and to 'adults,' and hence to the construction of the identity of the middle-class, American child in contrast to the middle-class, American adult/parent. What the commercial world proposes in terms of belonging to or targeted for children, adults in the household reinforce and make tangible in their attempts to sort the good from the bad, the proper from the improper.

Children's voices here are refracted through mothers' perspectives and narratives who sometimes assumed something of a defensive posture toward me in the effort to illustrate their efforts at producing order and hence a healthy environment in this study, even if these efforts had failed or were ongoing. All the women with male partners/husbands downplayed their role in feeding children and, indeed, often saw them as another source of disorder to their efforts, echoing what Curtis, James and Ellis (Chapter 5 in this volume) found in the United Kingdom as reported by children. Speaking with children and observing directly children and parents would expand the scope of the inquiry and offer insight into the varied understandings and the process of the negotiations taking place. The inclusion of mothers and children from varied class and ethnic backgrounds would, as well, no doubt reveal a variety of practices that would contrast in some way with those discussed above.

These admittedly important caveats to the present discussion notwithstanding, I nevertheless stress the central thrust of this chapter – namely, that children's identities are bound up in dynamic interplay that involves food, commercial meanings and the interpretive provisioning of mothers and caretakers. If the desire is to move toward new kinds of understandings about the importance of food in children's lives and well-being, then one must be willing to contemplate and investigate the constitutive aspects of economic consumption in the making and remaking of childhoods and motherhoods and refrain from the simple and simplistic reflex to see anything commercial as essentially 'outside' childhood and the family. Effort in this regard must be placed on conceptually moving beyond an either/or stance and toward a both/and posture. All the while, I hasten to add, keeping a critical eye on the disturbingly successful ability of marketing and media interests to provide some of the semantic materials with which families use to forge their everyday lives.

Note

*A version of this paper was presented at Re-Presenting Childhood, 2nd International Conference, 10 July 2008. Sheffield, United Kingdom. This research was made possible by a grant from the University of Illinois Research Board (2005–2006) and by in-residence support from the ESRC Cultures of Consumption Programme, Birkbeck College, University of London in the Spring of 2007.

References

Banet-Wiser, S. (2007). *Kids Rule! Nickelodeon and Consumer Citizenship*. Durham, NC: Duke University Press.

Casey, E. & Martens, L. (eds) (2007). *Gender and Consumption*. Aldershot: Ashgate.

Charles, N. & Kerr, M. (1988). *Women, Food and Families*. Manchester: Manchester University Press.

Chin, E. (2001). *Purchasing Power: Black Kids and American Consumer Culture*. Minneapolis: Minnesota University Press.

Clarke, A. J. (2004). 'Maternity and materiality: Becoming a mother in consumer culture', in S. Taylor, J., Layne, L. L. & Wozniak, D. F. (eds), *Consuming Motherhood*. New Brunswick, NJ: Rutgers University Press.

Coffey, T., Siegel, D. & Livingston, G. (2006). *Marketing to the New Super Consumer: Mom & Kid*. Ithaca, NY: Paramount Market Publishers.

Cook, D. T. (2003). 'Spatial biographies of children's consumption'. *Journal of Consumer Culture* 3(2):147–169.

Cook, D. T. (2004). *The Commodification of Childhood*. Durham, NC; Duke University Press.

Cook, D. T. (2009). 'Semantic provisioning of children's food: Mothers, commerce and care'. *Childhood* 16(3):317–334.

CSPI. (2003). *Pestering Parents: How Food Companies Market Obesity to Children*. Washington, DC: Center for Science in the Public Interest.

DeVault, M. (1991). *Feeding the Family*. Chicago: University of Chicago Press.

Douglas, A. & Michaels, M. (2006). *The Mommy Myth*. New York: Free Press.

Douglas, M. (1966). *Purity and Danger*. London: Ark Paperbacks.

Douglas, M. & Isherwood, B. (1979). *The World of Goods*. New York: W. W. Norton.

Hayes, S. (1996). *The Cultural Contradictions of Motherhood*. New Haven, CT: Yale University Press.

Hochschild, A. R. (2003). 'The commodity frontier', in *The Commercialization of Intimate Life*. Berkeley: University of California Press.

Hochschild, A. (2005). ' "Rent a mom" and other services: Markets, meanings and emotions'. *International Journal of Work Organization and Emotion* 1(1):74–86.

James, A. (1982). 'Confections, concoctions, and conceptions', in B. Waites, B. Bennett, T. & Martin, G. (eds), *Popular Culture: Past and Present*. London: Open University Press.

Kaplan, E. B. (2000). 'Using food as a metaphor for care: Middle school kids talk about family, school and class relationships'. *Journal of Contemporary Ethnography* 29(4): 474–509.

McCracken, G. (1988). *The Long Interview*. London: Sage.

Miller, D. (1998). *A Theory of Shopping*. London: Polity.

Murphy, E. (2007). 'Images of childhood in mothers': Accounts of contemporary childrearing'. *Childhood* 14(2):105–127.

Phillips, J. (2008). ' "Attention, shoppers – Family being constructed on aisle six!": Grocery shopping and the accomplishment of family', in Cook, D. T. (ed.), *Lived Experiences of Public Consumption*. Houndsmills: Palgrave.

Pugh, A. 2009. *Longing and Belonging*. Berkeley: University of California Press.

Rubin, H. & Rubin, I. S. (2005). *Qualitative Interviewing*. London: Sage.

Seiter, E. (1993). *Sold Separately: Parents and Children in Consumer Culture*. New Brunswick, NJ: Rutgers University Press.

Scarry, E. (1985). *The Body in Pain: The Making and Unmaking of the World*. New York: Oxford University Press.

Scheler, M. (1992). *On Feeling, Knowing and Valuing*, Harold Bershady (ed.), Chicago: University of Chicago Press.

Slater, D. (1997). *Consumer Culture and Modernity*. London: Polity.

Zelizer, V. (2005). *The Purchase of Intimacy*. Princeton: Princeton University Press.

7

Children's 'Becoming' in Frontiering Foodscapes

Helene Brembeck

On making observations in the grocery store close to the school where we are conducting our current research on children and food, I see ten-year-old Sima coming in through the door. She is jumping and dancing her way through the store with a happy face, her quick feet finding their way to the dairy counter. She grabs a package of milk, and swinging it back and forth dances away to the check-out counter. I can't help noticing the difference between her tightly veiled head and neck, and her freely moving children's body dressed in blue jeans, a sweater and sneakers just like the rest of her native-born school mates, announcing Swedish childhood.[1]

Introduction

In Sweden the relationship between immigrant children and food is generally considered problematic and the Swedish media links ethnicity to obesity and poor diet, especially in regard to children. 'Soft drinks and sweets are everyday food for immigrant children in Göteborg suburbs', reads a daily newspaper headline (Göteborgs-Posten 16-9-2003). A survey from 2003 proves that: 35% of immigrant children in the suburbs of Göteborg are obese or fat, as compared to 20% of the total child population; 44% had soft drinks at least four days a week; and 38% reported that they had free access to sweets and sugary food stuffs at home every day (Nordin 2003). Public statistics confirm this picture. Immigrant children have more soft drinks and sugary and fatty foods than do native children (SBU 2006). The reasons put forward include: 'culture' in terms of food habits brought from the home countries, such as sweet fruit juices and an abundance of oil in cooking, practices that are not in tune with up-to-date nutritionist knowledge, social segregation, the combination of deficits in economy, housing and health, like other 'marginal groups' such as lone mothers or families on social welfare, the clash of tradition and modernity, and the resultant generational gaps in families where children aspire to the lifestyle of their native peers and their parents want them to stick to the old, most notably witnessed when patriarchic fathers forbid the daughters the freedoms of the receiving countries. In the aforementioned Göteborg survey, the blame is placed on the parents: 'It seems that the parents do not draw clear limits for what is reasonable to eat during weekdays and what should be saved for festive occasions', the research leader comments. She also hints that the mothers are not able to organise the meals properly, since the families are generally large, mostly with three or more children (Nordin 2003).

What happens if you re-read these figures from a childhood studies perspective? What role do the children play in the construction of this heaven of sweets and soft drinks? Has it something to do with their attempts to rework their identities as immigrant children in a new country? In the ambition to answer such questions, this chapter draws on results from a study of Bosnian and Iraqi families in Sweden, all former refugees from the devastating wars in their home countries.[2] In the study the focus was on the woman in the frontiering space of food and eating,[3] and although no children were interviewed directly, sometimes teenagers acted as interpreters, commenting on their mothers' stories. Thus, children's agency, detailed in this chapter, emerges in the stories of their mothers, where the obvious role of the children as integration agents, through acts of food consumption, was repeatedly highlighted. This was an intriguing and unexpected finding, since the interviews focused on women's food memories from their own childhoods and their changing identities as women and cooks brought forth by the emigration.[4] In addition, most of the women were 50+ and their children had grown up and moved out of their parental home.

Theoretical frame

To be able to reframe the findings from a childhood studies perspective, I draw on the work of the Dutch philosopher Rick Dolphijn by borrowing the concept of foodscape. Dolphijn poetically explains foodscape as 'how food functions in immanent structures that are always in a process of change ... how food affects and is affected ... how we live our lives with food, according to food, and through food and what happens between the eating and the eaten' (Dolphijn 2004:8; also Johansson et al. 2008). Foodscape, according to Dophijn, emerges or evolves as you move to where food is, but in this chapter I use the concept in a very concrete manner to denote the various places where children encounter food and eating during the day and where their identities as food consumers are enacted. Furthermore, I use the concept 'frontiering foodscape', to refer to the border zone where immigrant children meet Swedish food habits and encounter places for food and eating, such as shops, school, cafeterias and fast food venues like McDonald's.

With a similar interest in border spaces, Aitken (2008) has studied the transformation of children's identities in Tijuana, Mexico, as packers in grocery stores (2008:113–129). Following Deleuze, Aitken discusses identities in terms of adultist designations or discourses, suggesting that certain ways of being and acting can be called 'I-ams'. These designations are decidedly modern and western, drawing on developmentalist notions of children as still growing rather than mature or finished human beings, and in need of adult supervision and guidance. These are, of course, the ways children are usually regarded from a generational perspective; as subordinated schoolchildren, playing children and children in families, behaving as children are supposed to. Children should, through socialisation, more or less become the same as their parents, and as other adults, in their surroundings. There is, however, Aitken argues, also a children's way of knowing themselves through their activities, claiming identity through material action as I-do. This is an empowering activity, which enables children to become other, different from their parents.

Aitken also uses Deleuze and Guattari´s (1988) differentiation between striated and smooth spaces. A striated space is hierarchical, crowded with adultist designations of children, and oriented to the changing faces of development and it should be noted that most of children's activities and spaces are striated. As James and James (2004) show, childhood social experiences are shaped and controlled by adults across many key social arenas of their everyday life, such mechanisms and processes constituting the cultural politics of childhood (James and James 2004:3–4). Of course, children also often do what they wish, even if it goes against the way they have been told or taught. In this case childhood appears less constraining and becomes a social space in which children learn to explore their environment and to experiment with their agency (James & James 2004:4). Thus, although James and James regard childhood as a social space, whereas Aitken's space is more physical, there are clear resemblances between James and James's less-contained social spaces and Aitken's smooth spaces. In smooth spaces adult designations are fewer or more diffuse, and they give more room for children's 'I-dos'. They are, in a way, forgotten spaces or hideaways not regulated by adults where children can learn about themselves more on their own terms. As this chapter will show, what is interesting about the frontiering food-scape is that it is relatively smooth or holds smooth spots that open up opportunities for children's becoming other.

Material and relevance

In the 24 households we encountered there were approximately 80 children, and most of them, on their arrival to Sweden, had been babies or between 10 and 12 years old. For the Bosnian families their entry into Sweden had happened several years ago, in the mid-1990s, but the Iraqi families had arrived only 3–4 years prior to when the study was conducted, in the early 2000s. Most of the families were Muslim, but religion did not come out as a major issue in the interviews. The Bosnian women were secular, having spent most of their lives in socialist Yugoslavia. In addition, many of the Iraqi women came from big cities like Baghdad, and had a 'western' appearance. They had all opposed religious categorisation and the religious totalitarian regimes of their home countries. Fasting during Ramadan was, for example, explained to us as 'custom, nothing religious, a good way to lose weight' and only one of the women wore a veil.

Children's influences over food seemed to have been most prominent from around the age of 6 to 11–12 years of age. These represent the first years of school, when the children learn to read and spend time outside of the home, and parents also expect them to begin to cope on their own, without their parents' constant supervision. Younger children generally spent their days with mother and siblings and, since all of the women with small children were housewives, they had little firsthand knowledge of the foodscape outside the home. The mothers also told us that they had been able to influence their children's eating when they were small, for example, when they were spoon-feeding them. Teenagers were not spoken of with the same pride and gratitude as their younger siblings. More often, they were considered a problem; for example, teenage girls who did not want to learn to cook the homeland specialties, much to their mother's sorrow, since this was an important part of the female role in the home country and a way to keep a link with the homeland, with relatives and with customs.

Since the mothers' stories were of incidents that, in many cases, had happened many years ago, their remembrances cannot be accurate in every detail. However the overall tenor of their stories is clear and can be relied on since the main focus of the interviews was on the mothers' experiences and practices as housewives and as cooks. They were aware that we were interested in issues of health and they were very keen to let us know that they knew a lot about unhealthy and healthy food. They also assured us that they tried hard to keep to a diet, since many of them were overweight. The stories they told us of their children were related as general concerns, women-to-women. They were accounts of their everyday worries about children not wanting to eat the healthy food they would have liked them to eat and so on and they did not seem to notice that, what appeared as 'common knowledge' for them, was not so from our Swedish perspective. These differences provide the food for thought about children as food agents in frontiering foodscapes.

Frontiering children as antennas

From the stories the women told it became obvious that the children were soon in their element in the new country. They quickly picked up information. They learned the language and were able to read the text on the packages of the supermarket shelves and help their mothers decipher the content. They went to school and watched other children, had school lunches and home economics classes where they learned to cook new food. They acquired new tastes and new food favourites that they wanted to try at home. In short, they soon were acquainted with their foodscape and learned to navigate it. The mothers were proud of their progress, relied on them and saw this decision making by children as the fulfilment of their dreams for their children in the new country. Much like parents of my own middle-age generation who tend to give up in the new digitalscape of computers and remote controls, leaving the management of DVDs, digital cameras and television sets to their children, the refugee children become clever test pilots in the new frontiering food space that opened up for these families. Bridging the old and the new, it allowed them a new agency, rendering them the gratitude and pride of their parents.

It is important to remember that these parents, like other refugee families, had left their home country to be able to live in peace and freedom and give their children a better future (see for example Bryceson & Vuorela (2002:13)). This accords also with Povrzanovic's (2002) findings of Croatian refugees from Bosnia-Herzegovina in Sweden. Children's well-being and a cluster of values connected to the family were recurrent themes in the narrations she recorded. 'We came to Sweden offering ourselves at the altar of the children', as one of her respondents put it (2002:129). The women in our study tried really hard, from the very start, to make their homes as 'smooth' as possible in order to enhance the children's possibilities to be happy and to lead a good life in the new country. Their lives should not become the same as their parents, but something different, requiring a new set of competences, desires and objects, which are hard for the parents to decide on. Instead, the children must choose.

In the following three stories the agency of the children shines through.

First story: 'If the children want it, you have to cook it'

'She decides lots, lots. I don't really like it, but I ask her and... if we don't eat, what shall I do? If it is only me eating and not her? I can't tell her 'You must eat!' When she was little, I tried to, when I spoon-fed her. But now I have to like what my daughter likes.'

Food is a special commodity. It is necessary for survival, and it is perishable. You cannot save it for very long, or bring it in large quantities from your home country when you leave. Instead, you have to go to the local shops, and pick something from their local assortment, bring it home and transform it into dishes that give nourishment and delight to the family. Food and eating is, therefore, a very practical and mundane way to get to know a new culture and, as Aviakan (1997) has maintained, downplaying the importance of their own food and adopting the food-ways of the new country is one of the ways that immigrants opt for integration. Already, in the initial interviews, it became obvious that it was largely the children (and grandchildren) who were the leading and most knowledgeable actors in this process. They decided what to eat at home. Although the women often remarked that they were the ones who eventually decided what to cook, they did this while considering the children's opinions. It was important for them to cook food their children liked in order for them to eat it, get full and be contented.

The women were, for example, not very happy about semi-manufactured or deep frozen foods, like French fries, fish croquettes or pizzas. However, they felt that they had to buy them anyway, because their children wanted them. 'We have to', the women argued. It was also common that the children had Coca-cola on weekends and on holidays, even though the women did not really want to buy it. But they still did buy Coca-cola because their children enjoyed it. They get it 'with meat', when the family is having something special for dinner; 'they decide', one of the women remarked. Her children were also allowed to have crisps on weekends. They like it and she buys them large bags.

Another woman was deeply concerned that her daughter had too many sweets. 'I tell her not to eat sweets, it is not good for your teeth, but she likes sweets a lot'. Her daughter does not eat any fruit at all, and she spends all her pocket money on sweets, loads of sweets. The mother also, reluctantly, buys pizza to take home now and then, since this is another one of her daughter's favourites. She gets sad thinking about this, she told us, but she feels that there is not much that she can do about it. Her daughter also likes deep frozen fish croquettes and meatballs with boiled potatoes, so she makes this, even though she herself prefers traditional Iraqi foods, which she considers to be healthier. She also buys deep frozen hamburgers and readymade hamburger rolls, although she really does not want to. It is just because her daughter fancies that kind of food.

Second story: 'I cook everything, Swedish, Bosnian, it doesn't matter'

> 'My daughter makes Swedish food. And Bosnian pie, for example. I have shown her how to make various sorts of pie. It is important to learn both Bosnian and Swedish cooking. Maybe half Swedish and half Bosnian foods. It can be any kind of food, just any kind.'

The children's delight in Swedish food is not presented as a problem by the mothers. With little trouble, the women are able to find compromises that are accepted by the family. One woman told us that her children did not like the soup that is often part of a Bosnian meal, but wanted a sandwich instead. For her it was no problem to put both soup and water and bread and butter with milk on the table. The children also liked milk shakes and they preferred meat or sausage on the table every day, which she did not consider healthy. But this is not a problem, she says. Although the family cannot afford meat on the table every day, they have it now and then to please their children.

Hybrid cooking is thus another dimension of the capacity to 'relativize' that the experiences of frontier families make clear; a little bit of this and a little bit of that in different combinations in different situations. Indeed, this is a marker of a frontier lifestyle (Bryceson & Vuorela 2002:29) and in our interviews there are several examples of the women creating their own dishes, combining Swedish and Bosnian or Iraqi food to please both the children and themselves. One woman offered her family Iraqi Samonbread (round, flat cakes of bread), together with Swedish hard cheese (hushållsost) for breakfast, but not on top of the bread the Swedish way, rather as a side dish. She has also learned how to make cinnamon buns, which are not made in Iraq, because her children like them.

School has influenced the children's Swedish food favourites. One of the women told us about her son: ' "Oh, mother, today it is spaghetti day in school!" Then he is really pleased'.[5] Other women told how their children wanted potatoes with their food, which they had learned to appreciate in school. By contrast, in Bosnia, potatoes are only eaten as an ingredient in soup or a pie and in Iraq they are hardly eaten at all. The children also learned to cook dishes in the Home Economics classes, which they wanted to try at home. That the boys also attended these classes was appreciated by the women. In Bosnia and Iraq men rarely cook, and such Swedish equality is felt by them to be much better. As one woman said: 'Yesterday my daughter made dinner for the whole family. Potatoes, onion, spices and cheese in a pan that she put in the oven. She had learned this in school, and it was very good.'

The most prominent feature found in the interview data is that it really did not matter, for the women, if the food was Bosnian/Iraqi or Swedish. Their main concern was that the children liked it and wanted to eat it. Most of them remarked that they made all kinds of food at home and that mixing Swedish food with Bosnian or Iraqi was no trouble for them: 'We eat Swedish food, Bosnian, sometimes we have pizza. It is not Swedish but we eat it. First time I had pizza was in Italy, but we make food from various countries. I like Swedish food, it is easy to make and good for your stomach.'

Third story: 'Come and watch me!'

'I want her to learn the special foods. I say "Come and watch me!". Sometimes she comes, but sometimes, no, it's only the computer that will do. I really don't know what to do!'

At the same time as the women take a great interest in Swedish food and mix Swedish and Bosnian or Iraqi dishes without any trouble, they are nonetheless eager to keep their homeland specialties, like the Bosnian pie or the Iraqi Brijani. They see these as very much connected to the homeland and, for their daughters, learning to make these dishes is part of the socialisation process. Such dishes are considered 'love food from mother to children' (see also Sellerberg 2008:61), since they hold so many values and memories for the mothers. Moreover, they are quite complicated and lengthy to make so that, in their making, the women need to invest lots of work, caring and love. Their wish is that their children (daughters) and grandchildren should learn to appreciate and make them; and their fear is that they will not be able to pass these skills and tastes on because of their children's lack of time and interest. This way a vital link to the home country and to the traditional women's role and its skills will be lost, they feel.

From the women's accounts, it is obvious, however, that these foods of the home country are treated as secondary to Swedish food. They become 'special foods' for holidays and family occasions. The Swedish or hybrid foods, by contrast, now act as the normal everyday food. The homeland food becomes 'othered' since the 'love food from mother to children' cannot compete with the Swedish fast foods the children like. This means not only new roles for children, but also for mothers. For mothers to show affection now means not only making the difficult special 'love foods' but buying and cooking what the children like and even liking what they like. This can be a hard lesson to learn, that transforms mother into more of a supporter, than a guide, in the foodscape. Thus, the children take up the role of food guide and teacher for their sometimes stubborn, but also admiring, parents.

Relativising and synchronising tastes

Since the inception of the discipline, anthropologists have demonstrated how food is a profound medium of reciprocity that marks and distinguishes persons and relations through acts of sharing, giving and receiving (Malinowski 1922; Mauss 1925). Today there is a broad consensus that food is about commensality, and that it is the capacity of food to make connections that is its most essential function (Lien 2004). It thus comes as no surprise that the relation-building potential of eating together is pronounced in frontiering families. Eating together is part of what Bryceson and Vuorela (2002) call relativising, referring to the variety of ways individuals establish, maintain or curtail relational ties with family members. Relativising refers to modes of materialising the family as an imagined community with shared feelings of mutual obligations and is intended to stress the sense of relativity, of being related, that occurs in transnational families (Bryceson & Vuorela 2002:14) This is what food and meals are very much about. As shown in the narratives above, the children and their desires are the antennas in this process and the mothers try their best to accommodate their children's feelings and tastes in their decisions. Even if this means accepting food on the table that they themselves do not like or think is unhealthy they succumb to their wishes and even try to like the same food themselves. The children decide and they follow.

In contrast to this, the family meal is generally considered a main site for socialisation. The children have to learn 'food rules' (Counihan 1999), not only with regard to manners at the table, but they also have to learn to restrict their own food tastes and desires. They have to learn 'family tastes' and what are considered the normal food choices. This process is what Swedish sociologist Sellerberg (2008) calls the synchronisation of tastes. To be able to talk of yourself as a 'soup family', or to be able to say 'in our family we always have steak on Sundays', is very important, she argues. This is (primarily still) mother's work in all families, but the process is of special significance in immigrant families, Sellerberg maintains, because there is such a huge difference between the food of the old country and the food in the new country that the children like. In her own study of mothers with young children from countries like Lebanon, Iraq and Afghanistan, the 'cognitive engineering' the women engaged in to continually maintain proper eating, while also being flexible to the individual projects and preferences of the household members, is highlighted.

From the perspective of children's agency, however, it is obvious in our study that the synchronisation of tastes is very much what children do. Where it is normally considered that the children are the ones who are supposed to change – to restrict childish or egoistic tastes and mature to appreciate a broader range of healthy foods that are considered socially acceptable and 'normal' – in frontier families this synchronisation is to a large extent in the hands of the children. The whole family has to like what the children like. Families have to synchronise tastes to go on being families since synchronising tastes is a concrete way of materialising their unity as a family in new circumstances.

It is important to note, however, that this synchronisation should not be taken as a mark of bad parenting; rather, it is about putting the relation-building capacities of food before aspects of health. Neither is Swedish food always represented by food the women consider unhealthy; on the contrary, many mothers saw Swedish food as good food, because it is not as fatty as Bosnian or Iraqi food. One of them told us how 'Swedish slim food' like corn, lettuce, and filet of chicken and boiled potatoes are her children's favourite dishes, and another one tells how her daughter adores Swedish crisp bread and eats it every day.

Normalising Swedish food

As is clear from our earlier examples, much of the food that is considered by our interviewees as Swedish has very little to do with what is 'originally Swedish'. Instead, 'Swedish food' is the everyday cooking for families with children today and is what is considered children's food, probably not only in Sweden but in many other parts of the world (Roos 2002, Johansson et al. 2008, Vallianatos & Raine 2008). In this sense, it is Swedishness or normality as viewed by the children. In Sweden 'children's foods' – foods children generally like – are pizza, hamburgers, hot dogs, tacos, pasta. This is the kind of food the refugee children wanted at home, together with crisps and sodas. In Sweden, parents offer their children this kind of food to please them or to make sure they get full, but it is not considered very healthy food. Rather it is regarded as exactly the kind of food that children should restrict themselves from liking too much, in order to learn to eat a broader variety of healthier, more grown-up food. However, the children in our study also liked traditional Swedish foods, usually served in the school canteen, such as potatoes, brown sauce, meatballs, lingonberry preserve, rye bread and milk. They sometimes also wanted the privilege to take crisps, candy and soft drinks to their rooms to eat by themselves on weekends, and not in the company of their families. This was something they were generally allowed to do, much to their parents' reluctance, since this was considered the Swedish way. For the parents (like for Swedish parents), food is about sitting and talking together while having a tasty and nourishing common meal, and not to be consumed in solitude.

Thus, the argument of this chapter is that the refugee children are given agency, not only to decide what to eat, but to decide normality and Swedishness. This agency is, largely, derived from their expertise within the local foodscape, and the many smooth spots where they can exercise I-dos. Sima, described in the introduction, does not only know how to buy milk for her mother, and about expiry-dates and prices, she is also well accustomed to the burgeoning shelves with sugary cereals that are the favourites of her and her native born friends. Among the Coco Pops, Coco Pops Rocs and Frosties her personal favourite is Breakfast Hearts. The foodscape that evolves around her also includes, among other things, the school canteen, the healthy foods at the after-school centre and the candy-talk of the school breaks.

That mothers adhere to their children's demands for food from the new country and adapt their cooking is a common experience, as data from other European countries demonstrates (see Ruud 1998 for a Norwegian example, and Vallianatos & Raine 2008 for a Canadian one). This gives frontier children a unique position, responsibility and self-confidence. It might be too big a responsibility for them to carry; they might get into bad company, become one of 'the lads', circulating in the schoolyard eating crisps and candy instead of proper school meals. But during this process they also get access to 'Swedish childhood', something that helps them integrate.

Smooth spaces and striated spots of the foodscape

As argued above, eating Swedish food is a direct way of incorporating Swedishness, by relating the self to the territories of food and space (Sweden), or by incorporating food and space into what we call 'the self' (cf. Dolphijn 2004:55). One reason that immigrant children are given such apparent food agency is that it occurs in the smooth and almost neglected foodscapes of women and children – the local space of food and eating in the family, nearby shops, playground, school yard and afternoon centre, places where the mothers are at a loss, staff or other adults don't care, and the children are experts. And it is the very ordinariness of food, and the relative invisibility of the childish foodscape to authorities, such as teachers and health experts, that becomes an important factor supporting children's agency. These foodscapes prove to be a free zone for experimentation and confirmation of I-dos.

The foodscape of the children is, however, not altogether smooth as we have seen. At home it becomes to some extent striated through the mother's ambition to restrict the children's eating of meat, crisps and soft drinks to weekends, and their insistence that their daughters shall learn the special foods of their home country. While the latter points in the direction of the children becoming-the-same (as their mothers), the mothers, also actively turn the family foodscape in the direction of modernity, that is towards becoming-the-same as (their image of) Swedish children. They do this by helping their children to conform to the lifestyles of their peers and giving them certain kinds of 'modern' commodities and fashions. This resonates well with Salih's (2002) study of Moroccan women in Italy, who felt it very important to buy the things their children desired as a way to contribute to the stronger personality type of their children that they considered Italian children to have.

In Salih's study the commodities that the children desired were often school bags, clothes, shoes and toys, which would confer on them a status of equality with their schoolmates, and we also found examples of this in our study. One mother told us about her daughter: 'She likes clothes and shoes a lot. She says: "look at my friends, they have clothes, nice clothes and shoes. Mother, why don't I?" I have to buy. So I say "OK".' It is very important for her that her daughter should have 'everything the same as her friends', that she should have 'a good life'. While in some cases parents simply cannot afford these items, in others, through directing their choices to those specific objects of consumption, the women engaged in what Salih (2002:56) describes as a politics of negotiating difference to cope with the mainstream values of a society which emphasises conformity to certain fashions The consumption of 'modernity' or of choosing certain 'modern' items, like a certain brand of jeans, is one way for frontier women to solve the children's difference from mainstream society. The woman in the quote above managed this, she told us, by 'picking special things in the store', the ones with a great symbolic value for her daughter, and she hardly begrudges her anything. Sometimes she goes to Ullared (a discount store) and buys a lot. This is a way that mothers engage in childhood politics, by limiting their children's choices and directing them to items that are decidedly 'modern', that speak of development and 'becoming-the-same'. They have the purse, but it is up to the children to decide modernity and normality. Similarly, this may be another reason why crisps, soft drinks, candy, Coco Pops Rocs and other items from a childish and decidedly modern fast-foodscape find their way into immigrant family kitchens and living rooms.

Eating modernity

Another ingredient in the children's foodscape is McDonald's. As all the mothers told us, they take their children there occasionally. Their mothers are not fond of McDonald's. They do not like the food. But their children do. 'My daughter says, mother, I like McDonald's, so I go with her'. There are many reasons why the mothers accompany their children there, but the main reason is that the children want to go there and the mothers want to accompany them. It is also considered fairly cheap, they have halal meat and McDonald's is also well known from their home countries. One of the teenage daughters acting as an interpreter and fluent in both cultures explained to us that in her home country (Bosnia) McDonald's was considered an OK place to go, a proper restaurant. In Bosnia, restaurants were not as fancy as 'proper restaurants in Sweden with white table cloth and waiters taking the orders by the table', she told us. Instead, they looked much like McDonald's. The ordinary Bosnian family took their children at least once a week to the simple cafeteria or taverna 'around the corner', where they had a nice and not very expensive meal and a chat with family, friends and neighbours. In their eyes, McDonald's serves much the same function in Sweden.

Thus, not only are hamburgers, pizza and meatballs liked foods for Swedish children, McDonald's visits are also part of a normal Swedish foodscape for children. Swedish families with small children visit the restaurants almost twice a month on average and the restaurants are eager to adapt to the values and behaviour of Swedish families (Brembeck 2005a). McDonald's visits are part of what families, also with low incomes or out of work, try their best to give their children (Hjort 2004). McDonald's is, in fact, connected to modernity in many parts of the world (Watson 1997), as my own brief study of parents and children at McDonald's in Singapore, suggested. I learned that, at least for the upwardly middle class, the rice-based meal was considered traditional and old fashioned, while French fries symbolised modernisation, modern lifestyles, college education, high-salary jobs and high standards of living (Brembeck 2005b). Maybe this is part of the reason why the mothers in our study so willingly accompanied their children there, and put aside enough money to be able to do so.

Integration through food consumption?

There are, of course, categorisations of child shoppers and how to behave as a child in shops and other places within foodscapes. Such designations are, however, not very regulated, and are generally described in ethnic terms. The dancing Sima, who appears at the start of this chapter, with her 'Swedish' child body and her Iranian headscarf was exploring her own way of moving around in the shop, without anybody caring or even noticing her. However, as Salih (2002:56) argues, although immigrants' consumption patterns denote a model of integration, they do not reduce the migrants' social and political marginalisation. Maybe, then, for children it is not as easy to become a citizen as it is to manage the foodscape. Experiences from school seem to confirm this.

Sima is fluent in Swedish and very good at reading and writing, she is in fact the emblem of a clever schoolgirl. Still, her eating preferences are considered problematic by the teachers, especially the fact that, at only ten years old, she wants to fast at Ramadan. Her teachers can't understand why, and she tells me that this is nothing her parents demand of her. The teachers are worried that she will not get energy enough to take her through the school day, that she will get tired and not perform to her usual standard, and they are secretly content that she regularly 'falls through' and has some fruit to eat in the afternoon. Thus, her eating habits, which also include not eating pig's meat, make her not only ethnic, but also a problem.

In Sweden, the school is a firmly striated space for children, even though its food and eating spaces, like the canteen, the after-school centre or lunch breaks, are less regulated, Thus, for example, in a study of ethnic minority children in Denmark, Gitz-Johansen (2004) shows that they were often defined as not living up to the standards of the school culture and were thus considered incompetent. The children's lack of language competence was highlighted, but the teachers also expected these 'problems' to spill over into areas other than reading and writing. Moreover, while the majority children's deficits were considered appropriate responses to modernity and to their growing up in the intense stimulation, flow of information and general flux of modern society, the minority children's incompetence was attributed to tradition. At best they were regarded as 'exotic', perhaps most visible when the minority ethnic children and their families were invited to display their traditional costumes, food and dance at school. We, too, witnessed such exoticisation in our study, when the women made large quantities of pies for a 'Bosnian day' at the local school.

Frontier children are thus caught in a trap between tradition and modernity; they exist in a sort of no man's land, caught between two cultures that cause them a huge problem to present themselves as human and as becoming-Swedes (see also Wikström 2007). In our study, for example the mothers were eager not to be considered 'ethnic'. They regard themselves as individuals with separate life histories. Some are from cities, like Sarajevo, Banja Luka and Baghdad, some from the surrounding countryside; they have different occupations and family backgrounds. They argue that Bosnians have always been very 'European', and that religion meant very little in the socialist Yugoslavia, or that Baghdad was always an international city; the pearl of the Middle East. Bosnianness and Iraqiness is in their bellies, their palates and their skills as cooks.

Their children also fight ethnification, I would argue. By choosing 'Swedish foods' and by going to McDonald's, they display their normality and Swedishness. Sima tries to create her own Swedish way of being Muslim by eating fruit, which she tells me she does not consider food. Her mother also helps her (or restricts her if you choose to see it that way) by making her bags of dried fruits to bring to school. This way she can sit at the table in the canteen and at the after-school centre with her friends and, like them, have something to eat (cf. Vallianatos & Raine 2008).

But, at the same time, Sima has long ago noticed that she is different, and that this difference has something to do with ethnicity. When I ask her about the coming Eid al-fitr, the feast ending Ramadan, and what she is going to eat, she enthusiastically starts telling me about the sweet drink children get, but suddenly stops and turns silent as the girls at the opposite side of the table start giggling – and I feel like a really clumsy adult interfering in her ways of making the I-dos fit the I-ams in the relatively smooth space of the of the after-school centre.[6]

Conclusion: Becoming other in frontiering foodscapes

This chapter has shown that children's 'becoming other' in frontiering foodscapes needs to be highlighted in order to better understand processes of integration, as well as children's agency more generally, and the importance of food in this respect. The space that opens up in between the old and the new of foodstuff, images, brands and people offers possibilities of an agency that is seldom ascribed to children in general. Although the sweet tooth of immigrant children might be considered as a health problem, our study suggests that is does offer them the possibility to introduce the family to the new country's foodscape; the childish foodscape of the new country gives them an important, albeit slender, opportunity of integration. Whether the recent Bosnian and Iraqi immigration will be a success story and whether the children will become Swedes in their own way, as Sima might, or be pushed into ethnification and otherness, is dependant on the capability and willingness of Swedish society to embrace the newcomers and offer support in all parts of social life.

Notes

1. The project is called *Barn som medforskare av matlandskap, BAMM* (Children as co-researchers of foodscapes) and it is conducted at Center for Consumer Science (CFK) 2008–2010 www.cfk.gu.se. The story of Sima runs like a brief parallel story in this chapter, which is otherwise drawing on results from the project 'The Multidimensional Food Consumer'.
2. The project was called 'The Multidimensional Food Consumer' and it was conducted at CFK 2004–2007 supported by one of the Swedish national research board Formas. The researchers that took part in the project were Helena Shanahan, Lena Jonsson and Kerstin Bergström from The Department of Home Economics, Eva Ossiansson from the Department of Marketing and MariAnne Karlsson and Pontus Engelbrektsson from Chalmers University of Technology, and I am of course deeply indebted to my colleagues in writing this chapter. During three years we studied three different groups in relation to food and eating: wealthy inner-city dwellers, new Swedes and households in a sparsely populated area in West Sweden. A brief English summary of the

project is Brembeck et al. 2007. Another article in English of the refugee families is Brembeck 2008.

3. Attempting to focus on the family as a node for creating familial space and networks in a transnational situation, Deborah Bryceson and Ulla Vuorela coin the concept frontiering defined as 'agency at the interface between two (or more) contrasting ways of life' (2002:12).
4. The study was of values and behaviour in regard to food, and not primarily on children. Twenty-four households, represented by the women, were interviewed, mostly with the help of an interpreter; they were given food diaries to complete and disposable cameras with which to photograph their cupboards, cooking and dining. They were then interviewed for a second time with reference to the content of their diaries and snapshots and dining, and finally we met them for a third time to discuss the future (Brembeck et al. 2006).
5. Spaghetti is of course not an originally Swedish dish, but a food favourite for Swedish kids, like for many children around the globe, and a part of the Swedish kitchen.
6. In one Göteborg school all the pupils are served soft drinks and chocolate biscuits the first morning after Ramadan to celebrate the end of feasting, just as they are served 'Lucia cats', a kind of saffron bun, and 'julmust', root beer, on Lucia day, 13th December (Göteborgs-Posten 04-10-2008). To be invited to join the party seems to me a good way of making Ramadan and Muslim children popular among their native peers.

References

Aitken, S. C. (2008). 'Desarollo Integral y Fronteras/Integral Development and Boarderspaces', in S. Aitken,S., Lund, R. & Kjorholt, A. (eds), *Global Childhoods. Globalization, Development and Young People.* London and New York: Routledge.

Aviakan, A. V. (1997). *Through the Kitchen Window. Women Explore the Intimate Meanings of Food and Cooking.* Boston: Beacon Press.

Brembeck, H. (2005a). 'Home to McDonald's. Upholding the family dinner by the help of McDonald's'. *Food, Culture & Society* 8: 215–226.

Brembeck, H. (2005b). 'Hello Kitty in Singapore. Bridging the human-artefact division', in Ekström, K. M. & H. Brembeck, (eds), *Elusive Consumption in Retrospect.* CFK-rapport 2005:01. Göteborg: Center for Consumer Science www.cfk.gu.se.

Brembeck, H. (2008). 'Mediating lifestyles: Food in the life of Bosnian refugee families in Sweden', in Romaniszyn, K. (ed.), *Culture and Migration: The Cultural Implication of International Migrations in the Light of Fieldwork Evidence.* Krakow: Nomos.

Brembeck, H. et al. (2006). *Maten och det nya landet.* CFK-rapport 2006:05. Göteborg: Center for Consumer Science www.cfk.gu.se.

Brembeck, H. et al. (2007). 'Enjoyment and concern. The importance of food and eating for ageing consumers' *Proceedings of the Nordic Consumer Research Conference 2007.* Helsinki, 3–5 October 2007 www.consumer2007.info.

Bryceson, D. & Vuorela, U. (2002). 'Transnational families in the twenty-first century', in Bryceson, D. & Vuorela, U. (eds), *The Transnational Family. New European Frontiers and Global Networks*. Oxford: Berg.

Counihan, C. M. (1999). 'The social and cultural uses of food', in Kiple, K. F. & Ornelas-Kiple, C. K. (eds), *The Cambridge World History of Food and Nutrition*. New York and Cambridge: Cambridge University Press.

Deleuze, G. and Guattari, F. (1988). *A Thousand Plateaus*. London: Althone Press.

Dolphijn, R. (2004). *Foodscapes: Toward a Deleuzian Ethics of Consumption*. Delft: Eburon Press.

Gitz-Johansen, T. (2004). 'The incompetent child. Representations of ethnic minority children', in Brembeck, H., Johansson, B. & Kampmann, J. (eds), *Beyond the Competent Child. Exploring Contemporary Childhoods in the Nordic Welfare Societies*. Frediksberg: Roskilde University Press.

Göteborgs-Posten (16-09-2003). 'Läsk och godis vardagsmat för barnen i invandrartät förort till Göteborg'.

Göteborgs-Posten (04-10-2008). 'Hjällboskolan bjöd på morgonfika efter fastan'.

Hjort, Torbjörn (2004). *Nödvändighetens pris. Konsumtion och knapphet bland barnfamiljer*. Lund dissertations in social work 20.

James, A. & James, A. L. (2004). *Constructing Childhood. Theory, Policy and Social Practice*. Houndsmill, Basingstoke: Palgrave.

Johansson, B., Hillen, S., Mäkela, J. et al. (2009). 'Nordic children's foodscapes: Images and reflections'. *Food, Culture and Society: An International Journal of Multidisciplinary Research* 12(1):25–51.

Lien, M. E. (2004). 'The politics of food: An introduction', in Lien, M. E. & Nerlich, B. (eds), *The Politics of Food*. Oxford: Berg.

Malinowski, B. (1922). *Argonauts of the Western Pacific. An Account of Native Enterprise and Adventure in the Archipelagos of Melanesian New Guinea*. London: Routledge.

Mauss, M. (1925). *The Gift. The Form and Reason of Exchange in Archaic Societies*. London: Penguin.

Nordin, E. (2003). 'Läsk och godis vardagsmat för barnen i invandrartät förort till Göteborg', *Dagens Medicin* 03-09-2003.

Povrzanovic F. M. (2002). 'Homeland lost and gained: Croatian diaspora and refugees in Sweden', in Al-Ali, N. & Koser, K. (eds), *New Approaches to Migration? Transnational Communities and the Transformation of Home*. London: Routledge.

Roos, G. (2002). 'Our bodies are made of pizza – food and embodiment among children in Kentucky'. *Ecology of Food and Nutrition* 41: 1–19.

Ruud, E. M. (1998). 'Matlagning på schemat'. *Invandrare & Minoriteter* nr. 3 2002: 37–39.

Salih, R. (2002). 'Shifting meanings of "home": Consumption and identity in Moroccan women's transnational practices between Italy and Morocco', in Al-Ali, N. & Koser, K. (eds), *New Approaches to Migration? Transnational Communities and the Transformation of Home*. London: Routledge.

SBU (2006). *Sammanfattningar och slutsatser*. Statens beredningar för medicinsk utvärdering, Stockholm: SBU (The Swedish Council on Technology Assessment in Health Care).

Sellerberg, A. (2008). *En het potatis. Om mat och måltid i barn- och tonårsfamiljer.* Research Reports in Sociology 2008:03. Department of Sociology, Lund University.

Vallianatos, H. & Raine, K. (2008). 'Consuming food and constructing identities among Arabic and South Asian immigrant women'. *Food, Culture & Society* 11(3): 335–353.

Watson, J. L. (ed.) (1997). *Golden Arches East. McDonald's in East Asia.* Stanford, CA: Stanford University Press.

Wikström, H. (2007). *(Im)possible Positions. Families from Iran & Postcolonial Reflections.* Department of Social Work, Göteborg University.

8
Food and Relationships: Children's Experiences in Residential Care

Samantha Punch, Ian McIntosh, Ruth Emond, Nika Dorrer

Children's access to food, and the negotiations that take place around it, extend beyond the realm of immediate family relations to children's social and educational worlds. Food can thus play an essential part in their experience of other social and institutional arenas such as schools, hospitals or residential care. Food is both an essential and mundane part of everyday life and our familiarity with it can mean that we often pay little attention to the meanings and actions that surround it. However, the study of food within institutional contexts can offer a fascinating insight into the inner life of the institution and the relationships that can revolve around food practices. Food, we suggest, works not only functionally, as sustenance, but also symbolically and as a way to show care and build relationships. It becomes a means by which children can navigate through much of their daily life. Food practices can also be sites of tension and conflict around which a range of emotions and the multifaceted nature of relationships may be exposed.

In this chapter we argue that food and food practices offer a dynamic and symbolic medium through which children living in residential care create, sustain and mark relationships with each other and with the adults who care for them. Formalised relations between staff and children can be transformed into more clearly affective relations via food and, as such, can have a significant effect on how children see themselves, the development of particular identities and their relations to adult carers.

Despite the growing recognition of the diversity of childhoods, research has tended to locate children within a familial setting. There has been relatively little research carried out in relation to children and food within an institutional context with the exception of studies in schools (e.g., Valentine 2000; Nukaga 2008; Pike 2008; Salazer et al.

2008). This is somewhat surprising given the importance attached to the often highly ritualised nature of food preparation and mealtimes within a range of institutions (e.g., Goffman 1991). For example, in the institutions for older people described by Sidenvall (1999), the precisely organised procedures carried out by nurses during every mealtime, although depicted as bringing about a homelike feel, prioritised the values of order, cleanliness, responsibility and efficiency and functioned as a means to maintain a clear distance between nurses and patients. Prison studies (Valentine & Longstaff 1998; Comfort 2002; Smith 2002; Godderis 2006) have documented the great significance food acquires for inmates as a legitimate outlet for anger and a means for subversion and assertion of power and autonomy. Food becomes a physical and symbolic manifestation of the boundary between 'inside' and 'outside', which inmates and their visitors attempt to bridge through bought food, the smuggling in of homemade food and eating something together during visits.

While there are some parallels between the uses and meanings of food in a prison or nursing home context and that of residential children's homes, there are significant differences. For example, within residential settings for children, particularly those that define themselves as 'therapeutic' treatment centres, food interactions between staff and children, and the children's participation in food-related tasks, have been construed as having emotionally healing and nurturing poten-tial (Rose 1997; Ward et al. 2003). These different views of the role of food in adult and child environments can be seen as a reflection of the dominant association between food, feeding and intimate relations as located in infancy, as well as a perception of institutions for children as places of personal and social development.

Marshall (2005:75), citing Lalonde (1992), draws attention to the two forms in which the meal can be thought of as creating meaningful pat-terns and distinctions in the course of everyday life, that is 'as both an object (a timely repast and structural entity) and an event (scripted purposeful action and meaningful social event)'. In the latter form, the meal marks not only the passing of time but gives momentum to a special occasion, often the passing over into something new. Many of the food rituals shared in society are about the marking of transitional points in life (Visser 1991).

In order to explore these and other issues, we draw on emerging data from an ESRC funded ethnographic study entitled *Food Practices in an Institutional Context: Children, Care and Control* which sought to address some of the gaps in our current understanding of residential child care.

This chapter focuses on one element of these food practices; namely, examining the role food plays in children's experiences of relationship building within residential care. In particular, it considers the use of food as a medium through which relationships between care workers and children can be conveyed, contested and maintained. To this extent, we explore the building, entering, testing and sustaining of relationships within three residential care homes in Scotland.

Food practices and residential care

Residential care for children has long been the subject of academic, social and political debate (Berridge & Brodie 1998). That children are 'brought up' outside the norm of family life, coupled with the long-standing stigma and stereotyping attached to residential institutions, has resulted in this form of provision becoming regarded as a 'last resort' for children in need of care and protection (Cogdell 1989; McPheat et al. 2007). However, the apprehension displayed towards residential child care (Kendrick 2008) by both government authorities and the general public, stems not only from concerns over the damaging effects of such care but also from a long-standing ambivalence towards the children for whom it is provided.

Arguably, the identities of children living in residential care have been problematised as 'other'; as children in need of being rescued but also regulated and reformed due to the neglect, abuse and 'contamination' they have experienced (Abrams 1998; Ferguson 2007). Children in public care embody the notion of both 'victims' and 'threats' to society. They tend to be perceived as children who have not been cared for or controlled 'adequately' within their own families, thereby representing, sometimes simultaneously, the child as 'innocent' requiring protection from society and the 'evil' child from which society requires protection (Davis & Bourhill 1997). While such moral and pathologising constructs have been challenged in critical research and approaches to child welfare, they have not erased such attitudes and responses to children in public care.

Research on residential child care has undergone several trends since the first studies into institutional life in the 1960s. Empirical research on residential provision has most often been concerned with the 'functional' aspects of this type of care linked to policy and planning for services: evaluation of staff practice, models of practice, effectiveness, demographic mapping, and the place of residential provision in the broader continuum of care for children (see, for example, Aiers & Kettle 1998). In some ways, the approach taken to the study of residential care has mirrored broader shifts in the study of children's lives. Within social science, research has moved from being conducted *about* children, to being *on* children, to current research that is undertaken *with* children. There is now recognition that children are active social agents whose lived experiences are worthy of study in and of themselves (Mayall 2002). This has resulted in a growing body of research into the everyday lives of children and staff who live and work in residential care. However, in their 2006 review of empirical research conducted on residential child care Clough et al. (2006) concluded that

> residential child care is a field which has been adequately researched but inadequately theorised. To be more precise, we now have a reasonable baseline of information about the structure and nature of existing services, about whom they are for and what happens in them, but we still know little about the details of the processes involved, their outcomes or about how these outcomes may best be achieved. (Clough et al. 2006:15)

This emphasis on gaining a better understanding of the interactional patterns of care is beginning to influence the way in which residential care is being researched. However, there is still little known about the conditions for, and characteristics of, good relationships between carers and children. The call for attention to the qualitative details of interactions resonates with a so-called 'lifespace' orientation to practice, which suggests that in the context of residential child care therapeutic intervention needs to be located in all aspects of everyday life (Smith 2005). Food constitutes one of these everyday facets of life. It pervades the daily routines of residential homes in such a mundane way that it is often overlooked and dismissed as a basic and commonsense part of care that sometimes just needs to be 'gotten on with'.

Children in residential care live relatively public lives in that they are under surveillance from a range of adults (social workers, residential workers, parents, etc.) and agencies and they can experience limited power and control in relation to the institutional system (Mayall 1996). Clough (2000) argues that the move into care can threaten an individual's sense of identity and sense of self. It may be the case that, for these children, their care status becomes the defining feature as it influences not only how they see themselves but also how they are viewed by others (Emond 2003). However, we would argue that governance, or power, is never total, even within the context of an institutional environment such as a residential care home (Foucault 1983; Goffman

1991; Bevir 1999; Lukes 2005). Patterns of consumption around food practices are thus a good way in which to explore the limits, extent and interplay of power and resistance. Given this, there can exist the potential for children to exert a degree of agency or 'local reasoning' (Bevir 1999) and to create the space to indulge in 'strategic interaction' (Goffman 1970).

Our research project is not concerned with issues of nutrition, healthy eating or the effects of types of food on behaviour but instead considers food and eating as an everyday practice which plays a central role in the daily interactions and routines carried out by staff and children in care homes. More specifically, food is central to children as a medium to negotiate uncertain relationships. Not only is food a means to contest positions of power but it is also a means for communicating care, and building and developing relationships over time. Food, then, is intimately linked to relational experiences within a care and institutional context.

Methods

The research methods were selected with several objectives in mind. We wanted to be able to observe the dynamics that existed between carers and children around food over time. Secondly, we were concerned with gaining an understanding of these dynamics and the meaning given by children and adults to these interactions with and around food. Consequently, the research included 36 weeks of semi-participant observation across three residential children's homes as well as 12 group and 49 individual interviews (plus 48 unstructured or spontaneously recorded interviews) with the staff and children of these homes.

Given the small and close-knit residential community in Scotland, the identity of the children's homes and our participants need to be protected. Therefore specific ages are not stated, pseudonyms are used and only a pen picture can be given of the homes involved, which we have called Lifton, Wellton and Highton. Each home provided space for six full-time residents (with one of them providing two additional spaces on a part-time basis) although numbers could be lower depending on the timing of children moving in and out. Twenty-one children (14 boys and 7 girls) resided at the three homes during the fieldwork phase. At the time of data generation the homes catered to different age groups, the youngest group being 9–13 years of age, a middle group of 12–16 years, and a slightly older group ranging from 14–18 years. The data was gathered during the course of three 12-week blocks of ethnographic fieldwork in each home (between three and six day-long visits per week, including some overnights) and collected in field notes, overt audio recordings of mealtime interactions, semi-structured interviews and focus groups with the children and members of staff. Sixteen children (11 boys and 5 girls) and 46 staff members (26 women and 20 men including managerial staff, care workers, three cooks, administration and domestic staff) participated in an individual interview and/or a focus group.

Food and building relationships

Institutions, just as families, develop their own cultures and rituals, rules and routines imbued with meaning that may not be readily accessible to outsiders (Ward 1993). What adults and children entering institutions share is the experience of having to conform to food practices that they are not necessarily familiar with or do not, at least initially, recognise as meaningful. In all three of the residential homes food practices punctuated days and weeks into different segments of time and activity through fixed mealtimes and rules around what food can be consumed when, where and in what way (see Table 8.1). Each home provided breakfast, lunch, tea and supper, with tea being the main structured mealtime of the day. A professional cook prepared most of the main meals in each of the residential homes. Children were able to participate in the choosing and preparation of food to varying degrees across the three units.

Food was looked to as a means of overcoming a number of interpersonal and institutional barriers within the residential home. For example, it was noted by several members of staff that ways of actively showing care have become increasingly circumscribed within a residential setting. In particular, the use of physical affection has become much more regulated. Thus, food was perceived to provide a 'safe' medium through which emotional care could be communicated as Eddie suggests: 'I think within the residential world there are only so many ways you can show you care and food is one of them. A lot of other things have been taken away' (Eddie, Care Worker, Interview, Highton).

Amongst the staff, there was a dominant view that eating should be an inherently social activity. The socialising dimension of food seemed to be such a taken for granted cultural norm, something 'natural' and 'fundamental', that the socially constructed nature of rules and expectations was often uncritically accepted and acted out. This was particularly the case regarding the expectation that people converse about their day while eating together. Residential staff repeatedly stated that mealtimes and related chores could provide temporal scaffolding around which a relaxed and informal atmosphere could be created, thus enabling people to interact, get to know each other, and build relationships:

> it's the one point in time where everybody has a gathering point at lunch and evening meal where we sit and talk about our day and what's gone on and we tell jokes and we laugh and we moan about this, that and the other, and it's, it's a point in the day where everybody sits and that's the cook, the cleaner, the manager, the kids, everybody sits [...] which is great. (Derek, Unit Manager, Interview, Lifton)
>
> They come in from school, they sit, they sit down and you have a wee conversation over tea about how their day went, what did they do at school, just stuff that would have happened. (Rory, Care Worker, Interview, Wellton)

Many of the staff talked positively about the role of mealtimes as an opportunity for both children and staff to develop their relationships; a hoped for backdrop against which relations that are seen to be spontaneous and 'natural' can evolve. The coming together and sitting around the table created a space for conversation between and within the generations: 'it's like a social trigger, if you like. It's like you have permission to chat' (Eric, Care Worker, Interview, Highton).

However, it was widely recognised across the three residential homes that mealtimes around the table not only facilitated opportunities for relationship building but also carried the potential for conflict. Some residential staff described them as the most stressful times of the day: 'in the five years I've been here I find probably teatimes the most difficult time' (Sandra, Care Worker, Focus Group, Wellton). Mealtimes could be experienced as anxious occasions and as a setting in which children sought to exercise control:

> It can actually be a place, because all the kids are together and because all the staff are together, it can be a place that a young person will orchestrate conflict because they have the biggest audience. (Alana, Care Worker, Focus Group, Lifton)

In the same focus group, Bernice referred to mealtimes as children's 'platform for conflict'. This means that children's approach to mealtimes as providing an 'audience' for the expression of anger was not in line with the staffs' perception of mealtimes as an informal and democratic 'forum' for all to have a say. In the face of these challenges, the

Table 8.1 Main food practices across the three residential homes

Food Practices	Highton	Wellton	Lifton
Shared mealtimes around the table	Lunch and tea	Tea (children make their own lunch supervised by adults, and then chose where to sit)	Lunch and tea
Attendance at the table	Highly encouraged – adults try to coax children to the table	Enforced – children must sit at the table for teatime	Voluntary – less adult pressure to sit at the table
Who participates in the main meal (i.e., tea)	Care staff, cook, assistant managers and children	Care staff and children	Care staff, cook, managers, domestic and admin staff and children
What is eaten	Variety of dishes: usually something 'unhealthy' which the children want (i.e., chips), a traditional British dish (e.g., casserole) and new cuisine (e.g., vegetarian dish)	One main meal on offer, e.g., steak pie, mash potatoes and carrots (a variation such as chicken may be provided if the main dish is not liked)	Some variety, usually two choices, such as mince and potatoes or pasta and salads
Conversational approach during main meal	Focus on keeping it positive and upbeat, encouraging children to lead the conversation and suggest plans for the evening	Fairly structured – tends to start with staff asking questions about the children's day and ends with plans for the evening. The middle section varies depending on who is present and their mood	Anecdotes and stories about their shared history, current issues and their imagined futures
Cleaning tasks	Children would be expected to clean their own dishes but not each other's	A cleaning rota was in operation for each teatime whereby children would take turns in doing all the dishes	No expectations around children cleaning their own nor others' dishes
Breakfast	Maybe provided in their bedroom or they could grab something to eat on way to school	Children's breakfasts organised at staggered intervals in order to make sure they are ready on time for school	Individualised routines between particular children and staff
Supper	Toast and cheese in the dining or living room. Prepared by children or staff	No food, just juice in children's bedrooms as a means to help them settle for the night	Tea and toast in the living room. Other snacks if requested. Prepared by staff

staff often reverted to rules and the sanctioning of privileges as a system of control to ensure that the aims of the 'good mealtime' were achieved. In turn, this sometimes led to children perceiving mealtimes in a negative light. Thus, at times, the therapeutic potential of bringing people together across a dinner table and building relations could collapse when there was a mismatch between children and staff's expectations and interpretations surrounding the role of mealtimes. Given this, aspects of both care and control could be played out through the daily routine of sitting around the table to eat.

In two of the residential homes, members of staff gave examples of offering cups of tea or making something to eat on request, outside normal mealtimes, as a key way of demonstrating care and relationship building. The explanations that some members of staff provided regarding the meaning of this gesture suggested that the act held heavy symbolic significance and shared cultural understanding that they could draw upon and utilise. For most staff a primary function of the offer of a cup of tea, and the associated rituals accompanying the making and giving of it, was a way of acknowledging children's presence, giving them attention, responding to their needs (physical or emotional) and developing and maintaining relations. As the quotations below indicate, a cup of tea can open up an opportunity to chat informally with the children:

> If you're sitting there, you know, having a cup o' tea and cake or whatever and just chatting away about school or football or soaps on TV [...] it's more relaxed. (Claire, Care Worker, Focus Group, Wellton)
>
> I suppose it's just a way of caring, eh? 'Do you want a wee cup of tea? I'll fix ye a wee cup of tea', ken what I mean and, I suppose it's just a way. You know, a cup of tea solves everything in Scotland! Have you no' heard that yet? Watch all thae auld sitcoms. 'Wee cup of tea, hen'. And it disnae solve anything but I suppose it's just the way of showing, aye, I dae care have a wee cup of tea. 'Cause I suppose that offers the opportunity of...when you're making them a cup of tea it also offers the opportunity for to have a chat as well I suppose. (Iris, Care Worker, Interview, Lifton)

Making a cup of tea was a tangible demonstration of having made a compassionate effort and created a brief, but meaningful and readily understood, affirmation of caring. It also held the potential for initiating and developing a relationship. The simplicity and clarity of the cup of tea ritual lends itself to becoming part of a regular and commonplace occurrence within the care home and, as such, these apparently mundane acts and routines can be infused with positive elements relating to relationship building and maintenance.

Nevertheless, intersubjective meanings of particular acts are not routinely understood uniformly by all and, in the present study, children were not always familiar with the rituals such as the sharing of cups of tea between staff and children when they moved in. Similarly, some staff also had a more practical understanding of making cups of tea, as one care worker put it: 'I don't know, I am not really conscious about the reasons I do it. I just do it'. (Aaron, Care Worker, Interview, Wellton). However, it could be an important step in the process of getting to know a resident, as the following quote illustrates:

> For example, Lucy, a new young person who was in for the first time last night, I was making a cup of tea for people and Lucy turned round and said 'I don't drink tea or coffee. I do drink hot chocolate' and I says 'well I'll make you a hot chocolate then' and she said okay. Now I don't know anything about Lucy, obviously there was nothing I could help with her last night about her life because I've got the whole file of her and I've never read it all, but there's nothing, 'cause there's nae relationship developed, that I can help with her there but the message I give her by doing an individual hot chocolate is, you know, 'I do care for you' and 'I'll make something for you that you specifically asked for'. So it's a good kind of start to communication you know. (Will, Assistant Manager, Interview, Lifton)

In general, food objects and practices can thus gain the quality of a 'symbolic resource' that can be used to 'sustain or scaffold the work of reframing and reorganising' the changing experience of social relations (Zittoun et al. 2003:419). This could be particularly important in the early period of a child entering a residential care home.

Entering care

Food as a means for showing care often took on a more formalised role in each home's induction process for children. It offered a means for the 'orienting responses', which Brendtro (1969), in his analysis of relationship building in the everyday communicative exchanges between residential staff and children, identified as pivotal steps in coping with the new and unpredictable environment. Hence, very soon after a child's arrival, establishing what his or her 'likes and dislikes' often became a focus of staff–child interactions. In the course of the first week, food preferences were further documented either through the use of a questionnaire or the writing of a list with a key worker or cook. Finding out what a child likes to eat was thus invested with much meaning. Apart from making it easier for children to eat and relax, a primary function of acknowledging 'likes and dislikes' was to show an interest in the child as an individual. Through obtaining the kind of knowledge a parent may have of their child, the staff could define their care role as 'family like' and set themselves apart from impersonal forms of care associated with 'an institution':

> If you're in your own home your mum or somebody tends to know 'Oh they'll never touch that', 'Oh they'll eat that'. (Nicole, Care Worker, Focus Group, Highton)
> And I suppose in a family home you would have that communication with your significant care-giver, whether it be your mum or your dad, what you like and what you dislike. (Linett, Assistant Manager, Interview, Lifton)

However, some children viewed eating preferences as something personal, and only to be shared in the context of close relationships. Questions about what they liked to eat could be viewed by some with suspicion and as being as much about control as about caring. Demi describes how she experienced questions about her food preferences when she moved in: 'It's annoying 'cause it's like: "I'm no' telling you. I hardly ken [know] you" ' (Demi, Young Person, Interview, Highton). Eating in close proximity to people and accepting food from the residential staff was at times experienced as difficult by many of the children who participated in this study. This seemed to be particularly acute in the initial period following their admission to the residential home. For many, these difficulties were less about the food as functional sustenance and more about the lack of certainty about expected practices and the tentative nature of the relationships with other children and adults. Abbey, for example, displayed the gaining of membership in the resident group through performing what constituted a regular pre-dinner ritual of the girls. The girls in this residential home, either by themselves or in pairs, would frequently approach the cook shortly before the meal was going to be served with declarations such as 'I don't eat any of that!' 'What have you made for me?' (Field notes, Highton). By joining in on the complaining ritual, Abbey began to be more accepted into the girls' group.

Furthermore, eating within the gaze of others can be experienced as a personal disclosure, thus rendering the individual young person vulnerable and exposed. As already mentioned earlier, the move into care can threaten an individual's sense of identity and sense of self (Clough 2000). The following extract is illustrative of this:

ANNA: You know what I like about here? That everybody sits
           down and has dinner together.
GRAHAM: My best meal in here was when I just moved in and I got
           a big plate with mince and tatties brought to my room.
           And I was sitting there looking at it … hmm should I eat
           it or not? And then I just munched away on it. And I hid
           the plate on top of the cupboard.
NICOLE: Why?
GRAHAM: So that they didn't know if I ate it.
NICOLE: Why did you not want them to know?
GRAHAM: 'Cause I was embarrassed. (Anna, Locum; Nicole, Care
           Worker; Graham, Young Person; Field notes, Highton)

Food can, nevertheless, be a powerful medium which can ease the transition from 'outside' to 'inside', despite an initial resistance to eating or being seen eating. For example, as one member of staff suggested 'it's almost like they're being accepting of being looked after and allowing us to care for them' (Rachel, Assistant Manager, Interview, Highton).

Exploring and testing relationships

In the course of their transition into residential care, however, children began to actively draw on cups of tea, and other food objects, to develop, display and test their relations to staff and other children. For example, Ryan maintained a preference for hot chocolates at certain times of the day throughout his residence at Lifton. Ryan was introduced to the making of cups of tea for staff and children by an older resident:

Ryan's second day

Ryan helps Melanie make a round of tea and coffee for the children and staff. Melanie initiated the tea making and invited Ryan to come to the kitchen with her. Ryan comes to the office door to ask the mangers if they take sugar.

Fourth week

Angela brings through a tray with cups of tea for everybody. She got Melanie her new cup and extra milky tea. Ryan got one of the tall cups. Ryan requests more milk. Angela returns with the milk container and shares out refills.

Fifth week

I join Bernice in the kitchen where she makes a round of tea. Beth offers to make toast and puts several slices in the toaster. Melanie is standing next to Beth 'Oh could you toast me the bottom half of a roll?' Beth does. Ryan comes in to look into the cups of tea. Bernice shows him his. Ryan 'That's not milky enough, pal!' Bernice protests briefly. Ryan gets the milk container out of the fridge and pours more into his cup, then the one next to his, and checks the other cups sitting on the counter. 'Which one's Melanie's? Have you got enough milk in her's?' He takes his cup and the one next to it through to the lounge as he believes it is meant for Matt. Matt however declares he will make his own cup of tea. I inquire and Ryan answers 'cause he doesn't like Bernice!' and grins. (Field notes, Ryan, Melanie, Matt: Young People; Angela, Beth, Bernice: Care Workers, Lifton)

Such extracts from the field notes illustrate how Ryan, and other children, learnt the significance attached to the offering, requesting, and accepting of beverages. The simple interaction involving the giving and receiving of cups of tea or hot chocolate can be perceived and intended as acts of caring and relationship building.

The children and staff's interactions around food demonstrate that children enter into a dialogue using symbolic resources in such a way that they do not passively assimilate the meaning systems of staff but actively negotiate their positions and give new meanings to interactions. In the process of developing relationships the children's refusal to eat, complaining over food and requesting special foods or drinks could take on different functions and have varying consequences. Children could use such strategies to get attention and/or protection from staff (see also Valentine & Longstaff 1998) or invite staff into a 'getting to know you' interaction. Often the testing of the relationship was manifest in children giving instructions relating to food, something that was clearly understood by many of the staff we interviewed. The following quotation highlights this:

And you make the cup of tea and it's actually less about the cup of tea and more about that you're willing to do something *for* that young person and maybe *that's* what they're checking out – 'will I get my own way in this situation'? But it's not about that, you know. 'Do they still like me? They haven't been in for a week-and-a-half. Will they still make me a cup of tea if I ask for one? Will they remember how I take my cup of tea?' You know? And, 'if I ask for this cup of tea and I'm pissed off that they never said cheerio before they left a week-and-a-half ago I'll tell them that it's not milky enough and that'll make them feel like they've forgotten how to make my cup of tea' (laughs). You know, it's like 'there's not enough milk in this you've forgotten how to make my special cup of tea, I knew you would forget' (laughing). (Alana, Care Worker, Interview, Lifton)

Similarly, as can be seen in the example below, such detailed instructions for how to make a 'special hot chocolate' was a key way in which children made themselves known and tested care workers' willingness to know and remember them. Ryan's 'special hot chocolate' had to be made in the following manner:

Right, go and put milk full to nearly to the top then put it in the microwave for two minutes then put a scoop of hot chocolate in then two sugars then mix it well and then stir it really fast. Put, eh, the milk in the microwave first and then put the hot chocolate and sugar in when you've heated it up for two minutes and then stir it really like and then it will come out all frothy and then that's it. (Ryan, Young Person, Supper Recording, Lifton)

Equally, Carrie Ann felt that the adults should be paying more attention to what it is she means by 'cheese':

CARRIE ANN: I only like brie or Dairylea spread. And they buy cheddar and sometimes... they just ask me if I want cheese on toast and then I say, 'Aye,' thinking it's Dairylea or brie and then they come through with the cheddar.

NIKA: OK, so they don't get it right?

CARRIE ANN: No.

NIKA: How do you feel about that?

CARRIE ANN: Terrible because then I have to go through and make it by myself. Because staff don't think about turning round and say, 'What kind of cheese would you like on your toast?' (Carrie Ann, Young Person, Interview, Highton)

The children's uses of food were not restricted to unilinear acts of 'knowing'. In the process of establishing relationships, the children used the adults' responses, as well as observations of staff's food idiosyncrasies, as a means for getting to know individual adults. In one of our focus groups, children displayed their knowledge of each other and staff members through their account of how each person likes their cup of tea:

MELANIE: Aye. Ryan has two sugars and milk, Matt has two sugars and milk...
MATT: Ryan has two and a half.
RYAN: Nah, I have two now.
MELANIE: Ryan and Matt has two sugars and milk, and I just have milk...
MATT: Although they try and gie me nae sugars.
MELANIE: Naw, I give you sweeteners (laughs). Adam just takes milk, Linett takes just a wee drop water, Will takes milk, em, Derek takes one sugar and milk, Angus just takes a wee drop water. Who else is there?
MATT: And tea mind you he doesn't just drink water.
MELANIE: Shuddup!
MATT: Melanie has a lotta milk.
MELANIE: Hannah has two sweeteners and milk. Beth has the same. Who else is there? Erin has, em...
MATT: Nae sugar, with water.
MELANIE: Yep. Who else is there?
MATT: Wi' the teabag. Geoff, I dinnae ken [know] what he takes. (Melanie, Matt, Ryan, Adam: Young People; Linett, Will, Derek, Angus, Hannah, Beth, Erin, Geoff: Staff, Young People's Focus Group, Lifton)

These children placed a heavy significance on knowing how to make each person a cup of tea exactly how they wanted it. This could be perceived as an 'index' of their detailed knowledge of each other and the length and closeness of their connection. It highlighted people's individuality and differences as well as personalising relations between them, thereby emphasising that they are not just 'a resident' or a 'staff member' but they are 'Melanie' and 'Hannah' and they look after each other.

The making of cups of tea was just the most obvious and embedded of a range of food practices [e.g., coffee, juice, smoothies etc. could fulfil a similar function] which helped to foster relationships.

They provided a brief personal connection as well as a more powerful symbolic code through which closeness and personal knowledge could be communicated. Such interactions allowed for an exploration of the nature of the relationship, its limits and boundaries and the rules that governed it. Staff and children alike used food as a means of experimenting with, and reinforcing, the subtleties and strength of relationships.

Sustaining relationships

Often children used food to explore the extent and limits of the power they may have in relation to staff and each other. Many of these children had been removed from parental care because of a lack of consistent care and control or through abuses of power by adults. Thus, to passively accept the power and control of staff was to trust that their use of such power would be proportionate and beneficial and. for many children. This was a new and often problematic experience. Food practices provided a repertoire of rituals and regular interactions that children could draw upon to explore and navigate through these issues and to find ways to sustain relations.

Across all three of the residential care homes the children's appraisal of food or their acceptance of an offer of food or drink was thus often infused with perceptions of relationships with staff generally, or an individual staff member, as well as other residents. Food could be used to build trust and as a ready-to-hand and safe medium through which they could get to know others and maintain relationships. For example, when asked about *'what's good about food at their home'* Abbey praised one of the care worker's cups of tea as the best: 'Eric, Eric, oh his teas are gorgeous. Oh my God, they are the best!' (Abbey, Young Person, Focus Group, Highton). With the development of relationships, came a sense of connection to the residential home itself, and food practices were crucial in the mutual recognition of this process of belonging and attachment. The enjoyment of food could become inextricably intertwined with the sense of familiarity and trust associated with the person preparing the food. Colin, for example, explained how it makes him feel when he gets soup and egg rolls for lunch:

> It makes me feel happy. When I'm hungry I just think 'Yes, nice food!' But I think it's as well, if somebody cooks, you ken [know], you kind of think if it's somebody that you've had for a while and

kept on cooking nice food then you just automatically, just, you kind of eat it. I just think it's nice. I think it's like your brain's set up to think 'Oh this is wonderful food' because you've had ... because the person's cooked such good food for you in the past and your brain's set up to think 'Oh this is going to be nice whatever'. (Colin, Young Person, Interview, Lifton)

Such interactions indicate that both staff and children share an understanding of the role that food plays in daily interactions within the care home inasmuch as it can be perceived as a symbolic representation of their relationships around which often subtle negotiations over power, care and control are enacted and worked through. Food or cups of tea constitute a domain through which anxieties around relationships can be negotiated without putting much at risk. They lend themselves to this because they are simple acts which, on the surface, appear conventional and mundane. Consequently, little emotion or power is explicitly risked and vulnerabilities are less likely to be directly exposed. Little has to be brought to consciousness and spelled out verbally in a face-to-face interaction. Thus, the giving and receiving of food can be used as a safe way to play out, test and sustain relationships over time.

Generally, there were not clear differences in the ways in which staff and children used food symbolically. For example, both generations used food as a way of demarcating relationship boundaries. However, at times, children were more explicit and upfront about overtly using practices around food to demonstrate a change in their relationships, such as refusing to sit next to someone at the dining room table. Melanie indicates the impact that falling out with someone can have at mealtimes:

If like you're not talking to a young person, right, or something and youse are a' sitting at the table and joining in in conversation and that, you might feel a wee bit awkward, know what I mean. And that could make it feel like a bad mealtime and that, 'cause you cannae join in properly because you want to talk to them, but you're no talking to them. ... So that could make it feel a wee bit weird. So you might no even want to go to the table then. (Melanie, Young Person, Interview, Lifton)

Staff also mentioned that sometimes they might avoid sitting at the table or choose how long to remain seated, depending on who was present at the meal and their relationship with those people. The key difference with staff's use of food in this way, compared with the children's, is that staff would be less explicit and more subtle about concealing the link between their relationships and the sharing of food.

Requests and offers of food can form ongoing individualised routines, or rituals within routines. Unlike many of the rules and regulations imposed on children by staff, such rituals are often perceived as being co-determined and can become specific to relations between a child and staff member. This was particularly the case at the end and beginning of the day when children drew upon personalised routines revolving around food that further reinforced a feeling of reassurance and a sense of belonging. This is brought out by a staff member when she describes a night-time routine of one of the girls:

> ORLA: Abbey along there loves it when Elaine [night staff] comes in because Elaine'll make her a sandwich and she'll give her fruit and she'll give her juice and she'll spend time talking to her. Now, that's something that she asks for when Elaine comes in, she doesn't ask the same of me.
> NIKA: Why do you think that is?
> ORLA: Because she likes the contact that she has with Elaine. She has...she uses me in a different way. Like, she'll use me for, 'I don't know what DVD I want to watch tonight'. (Orla, Care Worker, Interview, Highton)

Food practices conducted between particular individuals can provide regular points of contact that help sustain relationships and a sense of identification with the care home. Melanie demonstrated her connection to a member of staff in the following extract:

> MELANIE: 'Cause when Angus was off I missed my toasted rolls. Ken [know] what I mean? So I had to get other people to make ma toasted rolls.
> NIKA: And was it the same?
> MELANIE: Nuh.
> NIKA: What was missing, do you think?
> MELANIE: Angus! (Melanie, Young Person, Interview, Lifton)

The interaction is very specifically about the person with whom the ritual is shared rather than about the content of the food. What is being expressed is the significance of a relationship to a person and a routine confirmation of this relation in a manner that may be more difficult to achieve through continual verbalising (a similar process takes place between staff). A staff member notes how on occasion a drink may be untouched by a young person but the power of the action and its meaning are still maintained:

> I don't know whether they like a wee bit of contact or they quite like….Because you go in in the morning and most of the food's untouched. Or the glass of juice that they wanted [...] Nick does that with me. He'll ask me to make him cups of coffee. It's not 'cause he gets a sick kick out of it or something. I do, I bring him a coffee and he's really grateful, but he never touches it. I don't know whether it's reassurance, I've no idea. I've often wondered that, though. (Liam, Care Worker, Interview, Highton)

In this study, refusing food was a common way to show emotion and attempt to exert some power and control in a range of situations. Carrie Ann described how she rejects offers of food when she is annoyed with people:

> Sometimes if I'm in a really bad mood and canny be bothered with naeone then I just go in a big storm off for nae reason. And then they come in and say 'Would you like this?' and I go 'No I wouldn't' and start shouting for nae [no] reason. (Carrie Ann, Young Person, Interview, Highton)

Crucially, the reverse is also the case in that offers of food can be one of the first ways in which conflict can be resolved within the care home. The following quotations reveal that both staff and children recognise that food can be used as a means of 'making up' without having to directly verbalise it:

> I think again it comes back to showing that you care. That you are willing to put out that extra effort to make something that they specifically like, and like Carrie Anne she likes her eggs cooked in a very specific way. I can think of times she has gone off at me and she's been really violent and horrible, she'll come back 'I'm really sorry, I didn't mean it' and 'OK I don't like the way you speak to me and don't do it again'. You have that conversation then 'Are you hungry, it's lunchtime. What are you wanting?' 'Oh I dinnae like any of this. I don't like it'. 'Right what would you like. Would you like an egg?' 'Oh aye, aye, aye' and then it's like 'remember I like it cooked?'

'Yes Carrie Ann I know. Right, I'll tell you what, you go and butter the bread and I'll get your egg on'. And it's that kind of dialogue of the shared experience of making up and then she'll do a bit and I'll do a bit and we'll come back together and we'll build our relationship back from her yelling at me and calling me every awful thing under the sun so it's been used to help make up. (Rachel, Assistant Manager, Interview, Highton)

Because then … like you dinnae have to go on and, 'Oh I'm sorry for daein' this and I'm sorry for daein' that' and then they have to go 'Oh, I'm sorry tae' and it's 'You just want a brew then, eh?' That way it's easier. (Melanie, Young Person, Interview, Lifton)

The above examples indicate that interactions involving food can be a useful way for children and staff to communicate with each other in an indirect manner. Food practices can help to avoid the difficulties associated with a more direct approach to resolving conflicts and articulating feelings.

Conclusions

This chapter has argued that food can be used symbolically, by both staff and children, to make, break, negotiate and sustain relationships. We have shown that food and the practices that surround it can be accompanied by a range of subtle and complex exchanges and negotiations. Food is a medium through which a complex web of relations involving power, conflict and care can revolve. Preparing and giving food to children within a residential home context can heighten the ambivalent nature of food provision as both a commonplace, routine and mundane activity and one which can take on a particular significance for providing care and building relationships between staff and children. Food practices not only enable the maintenance of relations over time but also create innumerable opportunities for developing such relationships in the first place. Furthermore, they can be a key way in which children assert their own sense of self and identities in relation to each other and staff.

People have to eat and it is the routine aspect of food that lends itself to relationship building. However, for the same reason, food can also be a site of misunderstanding and conflict as well as resolution and harmony. The experience of mealtimes was often complex and ambivalent, a potentially awkward interaction that was seen by staff to be a key way to develop relations with children but carried with it the potential to be misinterpreted and resisted by children. Mealtimes could be understood by children as a loss of control and a display of staff power. Often care workers' efforts to provide the best possible care and to make up for the losses experienced by the children – of 'family', 'childhood', and a 'normal' home – were in tension with their anxieties around losing control over children, containing the risks that children pose to others, setting unrealistic life standards (care being too good), and fostering the dependency of children who may take it for granted that everything is provided and done for them. As Coppock suggests there can be a 'thin line between methods used to control children and young people and the rhetoric of therapeutic intervention in their best interest' (1997:154).

However, it is clear from our research so far that food is central to the caring environment within each of the residential homes we studied and to the form and development of a range of relationships. This chapter has illustrated that issues of care, control, power and identity are played out through daily interactions around the giving and receiving of food. Food practices, as mundane, everyday aspects of residential child care, highlight the ways in which identities and relationships between children and staff can be initiated, developed and negotiated.

Acknowledgement

We would like to thank the Economic and Social Research Council for funding this research (ESRC award number RES-000-23-1581).

References

Abrams, L. (1998). *The Orphan Country: Children of Scotland's Broken Homes From 1845 to the Present Day*. Edinburgh: John Donald Publishers Ltd.

Aiers, A. & Kettle, J. (1998). *When Things go Wrong, Young People's Experience of Getting Access to the Complaints Procedure in Residential Care*. National Institute for Social Work/Selly Oak Colleges.

Berridge, D. & Brodie, I. (1998). *Children's Homes Revisited*. London: Jessica Kingsley.

Bevir, M. (1999). Foucault, power and institutions. *Political Studies* XL(VII): 345–359.

Brendtro, L. (1969). 'Establishing relationship beachheads', in Trieschman, A., Whittaker, J. & Brendtro, L. (eds), *The Other 23 Hours*. New York: Aldine De Gruyter.

Cogdell, K. (1989). *Long Term Fostering After Residential Care*. Norwich: Social Work Monographs.

Comfort, M. (2002). 'Papa's house': The prison as domestic and social satellite. *Ethnography* 3(4):467–499.

Coppock, V. (1997). '"Mad", "Bad", or Misunderstood'?, in Scraton, P. (ed.), *'Childhood' in 'Crisis'*. London: UCL Press.

Clough, R. (2000). *The Practice of Residential Work*. London: MacMillan Press.

Clough, R., Bullok, R., & Ward, A. (2006). *What Works in Residential Child Care: A Review of Research Evidence and the Practical Considerations*. London: National Children's Bureau.

Davis, H. & Bourhill, M. (1997). '"Crisis": The demonization of children and young people', in Scraton, P. (ed.), *'Childhood' in 'Crisis'*. London: UCL Press.

Emond, R. (2003). 'Putting the care into residential child care: The role of young people'. *Journal of Social Work* 3(3):321–337.

Ferguson, H. (2007). 'Abused and looked after children as "moral dirt": Child abuse and institutional care in historical perspective'. *Journal of Social Policy* 36(1):123–139.

Foucault, M. (1983). 'Body/Power', in Gordon, C. (ed.), *Power/Knowledge: Selected Interviews and other Writings 1972–1977* (pp. 55–62). Brighton: Harvester.

Godderis, R. (2006). 'Dining in: The symbolic power of food in prison'. *The Howard Journal* 45(3):255–267.

Goffman, E. (1970). *Strategic Interaction*. Oxford: Blackwell.

Goffman, E. (1991). *Asylums: Essays on the Social Situation of Mental Patients and other Inmates*. London: Penguin.

Kendrick, A. (ed.) (2008). *Residential Child Care: Prospects and Challenges*. London: Jessica Kingsley Publishers.

Lalonde, M. P. (1992). 'Deciphering a meal again, or the anthropology of taste'. Social Science Information 31(1):69–86.

Lukes, S. (2005). *Power: A Radical View*, 2nd Edition. Houndsmills: Palgrave Macmillan.

Marshall, D. (2005). 'Food as ritual, routine or convention'. *Consumption Markets & Culture* 8(1):69–85.

Mayall, B. (1996). *Children, Health and the Social Order*. Buckingham: Open University Press.

Mayall, B. (2002). *Towards a Sociology for Childhood*. Buckingham: Open University Press.

McPheat, G., Milligan, I. & Hunter, L. (2007). 'What's the use of residential child-care? Findings of two studies detailing current trends in the use of residential childcare in Scotland'. *Journal of Children's Services* 2(2):15–25.

Nukaga, M. (2008). 'The underlife of kid's school lunchtime: Negotiating ethnic boundaries and identity in food exchange'. *Journal of Contemporary Ethnography* 37(3):342–380.

Pike, J. (2008). 'Foucault, Space and Primary School Dining Rooms'. *Children's Geographies* 6(4):413–422.

Rose, M. (1997). *Transforming Hate to Love*. London: Routledge.

Salazer, M., Feenstra, G., & Ohmart, J. (2008). 'Salad days: A visual study of children's food culture', in Counihan, C. & Van Esterik, P. (eds), *Food and Culture: A Reader*, 2nd edition. New York: Routledge.

Sidenvall, B. (1999). 'Meal procedures in institutions for elderly people: A theoretical interpretation'. *Journal of Advanced Nursing*. 30(2):319–328.

Smith, C. (2002). 'Punishment and pleasure: Women, food and the imprisoned body'. *Sociological Review* 50(2):197–214.

Smith M. (2005). 'Rethinking residential child care: A child and youth care approach', in Crimmens, D. & Milligan, I. (eds), *Facing Forward: Residential Child Care in the 21st Century*. Dorset: Russell House Publishing.

Valentine, G. (2000). 'Exploring children and young people's narratives of identity'. *Geoforum* 31(2):257–267.

Valentine, G. & Longstaff, B. (1998). 'Doing porridge: Food and social relations in a male prison'. *Journal of Material Culture* 3(2):131–152.

Visser, M. (1991). *The Rituals of Dinner: The Origins, Evolution, Eccentricities, and Meanings of Table Manners*. New York: Penguin Books.

Ward, A. (1993). *Working in Group Care*. Great Britain: Venture Press.

Ward, A., Kasinski, K., Pooley, J. & Worthington, A. (2003). *Therapeutic Communities for Children and Young People*. London: Jessica Kingsley Publishers.

Zittoun, T., Duveen, G., Gillespie, A., Ivinson, G., & Psaltis, C. (2003). 'The use of symbolic resources in developmental transitions'. *Culture and Psychology* 9(4):415–448.

9
Discourses on Child Obesity and TV Advertising in the Context of the Norwegian Welfare State

Vebjørg Tingstad

Child obesity has become a hot topic in policy debates, media discourse and academic literature in recent years. Incessant media coverage reports that obesity is becoming an epidemic, with the phenomenon being spoken about as a *global epidemic* (Okie 2005), *globesity* (Dávidsdóttir 2005) and a *pandemic,* seen as by far the fastest growing public health crisis in the industrialised world (Shell 2003). In the European Union, 30% of the child population is estimated to have a serious problem with their weight and the health authorities' concern is that Europe will go in the same direction as the United States, facing an obesity problem 'out of control' (WHO 2006). In this chapter, I explore the reasons that are currently being offered in the public sphere in Norway to explain the increasing levels of child obesity and, maybe as equally important, the reasons that are not mentioned. As I shall argue, the ways in which these issues are talked about reveal the discourses that frame, for instance, the explanations and solutions offered, the location of responsibility and also how children's identities and childhood itself are understood in the Norwegian context (James 1993).

Media debates about obesity often conclude with claims about the individual consumer's morality and responsibility as a citizen – referring to the US context, for example, 'fears of an obese nation have led the last three Surgeon Generals as well as the current President to call for greater personal responsibility towards exercise and weight loss as part of the moral obligation of citizenship' (Julier 2008:482). However, in relation to children, interestingly, it is parents who are often held responsible for the growing levels of child obesity, in respect of their children's media use. The media is blamed in two ways; firstly for keeping children physically passive in front of their screens, and secondly, which is the focus in this chapter, for targeting children with advertisements for unhealthy food and drinks.

In recent years, this public interest and anxiety about a presumed close link between child obesity and TV advertising of unhealthy food and sweet drinks has escalated to dimensions that seem to be more extensive and heated, internationally, than any other issue concerned with children's diet and health and are particularly visible in Anglo-American and European public debates. This chapter, therefore, analyses Norwegian debates about child obesity and TV advertising against these wider debates in Western Europe and the United States and, in doing so, it identifies some of the similarities and differences in the various positions that are represented by asking the following questions: Who is speaking for what in these debates and what kinds of policy recommendations are proposed? To what extent are the media and advertising blamed for the child obesity problem? Finally, are some kinds of representations and definitions used more frequently than others in the Norwegian context, thereby constituting a hegemonic discourse, that in Foucauldian terms, makes them 'obvious' and 'natural', 'practices that systematically form the objects of which they speak' (Foucault 1972:49)?

The chapter's focus is therefore neither on obesity as a health problem as such, (even though obesity undoubtedly represents a serious problem for many children in contemporary societies), nor is it about the impact of TV advertising on Norwegian children's eating habits or obesity levels. Rather, it is about how the child obesity problem is talked about and explained in the public sphere; the kinds of reasons and solutions that are proposed; and the constructions of 'responsibility' that are implicitly at stake in the debates. As such, drawing on empirical research, it presents an analysis of how relevant experts in Norway understand the 'panic' about child obesity and the extent to which the construction of *individual responsibility* (Rose 1999) is woven into the solution to the child obesity problem. Thus, importantly, the chapter asks how the obesity problem, which is unequally distributed among different social classes, and as such inherently structural, is transformed into a discourse that locates the problem as a matter of children's individual consumer choice, moral, self-control and responsibility. Finally, the chapter considers whether this represents a new view of Norwegian childhood that contrasts with the traditional emphasis on protection by the state or whether it is, in fact, the logical outcome of the idea of children as active and participative Norwegian citizens.

Background issues: Child obesity and the media

In 2007, the British media regulator Ofcom started to implement new restrictions on the advertising of food and drink products in TV programs for children. In fact, these restrictions imposed a total ban on the advertising of food and drinks in the United Kingdom that are high in fat, salt and sugar (HFSS). This ban includes 'all programmes of particular appeal to children under the age of 16, broadcast at any time of day or night on any channel', restrictions seen as an explicit contribution to the government's attempts to reduce child obesity (Ofcom 2007).

The UK ban did not come from nowhere, however, but had its political and academic roots in a report from the World's Health Organisation and in 'evidence based research' (Hastings et al. 2003; Livingstone 2004, 2005, 2006; Livingstone and Helsper 2004, 2006; WHO 2006). In turn, this ban, and the political and academic work prior to its implementation, has informed the premises of a widespread contemporary global discourse about child obesity in which particular reasons for the 'epidemic' have gained status as self-evident, even if the evidence itself is rather questionable (Julier 2008; Buckingham 2009a). In this way, globally, the media coverage about child obesity has become an everyday discourse, with the 'problem' of obesity – the 'reasons' for it and not least the 'solutions' to it – being spoken of as simple and straightforward issues. The recommended solution is, as the quote above demonstrates, the strict regulation of children's access to TV advertisements for what is presumed to be unhealthy food and drinks. Claims made about the research are, however, rather vague and, referring to the UK context, Buckingham has argued that there seems to be a significant mismatch between the policy that finally appeared and the evidence that was adduced to support it (Ashton 2004; Buckingham 2009a). However, this fact does not seem to prevent public debates being influenced by a 'taken-for-granted' view that there *is* a close link between TV advertisements and child obesity and, in the next section, I explore these issues in the Norwegian context, the location for the study upon which this chapter draws.[1]

Context: The Norwegian welfare state

Norway hosted the WHO meeting in 2006 which placed the issue of child obesity and marketing on the political agenda. In 2007, WHO agreed to develop international guidelines for the marketing of unhealthy food and beverages to children and young people. This work is being directed by Norway.

On a national level, a series of political initiatives have been implemented in order to deal with child obesity as a health problem in different ways. A number of political documents have been published, in which children's physical activity, diet and health are the focus.[2] Figures that support such initiatives are reported in a survey that estimates an obesity/overweight rate of 21% of children in the age group 8–12 years in Oslo, the capital of Norway (Andersen et al. 2005). For the country as a whole this was estimated to be 10–15% in 2005. The highest child obesity rate appears in families with low education and in immigrant families (Kolsgaard et al. 2008). More recent figures report that 15–20% of children in the same age group have an overweight or obesity problem. These figures, which seem to be on the same level as in the other Nordic countries and the rest of Western Europe,[3] reveal variations across different parts of the population, demonstrating that child obesity is not equally distributed according to variables such as location (urban/rural), education and ethnicity.

These facts may be surprising, challenging some popular images about the egalitarian nature of the Norwegian welfare society as a strong state that offers its inhabitants a minimum standard of living and rights (Sejersted 2005). Contemporarily, Norway is at the top of the world list in terms of prosperity. Norway too has a ministry for children and equality that 'seeks to strengthen the rights of consumers, families, children and young people, anti discrimination and full equality between men and women'.[4] Indeed, Norway was the first country in the world with a child ombudsman (1981) who, together with the consumer ombudsman,[5] is supposed to act as a 'watch dog' for issues related to children and consumption, respectively. Thus, at the same time as children are objects of protection in Norway, there is also a growing emphasis on children as social participants and citizens that, since the 1990s, has merged with international children's rights discourses to give children, at least symbolically, a role as important actors in the renewal of Norway as a modern democracy (Kjørholt 2004).

Another feature that distinguishes Norway from many other countries is its media history and the level of its regulation. Norway has relatively strict regulations on TV marketing to children that have been so since the introduction of TV. This happened as late as 1960 and, in the first years, only in the southern parts of Norway. Additionally, another issue that makes the Norwegian context distinctive, compared to the US and UK, is the public broadcasting monopoly and the late introduction of commercial channels. The public broadcaster, NRK, remained the only TV channel until the early 1980s when the commercial TV channels were first introduced. Moreover, regulations prohibit TV companies that produce children's TV in Norway from showing advertisements in their programs. With the exception of an increasing number of spin-off products being promoted since the early 1990s, one consequence of this national restriction is that children, to a large extent, have been protected from direct marketing through the TV programs that are produced for them. However, despite this quite strict regulation, child obesity rates appear to be rising both in Norway and Sweden,[6] which suggests that, contrary to popular belief, advertising is not in fact a major cause. It is, therefore, in the light of these distinctive features of the Norwegian social and political context that the following empirical data and analysis have to be interpreted and understood.

Methodology

This analysis draws mainly on in-depth online interviews, carried out in the spring of 2008, with nine of the most prominent stakeholders who have been involved in the debates about child obesity from different positions in Norway, such as health, nutrition, government, media authority, food industry and marketing. Consumer and children's 'interests' were specifically represented by the consumer ombudsman, the ombudsman for children and the lobbyist organisation Barnevakten (Childaware). With the exception of the representatives from the media authorities and the one from the industry, all the informants had recently participated in public debates about the issue of child obesity and TV advertising, with some of them having a national mandate to deal with the issue – for example, The Directorate for Health and Social Affairs and The Norwegian Institute of Public Health.

Most of these informants represent their organisations, although one was recruited after having participated in a TV debate and another via a colleague. The questions sought to discover whether the informants thought TV advertising towards children should be regulated and if so, for what age groups. The informants were also asked whether their stated position was based on something they themselves had experienced, something they believed and/or something they had read. Other questions aimed to gain knowledge about how these different stakeholders evaluated the consequences of regulating TV advertising of unhealthy food and drinks and whether they thought it would prevent child obesity and influence children's eating habits. The informants were also asked how significant they thought the impact of TV advertisements was compared to other kinds of influences. Some other questions explored whether the organisations, represented by the various informants, had developed a plan for how to deal with the child obesity problem and, if so, what elements were included in such a plan. The interview also asked to what extent their standpoint(s) were influenced by debates and documents from other countries and international organisations and a final set of questions asked what they thought were the potential reasons for the increasing level of child obesity and who they believed was responsible.

All the informants were also the gatekeepers of relevant documents and media coverage and they were asked to give a detailed account of both the debates and documents in which they had been involved. Further sources used in the study were public reports, web pages from the different organisations, newspaper and online articles and reports, as well as links to TV debates. Online versions of these debates made it possible to listen, watch and transcribe them. Thus, the data set on which this chapter draws includes interviews, governmental documents, reports, TV debates, newspapers and online articles collected in a period of about 6 months, mainly in early 2008.

Who is speaking for what?

I begin this section with a table (Table 9.1) that summarises the different stakeholders' answers to the questions about what they think are the reasons for the increasing level of child obesity and, secondly, where they place the responsibility for this situation.

Looking closely at this table reveals some interesting features. One might have expected that, given the Norwegian media coverage of the UK ban, the WHO report and the guidelines about the marketing of unhealthy food and drinks, at least some of these informants would have reported TV advertising as one possible reason. Even the consumer ombudsman, who has given substantial comments on the proposed laws in the new marketing act, arguing for stricter regulations on marketing, does not mention TV advertising as a reason for child obesity. Instead, most of the informants give other reasons, with 'lack of physical activity' being mentioned by almost all of them. With the exception of the people from the marketing industry and media authority, the 'access and price of unhealthy and healthy food' are also mentioned as important issues related to child obesity. 'Screen activities' such as computer games, the Internet and TV are, somewhat surprisingly, emphasised little. This contrasts strongly with debates in newspapers and on TV where the media is regularly blamed for the 'obesity epidemic'. (Screen activities may, nonetheless, be an underlying explanation for the argument

Table 9.1. Reasons for 'the obesity problem' and responsibilities for solving it – cues from nine stakeholders

Stakeholders	Reasons	Responsibilities
Marketer	Too little physical activity, parents are driving the kids to their activities, computer games and watching TV.	The single household, how they practice lifestyle and dietary routines.
Industry	The diet and lack of exercise.	Parents and school.
Directorate for Health[a]	Sedentary lifestyle and increasing access to energy rich and nutrition poor products, development in society.	Public responsibility to organise society in ways that make it easy to live a healthy life, many sectors involved, such as public, private, voluntary.
Norwegian Media Authority	Internet, pc-games, prosperity, too little physical activity.	Parents and school.
Consumer Ombudsman	Access to more food, more unhealthy food and less exercise.	Parents, politicians who do not impose advertising restrictions, do not use the system of charges to make unhealthy food more expensive and healthy food cheaper, who reduce the time allocated to physical education and neglect to introduce school meals, industry that sells and advertises unhealthy products.
Children's Ombudsman	Sedentary lifestyle, cheap and unhealthy food, increased sizes of bottles for sweet drinks, the cultural norm to eat and drink sweet products when we are together.	Health authorities should do preventive work in families at risk, develop guidelines, but avoid other eating disorders.
Childaware	The combination of more sugar, easier access to cheap and unhealthy food, stress and less physical activity.	Collaboration between parents, school, public authorities and commercial actors.
Nutrition Research Medicine	Changes in lifestyle, less physical activity, social and genetic heredity, high price of fruits and vegetables.	Society and health authorities have the main responsibility, parents.
Nutrition Research	Complex set of reasons; increasing access to food, flexible work life, individualised food habits.	A collective 'we'.

Note: [a] This informant is a nutrition expert, representing the Norwegian health authorities.

about sedentary lifestyles among children and young people since children are assumed to be less physically active when they spend a lot of time in front of their screens. In this case, it could be argued that the media *is* being blamed – but only indirectly – for the obesity problem). However, the emphasis on sedentary lifestyle, rather than TV adverts, is probably picked out most often by the experts because regulation is already 'in place' in Norway and also because being active and outside is about being Norwegian. This contrasts with material from the United Kingdom (Sommer 2008), where exercise is not as high on the agenda as in Norway, and where the focus is instead on the need for regulation.

Lack of knowledge and evidence does not seem to trouble the informants a great deal. Only a few of them had read literature about obesity and, those who had, had read mainly about the 'evidence based research' that was used to support the UK ban and general literature about child development and advertising. Most of them trusted their own experience and what they believed, with the stakeholders confirming that they, and their organisations, are heavily influenced on this issue by public debates and documents from other countries or international organisations. The rationale for political arguments and recommendations in Norway thus seems, largely, to be informed by arguments derived from the wider international obesity discourse.

Responsibility

Other reasons given by the informants for the rise in child obesity, however, such as 'stress, changes in lifestyle and the development in society' are rather vague and relate to wider social issues, both at a structural and an individual level. In short, these reasons are closely linked to questions of responsibility and reflect the informants' evaluation of what they think should be taken care of by society and what is expected to be an individual's responsibility. One of the informants, for example, was worried that 'we know too little' about the relation between the various elements that cause child obesity, for instance 'social and genetic inheritance'. Another informant argues that the contemporary situation of child obesity is the result of the kinds of societal changes that have been given priority for decades. Modern life, including less physical exercise, flexible working patterns and, not least, unlimited access to food and entertainment, has left the individual alone to face the challenges of choice and responsibility.

Such views on the consumption of food in contemporary affluent societies thus reveal new kinds of identities and subjectivities; it places individual consumers as responsible for acting in healthy and morally acceptable ways. Indeed, the 1990s are said to represent a historical watershed with regard to the ways in which food is thought about, talked about and handled (Lien & Nerlich 2004). What previously was left to food-safety authorities and nutrition experts has hit the headlines of the news media and become a topic of expert controversy and public debate. In this respect, food is no longer 'just food', but has become linked to risks in new ways, reflecting both the *danger* and *possibility* that Giddens (1990, 1991) identifies as comprising contemporary identity projects. Emancipated from tradition and authorities, people in modern societies are both 'blissfully free' and 'terribly alone' in their identity formation. In this respect, food consumption represents new kinds of challenges for the individual, including children, in affluent societies.

If we look at who the Norwegian informants think are responsible for the child obesity problem, this pattern can be detected. The marketers, industry and media authority blame single-parent households and speak of parents' failure to cope with lifestyle and diet. These stakeholders thus emphasise individual responsibilities. However, other informants point to structural issues, recognising that some people are more vulnerable than others are:

> An increasing number of fat children and young people are, in my opinion, expressing features in our time and culture that, on the one hand, are obvious and, on the other hand, hidden for us. The increased access to food and the commercialisation of food are examples of the visible part of it. Children and young people's autonomous economy and leisure time without adults are another one. Besides these things, I understand obesity as an integral part of complex relations. These are all issues that in our time's emphasis on rational thought are not necessarily and easily recognised. (Nutritionist; author's translation)

With such a perspective, then, it is no longer possible to point the finger at 'who' is responsible. Rather, 'we' should approach the issue collectively, the nutritionist argues. Here the consumer's subject position is relational; the consumer is not an isolated and independent identity (Mead 1955). Responsibility, to different degrees, rests on 'society' – on the 'collective we', comprising politicians, health authorities and commercial actors such as companies and marketers. The logic here is that social structural arrangements, such as regulation, make it easier for the individual consumer to cope with challenges related to modern food consumption, and thus society is seen as responsible for preventing problems like child obesity. Thus, the blame is placed on society rather than on the individual.

Although these latter interviews appear as a relatively consistent voice on this matter, looking at the media coverage, the picture is not that simple, however. Data gathered from the media debates reveal huge controversies about the question of public or personal responsibility and, in the next section, I present an example of one such controversy. This reveals a real tension in Norway between the traditional and social democratic emphasis on the state's need to regulate and the new emphasis on 'individual responsibility'.

The school meal: The key battle ground?

Although Finland and Sweden have had school meals since 1938 and 1948 and this is part of the curriculum in primary education (Kjørholt, Tingstad & Brembeck 2005) in Norway, school food has historically had a lower priority. It is significant, therefore, that one of the hottest topics in the more recent media debates about child obesity is the school meal provided in child-care institutions and schools (see Chapter 4 by Dryden et al., this volume).

It is routinely reported in the media, for example, that children often go to school without breakfast; that a proper lunch is being substituted with nutritionally poor food and drinks; that the traditional family dinner is being increasingly replaced by individual meals that are supposed to be less healthy; and that children's consumption of sweets and sweet drinks has expanded greatly during recent years. In 2005, for instance, the Consumer Council introduced a 'sugar calculator', aimed at reducing children's intake of sugar in day care institutions and schools in particular.

These anxieties about children's health can be contextualised within a set of policy issues related to child obesity in the Norwegian context. For example, from the fall 2007, the Ministry of Education introduced free fruits and vegetables for students in some primary schools and all secondary schools. Parallel to this, the government introduced the school meal as an experiment in some municipalities, offering a hot meal, three days a week, and breakfast every day. (This was initially part of the school reform Kunnskapsløftet, implemented in August 2006 after the declaration from a new government, aiming at extending the length of the single school day, but also aiming at equalising social differences).

However, in a TV debate about the problem of obesity,[7] the government, represented by the Ministry of Health and Care, was accused of not having given economic priority to this issue since such initiatives are both few and fragmented. The experiment with the school meals, for instance, is just for some students and, in one TV discussion, a marketer argued that if the Norwegian health authorities really wanted to combat child obesity, they could easily do this by using a complex set of approaches and tools that could be employed systematically, at the same time all over the country. One could, he suggested, promote the negative consequences of obesity, like in the 'smoking kills' – campaign, since this initiative changed people's attitudes and practices. The representative from the Ministry of Health and Care, however, rejected this idea and argued for 'positive information', like 'five fruits a day', rather than an approach that worked by 'frightening people'. Thus, once more, the key question is: What are the dominant debates in Norway about responsibility for child obesity? Is it the state, the parents or the individual child?

Measuring and weighting children: A good tool or adding to stress?

Given the level of public anxiety and the figures that confirm the increasing level of child obesity, a project has been implemented recently in Norway to measure children. As a part of the World's Health Organisation's program on child growth in 25 countries, The Norwegian Institute of Public Health, together with the Directorate of Health and the health service at a selected number of schools, have started to organise a national 'trend monitoring study' in which 4,000 children in the third grade (8 years old) are to be measured in terms of their height, weight and waist circumference.

On the institute's web page (www.fhi.no), this initiative is presented as a collective 'political and social effort' by the state to deal with the obesity problem. It is argued that since 'we do not know if the proportion of overweight children is also rising in Norway as we do not have representative national data to compare with, the results from this study will be important to get a picture of Norwegian children's growth and development, and also health'. Furthermore, it is suggested that 'the results will also help us to measure any effects of preventative actions aimed at children's well-being and physical activity, both nationally and internationally'. A newspaper article[8] about this study headlines the idea that weighing children is a social responsibility, that this kind of measuring should be a permanent project, that children are protected (since their individual results are not given to them) and that the health personnel are positive about the project. As part of this project some children are also to be interviewed, reporting on who is the tallest, smallest and oldest in the class. Significantly, however, this leaves who is the thinnest and fattest as an issue that is either seen as irrelevant or an issue that is not asked about or to be talked about 'in public' for ethical reasons.

However, according to media coverage and one of my informants, this project is regarded as controversial among nutritionists. In one newspaper article, for example, two health academics from the University of Oslo, argue that fat children should be kept away from stress about their weight.[9] Their argument is that the continuous pressure on children about bodily change and the requirement to be slim may, in itself, cause more eating. A young man, reflecting back to his childhood when he himself was obese, argues the same in a TV debate.[10] The newspaper article's authors support his argument by referring to international studies that show how both adults and young people, who have tried to lose weight, regain that weight after a short period. The long-term effects of individual slimming attempts are, according to these studies, questionable. The authors' concern is that the focus on weight and measuring may contribute to additional problems, such as eating disorders and other disorders related to food, body and exercise. They also ask why the evidence about documented effects of interventions is less reliable in the treatment of obese people when compared to other patients. Given this, they suggest, health authorities may risk introducing interventions that are neither healthy nor a good strategy in preventing child obesity. On the contrary, given the stigma of obesity and the war against obesity, such an intervention may risk creating new problems by constructing health as an issue of individual responsibility (Julier 2008).

Compared with many other health issues in public debates in the Norwegian context, it seems therefore that the obesity issue is largely infused with a range of conflicting ideologies. For example, one of the informants refers to the common assumption that families with obesity probably live a more unhealthy life than others, while acknowledging, at the same time, that there is insufficient evidence to make such a generalisation:

> We have to be honest and say that we have not yet got the truth about the explosive increase in the level of obesity. We should not encourage stigmatising, particularly in families where the resources are limited. (Author's translation)

And here, children's vulnerability is seen as an important part of the child obesity discourse. It is suggested that, although by employing such measuring strategies the health authorities are demonstrating that they are doing something. They may also risk not solving the problem of child obesity but simply add more stress to the lives of children who are obese.

Thus, while such measuring and weighing projects reflect traditional Norwegian patterns of close regulation by the state, through which health authorities attempt to identify fat children early on, they also indicate the emergence of a new emphasis on individual responsibility that now also includes children. In this respect, in modernity, there may be new child identities emerging in Norway through the discourses about obesity.

Changing images of children's identities: Protected and/or responsible?

The interview material reveals a general agreement about obesity as a growing problem among children and young people in Norway. Most of the informants, in line with the fact that many of them blame 'society', argue in favour of regulating TV advertisements, based on the assumption that children are not able to protect themselves from being influenced by commercials. One needs to regulate adverts, it is suggested, because the protection of children that was originally in place has now been lost, with the advent of more commercial channels and with children now watching things other than children's TV.

Such views seem, initially, at odds with the dominant Norwegian images of children as competent citizens with rights in matters that affect their lives (Kjørholt 2004). However, what the data show is an interweaving of discourses about TV adverts and obesity that indicate signs of new and diverse images of children and childhood in Norway. For example, with only one exception, the informants are positive about the need for regulation, even though, strangely, they are not at all convinced that strict regulation will have any effect in preventing obesity. They are also very unsure that this kind of regulation has much, if any, influence on children's eating habits. Even stranger, as already mentioned, none of them mentioned TV advertising as a reason for the increasing obesity rate! What does this mean? Why do these experts opt for regulation if they do not think it has any effect?

One explanation may be that, as citizens in Norway, these informants are very used to regulation, as part of the political system, and they believe in a statutory regulatory framework on TV advertising in general. In a comment made in the public hearing on the proposed new law on marketing, the consumer ombudsman argues that, even if children are protected in relation to the TV programs that are produced for them in Norway, they need special protection since they watch adverts in and between other programs. The consumer ombudsman, for example, argues that since the regulation of marketing with respect to children has so far been successful in terms of protection, due to general agreement being reached between government, consumers and marketing companies about appropriate limits, there needs now to be additional, special regulation for children. Secondly, and parallel to the previous reason, the informants may trust in the logic of influential advertising, based on the assumption that the industry would not spend huge amounts of money on commercials if these investments were not 'paid back'.

A third reason, however, why my informants talk about advertising is probably because it is an easy and visible target, thereby playing into the wider suspicion of 'evil' marketers and a common distaste for popular culture. Advertising becomes a kind of symbolic 'bad object' – a scapegoat (Reilly & Miller 1997) that, for politicians and experts with a public mandate to 'solve' the obesity problem, is useful since it directs attention to less complicated issues, and, as already mentioned, focuses attention on individual responsibility. Since child obesity has such a high media profile, calls for regulation may simply be an easy way to appear to be doing something.

Thus, these issues around marketing and childhood obesity illustrate the significant ambiguities that exist more generally about children's participation in Norwegian society. New childhood identities seem to be emerging from a former polarised view of children as either vulnerable and in need of protection or, on the other hand, as competent and empowered, to a view of children as responsible consumers, having the right to information about commodities in the commercial market. Through the 'politics of individual self-justice', one can ask, therefore, whether Norwegian children are still being protected or being made more responsible through a reconstruction of these old dichotomies?

Interdependence of panics: The Norwegian case of child obesity

In international debates about obesity, different claim makers draw attention in different directions. Referring to the US context, Julier argues that there are 'anti-fat scientists and activists who use science and the media to lambaste the food industry, Americans' sedentary lifestyles, and a variety of moral causes; on the other hand, there are fat acceptance researchers and activists, who question the links between body size and morbidity and advocate "for size acceptance" ' (2008:483). To different degrees, the claim makers justify their arguments and positions with 'evidence'. An obvious question related to Norwegian policymaking in respect of child obesity, therefore, is on what kinds of science are decisions now being based?

For example, critical reviews of traditional effect research in media studies, during the latest decades, challenges any close linkage between TV commercials and the development of children's obesity:

> In the absence of definitive proof (and even of the likelihood of definite proof), policy may have to be made on the basis of the 'balance of probabilities' – or in other words, 'erring on the side of caution'. Such decisions may be particularly difficult in situations where there is significant emotional investment in the issues, or where such interest is exaggerated and inflamed by media commentary. Government may need to be seen to act as a matter of urgency, and it may genuinely not have the time to wait for definitive evidence'. (Buckingham 2009a)

Thus, as Buckingham argues, the debate about children, obesity and TV advertising is essentially a political debate – both about the politics of academic disciplines and about the ways in which research is used in the policymaking process. This illustrates well what Rose calls the social formation of knowledge through 'the rhetorical use of the claim of evidence and facts' that allows certain things to be considered true at particular historical moments (Rose 1999:xi).

As we have seen in this study, the Norwegian data show that obesity is regarded as a complex phenomenon and that society, to a great extent, must take responsibility for it on behalf of consumers. This could be through different kinds of initiatives, such as providing a proper school meal for all pupils. Public debates, however, continue to focus on sedentary lifestyles and on the media as the main problems to be solved. Thus, the discursive focus on the relationship between TV advertising and obesity, particularly in the media coverage and in the debates around the new marketing law in Norway, seems to have much in common with previous anxieties about the harmful effects that media has on children and childhood (Buckingham 2000). It appears, therefore, as if the discourses about children, obesity and TV advertising are escalating into what can be conceptualised as an *interdependence of panics* (Cohen 1972; Jenkins 1992). Referring to Great Britain, Jenkins discusses the role of moral panics in the 1980s concerning what were characterised as social problems, such as drug and drink problems and violence. 'In each case', he argues,

> we find a number of influential claims-makers, each with a set of interest or a political agenda. There is evidence for the role of all types of moral entrepreneurs and interest groups: individuals, pressure groups, and bureaucratic agencies, with a complex and often shifting pattern of alliances between them. (Jenkins 1992:10)

This means, therefore, that problems and panics are closely interlinked with one another, and, indeed, are interdependent. One panic is 'fruitful' for another and vice versa.

In this case, the 'interdependence of panics' of the discourses around child obesity and TV advertising in Norway draws on at least three different issues, each of them already objects of anxiety in the public sphere: childhood, food and media. As I have shown, anxieties, particularly related to childhood and media, are often based on ideology, morality and 'custom' rather than empirical research. Comparably, the particular 'moral panic' about obesity builds on decades of what Chernin (1981) refers to as a 'tyranny of thinness' that has been 'aided by the moral entrepreneurship of doctors, pharmaceutical companies, and public professionals who, in the last two decades, began shifting obesity (a descriptor of a physical state) to a disease entity with the potential for contagion' (Julier 2008:483). Thus, in the mid-1990s, obesity became linked to mortality, when the World Health Organisation also issued a report that used new, lower BMI (Body Mass Index) benchmarks for overweight and obesity (Julier 2008).

However, in her analysis of the economic, political and cultural 'functions' of obesity in the United States, Julier argues that the obese facilitate the American political process and that the 'obesity epidemic' is more about social and political norms than about the scientific and medical realities of body size. The framing of obesity is, she argues, useful for those whose ideological commitments are focused on 'individual responsibility', rather than the provision of universal health insurance:

> Most importantly, it shifts the focus away from structural and cultural reasons for obesity and allows some groups in society to scapegoat

other groups, while avoiding questions about the nature of food distribution, poverty, lack of jobs at a liveable wage, and a time bind that
encourage people to work longer for less pay. (Julier 2008:494)

In the Norwegian context, the interdependence of panics seems to be
a fruitful discourse in the sense that it works as a focus for people's
concern whereas a more underlying and complex analyses of the child
obesity problem would, politically, have generated claims about higher
priority from the state.

Conclusion

For the purpose of this chapter, I have looked at the discourses of
child obesity as 'nurturing' anxieties that, in the Norwegian context,
seem to be merging with other anxieties. A question to ask is whether
media, and in this case advertisements through TV, are becoming easy
scapegoats to be blamed for causing problems that are far more complex a matter than one of single cause-and-effect. By oversimplifying
the issue of child obesity and underestimating the different elements
that affect people's diet and health in modern societies, the complexities of the 'solutions' proposed to solve the 'obesity problem' risk being
less visible and less publicly discussed so that, for example, attention is
directed to specific areas at the expense of others that could be more
relevant.

Another question this raises is whether the twin panics that
interweave – TV adverts and obesity – may also be a sign of some
changes in the Norwegian view of its children. The shift of emphasis
towards individual responsibility might be linked to the fact that children in Norway are positioned much more as citizens than they are
elsewhere so that now, as society is changing, children have more individual rights and thereby also responsibility for their own futures and
food consumption. From the assumption that rights also include obligations, the paradox is, then, that despite traditional high levels of protection through regulation, the 'Norwegian way' may be less protective
than the regulation 'entrepreneurs' intended.

Notes

1. The study is called *Discourses of the consuming child* and is a project under
   the umbrella 'Consuming Children, Commercialisation and the Changing
   Construction of Childhood', running at the Norwegian Centre for Child

Research from 2006 to 2009 (Buckingham & Tingstad 2007). Other publications from this sub project are Sommer 2008 and Buckingham 2009a, b.
2. In 2007, Norwegian Ministries published an action plan on nutrition, called Recipe for a Healthier Diet. The same year, The Directorate of Health published a report on the development of the diet in Norway and The Norwegian Institute of Public Health published a report on social inequalities in health issues (Næss et al. 2007).
3. Helsedirektoratet/Norgeshelsa (The Directorate of Health).
4. http://www.regjeringen.no/en/dep/bld.html?id=298
5. The Consumer Ombudsman is an 'independent authority' who monitors marketing activities and negotiates contracts between consumers and businesses. In addition, the Ombudsman can impose sanctions.
6. Nordiska Ministerrådet 2007 (The Nordic Council of Ministers).
7. The television program Puls, 19 May 2008, NRK1.
8. The newspaper Adresseavisen, 7 October 2008.
9. www.aftenposten.no/meninger/debatt/Article1371576.ece?service=print
10. The television program Standpunkt, 29 May 2007, NRK1.

References

Andersen, L. F., Lillegaard, I. T., Overby, N., Lytle, L., Klepp, K. I. & Johansson, L. (2005). 'Overweight and obesity among Norwegian schoolchildren: Changes from 1993 to 2000'. *Scandinavian Journal of Public Health* 33:99–106.

Ashton, D. (2004). 'Food advertising and childhood obesity'. *Journal of the Royal Society of Medicine* 97(2):51–52.

Buckingham, D. (2000). *After the Death of Childhood. Growing up in the Age of Electronic Media.* Cambridge: Polity Press.

Buckingham, D. (2009a). 'The appliance of science: The role of evidence in the making of regulatory policy on children and food advertising in the UK'. *International Journal of Cultural Policy* 15(2):201–215.

Buckingham, D. (2009b). 'Beyond the competent consumer: The role of media literacy in the making of regulatory policy on children and food advertising in the UK'. *International Journal of Cultural Policy* 15(2):217–230.

Buckingham, D. & Tingstad, V. (2007). Consuming children. Commercialisation and the changing construction of childhood. *Barn* 25(2):49–72.

Chernin, K. (1981). *The Tyranny of Slenderness.* London: Womans's Press.

Cohen, S. (1972). *Folk Devils and Moral Panics: The Creation of the Mods and the Rockers.* London: MacGibb & Kee.

Dávidsdóttir, S. (2005). Gener, savn og søtsaker (Genes, wants and sweets). Newspaper article in Morgenbladet, 25 February, 14–17.

Foucault, M. (1972). *The Archaeology of Knowledge.* London: Routledge.

Giddens, A. (1990). *The Consequences of Modernity.* Oxford and Cambridge: Polity Press.

Giddens, A. (1991). *Modernity and Self-Identity. Self and Society in the Late Modern Age.* Cambridge: Polity Press.

Hastings, G. et al. (2003). *Review of Research on the Effects of Food Promotion to Children.* London: Food Standards Agency.

James, A. (1993). *Childhood Identities. Self and Social Relationships in the Experience of the Child.* Edinburgh: Edinburgh University Press.

Jenkins, P. (1992). *Intimate Enemies. Moral Panics in Contemporary Great Britain.* New York: Aldine de Gruyter.

Julier, A. (2008). 'The political economy of obesity: The fat pay all', in Counihan, C. and van Esterik, P. (eds), *Food and Culture. A Reader,* Second Edition (pp. 482–500). London: Routledge.

Kjørholt, A. T. (2004). Childhood as a social and symbolic space: Discourses on children as social participants in society, doctoral thesis, Trondheim: NTNU.

Kjørholt, A.T., Tingstad, V. & Brembeck, H. (2005). Children, food consumption and culture in the Nordic countries. *Barn* 23(1):9–20.

Kolsgaard, M. L. P., Andersen, L. F., Tonstad, S., Brunborg, C., Wangensteen, T. & Joner, G. (2008). Ethnic differences in metabolic syndrome among overweight and obese children and adolescents: the Oslo adiposity intervention study. *Acta Paediatrica,* 97(11):1557–1563.

Lien, M. E. & Nerlich, B. (eds) (2004). *The Politics of Food.* Oxford/New York: Berg.

Livingstone, S. (2004). *A Commentary on the Research Evidence Regarding the Effects of Food Promotion on Children.* London: London School of Economics.

Livingstone, S. (2005). Assessing the research base for the policy debate over the effects of food advertising to children. *International Journal of Advertising* 24(3):273–296.

Livingstone, S. (2006). *New Research on Advertising Foods to Children: An Updated Review of the Literature.* Annex 9 of Ofcom, Television Advertising of Food and Drink Products to Children. London: Ofcom.

Livingstone, S. & Helsper, E. (2004). *Advertising Foods to Children: Understanding Promotion in the Context of Children's Daily Lives.* London: London School of Economics.

Livingstone, S. & Helsper, E. J. (2006). Does advertising literacy mediate the effects of advertising on children? A Critical examination of two linked research literatures in relation to obesity and food choice. *Journal of Communication* 56:560–584.

Mead, G. H. (1955). *Mind, Self and Society. From the Standpoint of a Social behaviorist.* Chicago/Illinois: The University of Chicago Press.

Nordiska Ministerrådet (2007). Söt reklam och feta ungar (Sweet advertisement and obese children). *Nord 2007*:002. Copenhagen: Nordiska Ministerrådet (The Nordic Council of Ministers).

Norwegian Ministries (2007). Recipe for a healthier diet. Norwegian Action Plan on Nutrition (2007–2011).

Næss, Ø., Rognerud, M. & Strand, B. H. (2007). Sosial ulikhet i helse. En faktarapport, Folkehelseinstituttet (Social Inequalities in Health. A Report on Facts. Institute of Public Health). *Rapport* 2007:1.

Ofcom (2007a). Final statement on the television advertising of food and drink products to children http://www.ofcom.org.uk/media/mofaq/bdc/foodadsfaq/

Okie, S. M. D. (2005). *Fed Up! Winning the War Against Childhood Obesity.* Washington, DC: Joseph Henry Press.

Reilly, J. & Miller, D. (1997). 'Scaremonger or scapegoat? The role of the media in the emergence of food as a social issue', in Caplan, P. (ed.), *Food, Wealth and Identity* (pp. 235–251). London and New York: Routledge.

Rose, N. (1999). *Governing the Soul. The Shaping of the Private Self.* 2nd Edition. London: Free Association Books.

Sejersted, F. (2005). *Sosialdemokratiets tidsalder. Norge og Sverige i det 20. århundre* (The Age of Social Democracy. Norway and Sweden in the Twentieth Century). Oslo: Pax.

Shell, E. R. (2003). *Fat Wars. The Inside Story of the Obesity Industry.* London: Atlantic Books.

Sommer, M. (2008). Discourses of the consuming child. An analysis of the constructions of childhood and advertising in the UK debate about 'junk food' advertising. Master thesis, Norwegian Centre for Child Research.

WHO (2006). Marketing of food and non-alcoholic beverages to children. Report from a WHO Forum and Technical Meeting, Oslo, Norway, 2–5 May 2006.

10

'I don't care if it does me good, I like it': Childhood, Health *and* Enjoyment in British Women's Magazine Food Advertising

Joseph Burridge

Introduction

Advertisements included within women's magazines have often used portrayals of families, and of children, in the attempt to persuade readers to purchase the products depicted. As part of such attempts at persuasion, and consistent with advertising's more general tendency to put products forward as problem-solving devices (Dyer 1982:168–169; Cook 2001:49), particular versions of the relationship between childhood, food, and consumption are advanced in such material. For instance, children may be constructed as particularly 'faddy' in their food preferences, and resistant or uncooperative when it comes to eating healthily. Thus, advertisements for food products have often featured the 'voices' of such children, endorsing a product – evidence that it transcends 'faddiness' or circumvents a more generalised resistance to eating healthily.

This chapter focuses on adverts for food products that involve the depiction of children in some way. It explores advertising claims about the relationship of the products depicted to *health* and *enjoyment*, and the degree to which these are aligned differently with adults and children respectively. In exploring this, the chapter uses materials drawn from food advertisements featured in a corpus of women's magazines, between 1940 and 2006, to examine key aspects of the representations of childhood made in relation to food. Using a simplified coding procedure, and a thematic analysis of advertisements featuring children, it identifies a dilemmatic tension (Billig et al. 1988) between foods that can be 'healthy' *or* 'enjoyable'. In their key work on the gendered division of labour in food provision, Charles and Kerr (1988:94) noted that women's accounts of feeding their children often included references to a 'tension between social and nutritional needs'. Similarly, this chapter notes that the associated distinction between health (as nutritional) and enjoyment (as social) is often made, and shows that this is aligned with the adult/child distinction and viewed as a cause of conflict between the two groups in such a way that childhood is constructed as deficient (Lee 2001; Herrick 2007), and children positioned as deficient consumers. Health and enjoyment are constructed as in tension with one another, such that food provision *by* adults and *for* children involves balancing the tension that exists between the two.

As part of this argument, an extended discussion revolves around two key examples which put forward food products as devices that can resolve this very problem – balancing the competing imperatives of health and enjoyment – so that both groups (adults/children) can have their interests satisfied. These are an advert for St. Ivel Cheese from 1940 with the tagline 'I don't care if it does me good *I like it*' (which gives this chapter its title), and one for Glenryck Pilchards from 1967 which twice features the slogan 'Kids love pilchards even though they are good for them'.

The materials analysed have a clear relationship to the gendered expectations tied up with the caring dimensions role of housewife/mother (Charles and Kerr 1988; DeVault 1991; Parkin 2006), but also illuminate aspects of the culturally assumed irrationality of children, and the way that childhood agency (or a lack thereof) is constructed in relation to food. Therefore, the chapter begins with an account of some recent intense societal concerns that circulate with respect to the relationship between children and food.

Advertising, children and some key assumptions

Childhood is a social phenomenon that is defined perpetually as in crisis (James et al. 1998). At present, a significant proportion of public concern is directed at the relationship between children and food consumption as part of wider concerns and discourses about the risks of the so-called obesity epidemic.

In Britain specifically, the relationship between children and advertising has often been under intense public scrutiny, with the UK government announcing a 'review' of childhood in Britain as well as launching '10-year Children's Plan' in December 2007. Among the social and political concerns currently in circulation, several issues relating to media consumption are bound up together (Lee 2001). In relation to food consumption, a focus for concern is the issue of so-called 'pester power' (Hill & Tilley 2002; Dixon & Banwell 2004; Turner et al. 2006). This is the supposed tendency for advertising to stimulate children to 'pester' their parents for particular products until it becomes easier for those adults to say 'yes' rather than 'no' to their demands: 'a child's attempts to exert influence over parental purchase in a repetitive and sometimes confrontational way [...] with some degree of success' (Nicholls & Cullen 2004:77; also see McDermott et al. 2006:513).

A key focus for this latter concern has been the alleged influence of advertisements of 'junk food' upon children. This proceeds upon the assumption that children are stimulated by the attraction of such foods, which results in them pressurising and nagging their parents (Cook 2003; Marshall et al. 2007) to buy them, and that, because this is often successful, it works to the detriment of their health (see McDermott et al. 2006 and Livingstone 2005). Such worries have fed into the introduction of legislation which prevents the airing of adverts for 'junk foods' during children's television programming as a means to address concerns about the health of Britain's children.

Although this chapter does not address these concerns directly, it is related in so far as it considers the way that the *voices* of children are *used* in advertisements for foods directed at adults. That is, how claims about the likes and dislikes of children are mobilised in pursuit of the sale of food products – a rather more indirect form of pester power *within the text*. More importantly, it also connects with this literature concerned with pester power in so far as it explores something that tends to be acknowledged or assumed by many of the studies in this area – that children and adults/parents have systematically conflicting interests when it comes to food.

For example, in their account, Nicholls and Cullen (2004) acknowledge that the needs and wants of children and parents are often implied to be in conflict. On the basis of evidence obtained from surveys of UK retailers' marketing to children, they show that, for such retailers: 'children are seen as more concerned with fashionability and short-term needs and wants [...] parents, on the other hand, are more concerned about longer term value and the health of their children' (Nicholls & Cullen 2004:82). Similar tensions are identified by Gelperowic and Beharrell who claim that from the point of view of package design:

> healthy food products definitely have to be fun and attractive to appeal to children and show mothers their healthy aspect. The

challenge is to appear to both the final consumer – the child – and the buying agent – the mother with an 'appealing outside and a healthy inside'. (1994:7)

Marshall et al. (2007:167) argue that it tends to be assumed that 'parents have good nutritional knowledge, and would, if left to their own devices, prioritise healthy food in all cases'. While such assumptions are questionable, I would argue that, in the case of children, they are assumed to prioritise *enjoyment over health* if left to their own devices. When it comes to food, adulthood tends to be conceptually aligned with (or coupled with) health, whereas childhood is coupled with enjoyment, such that children are seen as acting with 'diminished autonomy' (Herrick 2007:98). Previous sociological work has identified the possibility that the status of certain foods, such as sweets, as proscribed (by adults/parents) can serve to render them more attractive to children (James 1982). The reverse process is often assumed – that endorsement of a food (by adults/parents) as healthy will automatically render it less attractive to children, and that its being considered healthy is insufficient to get children to consume it.

With this in mind, I turn to characterising the material analysed and the approach to analysis adopted, along with presenting an overview of the warrants for purchase offered for the food product advertisements featuring children that make up the sub-corpus of material.

Methodological considerations and an overview

This chapter is based upon materials drawn from a larger corpus of magazines assembled as part of the 'Food Provision and the Media' project within the *Changing Families, Changing Food* Programme at the University of Sheffield. A corpus of 2,544 magazine articles and adverts drawn from issues of *Woman's Own* (henceforth *WO*) and *Woman and Home* (*WH*) published between 1940 and 2006 was assembled in order to explore the construction of gendered responsibility for food provision. Despite acknowledging that definitions of 'proper' food are variable, this involved an inclusive definition of food, including sweets and cakes, which are often excluded culturally.

Once analysis was underway, it became clear that there were interesting regularities within adverts involving children, and the decision was made to explore directly those materials – and specifically adverts – featuring or mentioning children. Filtering out all irrelevant materials left a sub-corpus of 293 adverts, which amounts to 16.4% of the 1,786 advertisements featuring in the corpus – a considerable proportion.

Preliminary analysis of this sub-corpus proceeded through a process of thematic coding of the adverts in relation to the warrants offered for purchase – the claims that were made about what qualities they offer. That is, the answers given to the question: What are the ends that are claimed to be achievable via the product? This is similar to Warde's (1997:47) focus on 'principles of recommendation' with regard to magazine recipes (his chosen focus), and a total of over 60 individual codes were developed inductively.[1] Such coding is obviously a messy practice, which does violence to the complexity of such content, but can be helpful for broadly characterising a body of material and drawing out elements that recur, as well as giving some sense of their relative presence. To this end, adverts were coded according to the presence of *at least one mention* of a given theme, and the proportion of adverts in which each of the various warrants/ends featured was calculated to give a sense of their regularity of their use by advertisers within this material.

So, for illustrative purposes, here is an example of the textual content from an advert for Warburtons 'Riddlers':

What fills a lunch box in seconds but doesn't fill your kids with rubbish?
Now you can liven up the kids' lunchbox without lifting a finger. New Warburtons All-In-One Riddlers are bread rolls ready-filled with either cheese or ham flavour cheese spread.
Kids love them, and so will you, as Riddlers provide wholemeal goodness in a white roll, and they supply over 20% of a child's RDA of calcium.
A healthy lunch that kids love, with riddlers you've got it made.
Riddle solved. (Warburtons advertisement, *WO*, 30 January 2006:7)

This advert was coded as featuring each of the following themes: 'Easy to prepare', 'Health', 'Kids Love It', 'Specific Nutrition', 'Goodness'.

Information regarding the *ten most recurrent* ends featuring in the sub-corpus is contained within Table 10.1 (below). The sub-corpus provides insufficient material in order to make valid claims about diachronic change, something that is notoriously difficult to do in relation to advertising anyway (Cook 2001:222). Nevertheless, there is a noticeable drop in frequency of child-related content in such advertisements after 1970. Far more relevant material, for the present purpose, is included in those magazines published in the 1950s and 1960s. We could speculate that this is in keeping with various sociological narratives about individualisation (for example Giddens 1991), in that such material is less prevalent from 1970 onwards due to an increased focus upon the individual 'self' of the reader rather than the family. Nevertheless, rather than speculating, this deserves to be explored elsewhere with empirical material assembled specifically to address why this might be. After this preliminary coding process, it was clear that strong similarities between the two magazines, combined with unevenness in size, and temporal spread, of the materials, meant that is was sensible to treat them in aggregate rather than contrastively. Attention was focused upon regularities shared by them rather than any relatively minor differences. It should be clarified that no automatic claims are being made to any degree of generalisation across magazines – due to the unorthodox assembly of the corpus through a filtering process. The aim is, initially, descriptive, although some interesting regularities are certainly worthy of note.

It is clear from the table that the top three warrants/ends are identical across the two magazines, although the proportion of adverts containing each varies considerably. In both cases 'sensory taste' is the most common warrant for purchase, followed by 'specific nutritional

Table 10.1 The ten most recurrent ends/warrants offered

Ends of food provision, or qualities of product, identified	Percentage of sub-corpus containing	Percentage of adverts in WO	Percentage of adverts in WH
Delicious flavour/Sensory taste	**41.3**	36.7	54.3
Provides specific nutritional content	**39.9**	34.0	45.7
Kids love *it*/Happiness/Enjoyment	**38.6**	34.0	47.6
Kids love *you*/Shows motherly wisdom	**28.3**	28.2	28.6
Easy to digest/Enables good digestion	**26.6**	25.0	29.5
Goodness/Does good	**25.6**	26.1	24.8
Enables progress/Development	**24.2**	25.0	22.9
Health (Improves/Provides/Maintains)	**21.5**	20.7	22.9
Gives nourishment	**19.8**	20.3	19.0
Comfort/Soothing/Warmth	**19.8**	18.1	22.9

content', and the claim that 'kids will love it'. The remaining codes should be relatively self-explanatory, and I would argue that they can be combined at a meta-level to approximate to two even broader categories, which highlight something important about the way that the relationship between children and food is constructed.

One useful way of glossing the ends that were most recurrent, which divides them relatively neatly into two categories (with only one remainder that does not really fit), would be to see them as falling into two broad groups – those having implications for the bodily *health* of the consumer (health, goodness, nutrition, nourishment, progress, soothing, digestion) and those relating to *enjoyment*, or pleasure and desire (sensory taste, pleasing children – who like/love it). In her study of American magazine adverts, Parkin (2006:202) makes a series of assertions about the extent to which, throughout the twentieth century, mothers have been primarily constructed as responsible for family *health* and *happiness* as they pertain to food. So it is perhaps rather unsurprising that these sorts of themes were most prevalent.

The end which is leftover – relating to the 'kids love you' for giving the product to them – does not fit neatly into either of these broad categories. It is nevertheless related to the second category, but more directly concerned with the provider of food – the implications for (presumably) her self-esteem as influenced by food being positively received. Of course, this could also be considered to be related to 'enjoyment', but, because this is contestable, I have left it to one side as I proceed – despite its obvious connection to the gender division of labour, and the 'Sunny Delight' advert analysed by Cook (2001:144–145) which is discussed below.

The rest of this chapter concentrates upon the significance of these ten most recurrent ends and their relationship to childhood in terms of an apparent dilemmatic tension between, broadly speaking, *health* and *enjoyment*.

An antinomy or dilemma?

As stated, the ten most recurrent warrants/ends do largely seem to fit into two general groups – being broadly related to either *health* or *enjoyment*. Thinking in this way, the corpus of 293 adverts actually includes 124 which feature one or more member of each group in combination with one from the other (so either 'sensory taste' or 'kids love it' *and* one or more of the other seven warrants/ends relating generally to health). Therefore, 42.3% of the advertisements involving children feature references to *both* health *and* enjoyment in some form, many of which connect them directly, and imply that they are in a degree of *tension* with one another.

The notion that these broad imperatives – health and enjoyment – are often in competition with one another is clearly present in Alan Warde's work on 'culinary antinomies' – what he sees as the contradictory messages in circulation regarding the reasons that we should consume particular foods (Warde 1997:55). In fact, it closely approximates his health/indulgence antinomy (Warde 1997:78–96). As part of his work, Warde also makes claims about a trend towards 'women's magazines recommending dishes both because they promise good health and because they induce physical and emotional cravings' (Warde 1997:96). However, it is unclear here, both grammatically and on the level of meaning, whether he means that individual recipes are increasingly recommended on *both* bases *simultaneously* – that a recipe is both healthy *and* indulgent – or that both types of recommendation have (semi-autonomously) increased in incidence more generally in magazines.

'Health' and 'enjoyment' are, of course, not antinomies in the linguistic sense, despite Warde's use of the term to describe the relationship between health and indulgence. Disease or 'un-health' (see Jeffries 2007:115) would be rather more obvious candidates for the role with regard to health. However, I would assert that health and enjoyment are often used in such a way that they are constructed as implicitly or explicitly oppositional pairs (see Jeffries 2007:109–120) in relation to food. They are constructed as surprisingly co-present – as if their co-presence is a non-normative matter, a remarkable occurrence – as part of the construction of the problem-solving qualities of food products.

Rather than seeing this as a question of antinomies, I would prefer therefore to see the distinction as more akin to a *dilemma* in Billig et al.'s (1988) sense. In their work, Billig et al. (1988:146) argue convincingly that ideology produces 'dilemmatic quandaries' such that contradictory principles are set against one another, with individuals involved in managing them practically in some manner. What is at stake in relation to the mobilisation of health and enjoyment in these advertisements is an emphasis upon the need to practically manage and reconcile the competition between them, which arguably makes Billig et al.'s (1988) conceptualisation more resonant with the material. In fact, Warde himself does use the term dilemma to refer to what he sees as the 'counter-attractions of self-control and emotional comfort' (Warde 1997:92) that we face in relation to contemporary food consumption. Regardless of the specific analytical category into which we choose to place the distinction, however, what I am interested in is the ways in which the *combination* of these two imperatives works in examples that involve children, and what this can tell us about the assumptions about childhood identity that inform such materials, as part of their deliberately persuasive purpose.

The common alignments between 'healthiness' and 'enjoyment' and the concerns of adults and children respectively is ideological precisely because it is something that seems to be taken-for-granted (Billig et al. 1988; Cook 2001:178–179) in much of this material, along with the sense that the co-presence of health and enjoyment is somehow surprising or remarkable. Indeed the extent to which it also seems to inform research considering 'pester power', which I have already noted, also marks it as such. Moreover, such non-conventional oppositional pairs do tend to have a relationship to normative and/or ideological functions more generally (Jeffries 2007:119). Something interesting is going on when they are used together.

The incompatibility of the two imperatives is very often present in an implicit way, but some instances show it very clearly, and acknowledge it directly. For example, as part of a recurrent 'advertisement feature' in *WH* – 'Julie Jayne's Buying Spree' featuring the testimony of a housewife character regarding her experiences with certain products – a clear advertorial (Cook 2001:37) – we can find the following assertion:

> I LOVE blackcurrant drinks and my family were highly delighted when I started giving them Black Vel-Vit regularly. This tasty and satisfying blackcurrant syrup is so good for them in the winter. When I had a nasty cold recently I found it a wonderful help by having a warm gloss each night before bed, delicious and comforting. Black Vel-Vit health drink, made by Robinsons of Tenbury, contains a high proportion of important vitamin C as well as other natural nutrients – I believe it is used by many leading hospital groups throughout the country. It costs 2s. 9d. a bottle from chemists and grocers. *I find it a pleasant change for the children to love something that really does them so much good.* Why not add a bottle, or two, to your shopping list, now the cold weather is here. (*WH*, December 1962:114, emphasis added)

The key section for my present purposes has been italicised: 'I find it a pleasant change for the children to love something that really does them so much good'. This is a clear example of the separation of health and enjoyment, and the claim that they are regularly in tension with one another – the fact that both are achievable together through the use of the product is apparently non-normative in Julie Jayne's experience. Moreover, this clearly aligns the love of the product – the enjoyment part – with the children involved, and the concern for health (as doing them 'so much good') with the concerns of the adult/mother. In these materials, it is often implied that there is a problem regarding the compatibility of childhood imperatives and more adult concerns – that is, health is aligned with adulthood, and enjoyment with childhood. Children desire enjoyment from food, whereas adults are concerned about health on their behalf – a facet of mother knows best, or the more general ideology of childhood that claims that adults know better than children what is 'good for them' (see Jeffries 2007:187 and Lee 2001:89) and that children therefore require protection (Mayall 2002:21); often protection precisely from themselves. As such, children are clearly 'human becomings' in Lee's (2001) sense – they are incomplete and not to be trusted in relation to food and its health implications.

The resolution of this tension between health and enjoyment is therefore an additional reason offered for buying the product. It is not so much that such products are 'naughty but nice' in James's (1990:679) sense, but more a case of 'healthy *but* enjoyable' or 'healthy *and* enjoyable', as if it were rare for the two to coincide. The necessity of the conjunction implies as much, without the need for Julie Jayne's direct claim to it being a 'pleasant change' if and when they do. The fact that such a product can allegedly be both healthy *and* enjoyable is a cause for comment *precisely* because this is presupposed to be something that it is difficult to achieve. This is despite the fact that such a high proportion of the advertisements featured in the corpus do, in fact, claim to do both!

Noticing this issue of balancing health and enjoyment in connection with food advertising is not entirely without precedent. Similar ideas have been noted previously in an account of advertising as a genre and discursive practice. In his discussion of 'parallelism', Cook (2001:141–142) discusses a relatively contemporary American magazine advertisement for the soft drink 'Sunny Delight'. Within it, the product is claimed to reconcile two *identities* for the woman who purchases it – enabling her to be a 'good mother' and a 'great mom'. According to the text of the advert, the former is possible because the product is argued to be *healthy* and the mother will 'love the vitamins they get' (contrary to the common perception of the product). The latter is possible because the drink is allegedly *delicious* and children will 'love the refreshing taste' (Cook 2001:141). There is therefore a 'duality' when it comes to asserted perceptions of the product – it is both healthy *and* delicious, and perceived as such by mothers and children respectively. It therefore serves both of their interests, and resolves the dilemma for the mother (allowing her to also be a 'great mom' – and popular – while also concerned with health). The product is therefore doubly problem solving – allowing you to 'win two ways' (Cook 2001:142). This logic is present in several examples in the corpus – in relation to my broad categories of *health* and *enjoyment*.

I now move on to consider in detail two prime examples that distil the issue that I have been discussing. In these examples, not only are the products constructed as problem solving in the usual fashion, but the fact that they bridge a gap between two apparently competing imperatives – and balances the interests of the mother as purchaser and the child as final consumer – is portrayed as an additional higher level end that can be achieved via its purchase. Balancing health and enjoyment in relation to food is therefore constructed as a kind of 'meta-end' within them.

Some prime examples

These two prime examples share a range of features that deserve to be noted. Both address the dilemma I have identified in their headline slogans – the portion of text in largest type – and exemplify the coupling of health with adulthood and enjoyment with childhood that I have already mentioned. In common with many other advertisements, they generally assert that children will like or love the product advertised *despite* the fact that it is good for them, or does them good. Both also feature a picture – either a cartoon rendering or a photograph of a young boy, reflecting stylistic changes in the intervening 27 years. In both cases, the picture involves the boy happily consuming the product (see Cook 2001:182), and serves as an exemplar of the category of persons – children – who are asserted as liking the product. Moreover, in both instances, the health assessments made are 'objective' – direct statements about what is the case – 'they're good for them' and 'it does me good' respectively. The health properties are constructed as coming from the object, rather than being imputed to them as a matter of subjective opinion. Despite these similarities, there are also important differences between the two, and I now move on to consider them individually.

Glenryck and Puffin Pilchards – 'Kids love pilchards even though they're good for them'

This advert for Glenryck pilchards is full-page in size (see Figure 10.1) with the top two thirds taken up by a picture of a young child (subsequently

Kids love pilchards
even though they're good for them.

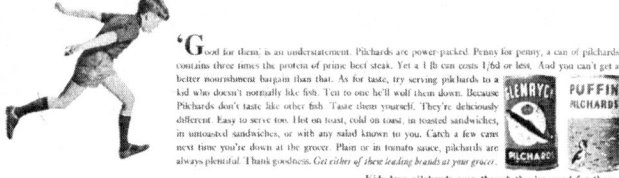

'Good for them,' is an understatement. Pilchards are power-packed. Penny for penny, a can of pilchards contains three times the protein of prime beef steak. Yet a 1 lb can costs 1/6d or less. And you can't get a better nourishment bargain than that. As for taste, try serving pilchards to a kid who doesn't normally like fish. Ten to one he'll wolf them down. Because Pilchards don't taste like other fish. Taste them yourself. They're deliciously different. Easy to serve too. Hot on toast, cold on toast, in toasted sandwiches, in untoasted sandwiches, or with any salad known to you. Catch a few cans next time you're down at the grocer. Plain or in tomato sauce, pilchards are always plentiful. Thank goodness. Get *either of these leading brands at your grocer.*

Kids love pilchards even though they're good for them.

60

Figure 10.1   Advertisement for Glenryck and Puffin pilchards (Reproduced with the Permission of Glenryck)

Source: *WH*, February 1967:60.

identified as male) in front of a plate containing the product. He is shown holding cutlery at the ready, and with mouth open far enough to expose teeth and a tongue poking through. It seems intended to connote eagerness on the part of the child for consuming the product, and therefore to be an example in support of the assertion that 'Kids love pilchards' – for this one clearly does.

Underneath this picture – which visually indexes the wider category of 'kids' – the rest of the page is made up of white space containing four other elements: an 'active' child on the left hand side, involved in the (male) child's world of 'high energy' (Parkin 2006:208–209); a depiction of the canned product on the right; a section of extended expositional text; and the heading 'Kids love pilchards even though they're good for them' in bold and in the largest font on the page. It is the latter of these elements that is of most interest analytically, and it also seems important to the advertising message, since it is repeated at the very bottom of the advert on the right, in smaller type, but again in bold. Nevertheless, these elements are all of importance to the rhetorical strategy being used to sell the product.

The paragraph of text begins by aligning itself both for *and* against part of the phrase 'Kids love pilchards even though they're good for them' in an interesting way. It constructs this is a claim made by someone else – as 'reported speech' (Vološinov 1973) – by disagreeing somewhat with the latter half. This disagreement concerns the intensity of the claim – which is constructed as an understatement. This is not simply a case of 'good', therefore, but *better than good*. The rest of the substantive content makes a set of claims about the virtues of the product – the ends/warrants that I have been discussing more generally. There is a claim to each of the following qualities: 'goodness', 'energy provision', 'economy', 'specific nutrition', 'nourishment', 'sensory taste', 'easy preparation', and 'versatility'.

In terms of the slogan that initially attracted my attention, it is the part-phrase/discourse marker 'even though' that is key to unlocking what assumptions are made about the relationship between children and food, and food that is 'good for you' (or, in this case better than good). Here, the conjunction 'even though' makes it clear that it is *despite* the fact that the product is healthy that it is also enjoyable – the degree of enjoyment overrides the aversion that 'kids' might otherwise feel towards foods that are healthy. The slogan is clearly orientated towards the dilemma of health and enjoyment that I have been discussing, and puts forward the product as one that successfully bridges the gap that is implicitly constructed between the interests of children (in enjoyment) and adults (in health). Just as with Cook's (2001:141–142) example, the product allegedly allows these two things to happen simultaneously – the dilemma is resolved as the product transcends the interests of the two groups. There is a (normative) discursive differentiation of health and enjoyment, with their de-differentiation promised by the product.

In a detailed analysis of food assessments in mealtime conversations, Wiggins and Potter (2003) focus upon some of the subtle rhetorical differences that assessing foods in 'subjective' and 'objective ways' can make interactively – for example intensifying praise, or minimising disagreement. While these adverts are not similarly interactive, it is nevertheless interesting to consider the differences that such nuances of assessment might make in relation to the strength of the claims being made.

In this regard, it is helpful to focus upon the 'Kids love pilchards even though they're good for them' slogan. Here we can see that although the first clause 'Kids love pilchards' does not make claims about properties of the 'object' pilchards – what they are like, what they consist of – it does contain information about the reaction that a whole category of persons (kids) will have to them – that they love them. The direct source of the claim, as has already been mentioned, is not available, but it is certainly asserted as a statement of what is the case, as is the second part 'even though they're good for them'. No doubt is acknowledged, and the statement therefore does not afford the possibility of it being available for disagreement as 'subjective'. Although the expositional text below does disagree with it in terms of the intensity of the *health* claim in the second clause of the slogan, the slogan is not identified as the *opinion* of someone. It does not afford the possibility of a differing opinion being easily accommodated on the same matter. It is not of the following form: 'It has been my experience that kids love pilchards' to which someone could easily reply 'Well I know children that do not love them', which does not question the original claim's truth content, but problematises it nonetheless. Of course, it would be possible to respond with 'Well I have encountered children that do not love them' to the claim 'Kids love pilchards', but that would arguably be a far more confrontational response, since it does directly problematise the original claim in terms of its truth content. I will return to this in my discussion of the other example – and advert for St. Ivel Cheese – because it is very different in this regard, and it is precisely the differences that exist between the two instances that should help to clarify matters.

St. Ivel Cheese – 'I don't care if it does me good I like it'

I DON'T CARE IF IT DOES ME GOOD *I like it*
  Of course he likes it – so do most children. The soft creaminess and distinctive flavour of St. Ivel Cheese are delightfully appealing – and it is so good for children, too.

> St. Ivel Cheese has all the nourishment of sweet fresh Somerset milk, special cultures which aid digestion and the vitamins 'A' and 'D' for promoting growth and resisting disease. In these difficult days this 'extra goodness' in St. Ivel Cheese is indeed a blessing. Give it to the children regularly – it spreads easily on biscuits or bread (saves butter) and combines deliciously with salads and fruit.
> A cool nutritious sandwich. Spread St. Ivel Cheese on slices of bread, complete with layer of shredded lettuce.
> The only cheese ever awarded a Gold Medal by the International Medical Congress, London.
> CHILDREN CHOOSE ST. IVEL CHEESE. THE NAME THE NATION KNOWS [...]
> St. IVEL CHEESE [...]
> FOR 30 YEARS IN POPULAR FAVOUR. (*WO*, 27 July 1940:26)[2]

The St. Ivel advert – the textual content of which can be seen above – is included on a page containing five other adverts, and is located centrally at the bottom. It takes up an eighth of the page space, and is itself made up of several sections. There is a heading in the form of 'reported speech' and an extended portion of expositional text, with a cartoon-style depiction of a child on the top right corner tucking in to a sandwich presumably filled with St. Ivel. Directly under that picture, there is a claim about an award received by the product. Finally, and directly under these last two, there is a restatement of the brand name and a claim about its longstanding existence and popularity, which is all in white, on a black background in the bottom right.

Again, the expositional paragraphs are of rhetorical relevance, and the advertisement displays a range of relatively expectable features. The content shows a fairly clear orientation to the significance of rationing, which is unsurprising given the time period. It refers to 'these difficult times' and portrays the product as a solution – a 'blessing' in relation to the problems that resulted (see Burridge 2008).

With regard to the coding procedures used to assemble the overview, the advert was coded in the following way, as featuring each of the following warrants/ends: 'kids love it', 'texture', 'sensory taste', 'goodness', 'nourishment', good digestion', 'specific nutrition', 'growth', 'disease resistance', and 'versatility'. The advert additionally asserts that the product has credentials in the form of an award – a Gold Medal – from an organisation that is both international (implying geographical scope) *and* medical (implying scientific expertise). The product is also portrayed as *unique* in this regard, as no other cheese has been similarly decorated.

As in the case of the pilchards advert, it was obviously the title or tag-line 'I DON'T CARE IF IT DOES ME GOOD *I like it*' which originally caught my attention. Interestingly, the slogan is, itself, split into two parts, by the fact that different fonts, and embellishments are used. The first clause is in capital letters, possibly connoting the strength of the assertion, while the second clause is in more orthodox lower case type, but italicised. Both parts of the slogan are also written in a rather scratchy type, perhaps implying that it was handwritten by a child – adding something of a 'personal touch' (Machin 2007:99). While this phrase, its rhetorical logic, and relationship to resolving the dilemma of health and enjoyment, is obviously very similar to that evident in the pilchards advert, it is nevertheless different in some subtle ways which also merit discussion.

Again, this slogan is clearly orientated towards both the issues of health *and* enjoyment, in much the same way as the pilchards advert. It claims to provide a solution to the likelihood that children have a preference for unhealthy foods. In fact, in this case, it is clearly the case that enjoyment overrides any aversion that may be brought about by the fact that the product is healthy. This time, however, the 'even though' is a silent one.

Returning to the issue of the types of assessment made – and whether they are 'objective' or 'subjective' – this time we have a clearly subjective assessment. Here, the slogan is presented as if said by a single individual – presumably the smiling boy depicted. It is worth considering whether the use of such a 'subjective assessment', focused upon a single child voicing the claim, serves to undermine the generality of the claim that the product successfully balances health *and* pleasure. According to the reported speech of the child, the product is not intrinsically or objectively likeable, and liking is therefore not an automatic result. Instead, the liking is less categorical, and comes from this single individual. This very much leaves open the possibility that other individuals may have very different positions on the likeability of St. Ivel. The implication is simply that he is a (highly personalised) example of success in regard to resolving the dilemma, but, coupled with the mitigated claim in the expositional text that only 'most children' like the product, it is clear that the claim to generality is less intense than in the Pilchards advert where 'kids' in general are claimed to love it.

The modality of the claim about the product's likely reception is relatively high, but also vague. There is no guarantee claimed that the product will be well received by all children for only 'most children' like the product. Of course, the claim is also less intense that in the case of Figure 10.1, since it is liking and not love that is at stake – a conventionally much lower grade of attachment. So, both in terms of breadth of positive response, and intensity of positive reception, this advert is making a less intense claim about the virtues of the product.

Now, it is certainly not part of my intention to adjudicate which of these two approaches is somehow more rhetorically successful. However, a few comments are appropriate with regard to what possibilities are afforded by these subtle differences. While this reduced intensity might seem misguided, it is also important to acknowledge that making extreme claims can be a rhetorically risky approach to take. Claims that are mitigated or that acknowledge a degree of relativity can actually be more difficult to counter than direct or extreme assertions that something is the case (see Edwards 2000). For example, in relation to the claim 'Kids love pilchards', all it takes to undermine the latter significantly is to present one child that does not fit with the claim – one child who does *not* love them. If the claim was, instead, that *most* kids love pilchards, then much more evidence needs to be garnered before the claim is brought into question. Similarly, if one individual is claimed to like a type of cheese, s/he can stand as an example – an act as an index of a category of persons with such a position. However, by making no direct claim that all individuals will be similarly approving, presentation of an individual or even several, does not undermine the general association made between the product and enjoyment for him or her (as well as health).

Therefore, there are differing potential advantages and disadvantages of both the approaches taken to claiming to solve the dilemma of health and/or enjoyment in relation to children's food consumption. It is important to note that these types of fine-grain difference are not captured well by any form of coding, but require close attention to the semantic, pragmatic and ideological dimensions of the specific arguments that are made. With such nuances acknowledged, I now return to the issue of where this leaves us in terms of the relationship between children, identity and food.

Conclusion

It is clearly the case that examining idealised cultural representations of this sort can bring to light some of the assumptions about children and food that underpin and inform the construction of these types of advertisements.

The key point that emerges from the preceding analysis is that in these food advertisements there is a dilemma of health and enjoyment constructed with a view to setting up various food products as solutions to that dilemma. Associated with this is the tendency for enjoyment to be aligned with children, and health with adults/parents/mothers, who are concerned about this on a child's behalf. A commercial solution is offered for the problem that is constructed – a means to manage, practically, the problem of the desires of children and the need to feed them healthy food. Products are constructed as solutions in so far as they can allegedly fulfil the requirements of both groups. This situation is something which constructs the relationship between children and adults as conflicted with relation to food consumption, and also portrays children as fundamentally irrational, incompetent or deficient, and does so in a way that may be ethically and practically unhelpful.

It could be argued that this health/enjoyment dynamic also brings to light another dilemma, regarding children – the degree to which they are deemed to be competent consumers within society, and the extent to which they can be allowed to make decisions for themselves, or require the overarching control of adults to ensure that they successfully do what is best for them (James et al. 1998; Lee 2001; Mayall 2002). In their discussion of child-centred approaches to parenting, Dixon and Banwell (2004:189–190) note the contemporary importance attributed to the acquiescence to children's desires. This may or may not be an increasing tendency in parenting practices, but the set of relations implied by the materials studied here is one that involves pleasing children through providing what they want, but trying to ensure that it is *also* healthy, on their behalf, because they would not choose to do so themselves.

This all implies a version of the child that is not quite a 'wilful, knowledgeable and desiring agent' (Cook 2003:126). Certainly, the child is viewed as wilful and desiring, but from the point of view of nutritional health, not knowledgeable. This is therefore an area in which the child is assumed to be lacking in competence as a social actor in James et al.'s (1998:93) sense. The point, however, is not that children should be understood automatically *as* knowledgeable about such things, but that the degree to which we might assume that they are not, and that adults automatically are, may be problematic in so far as it sets up this tension as normative, and aligns health and enjoyment automatically with adulthood and childhood respectively.

It does seem to be assumed that, if left to their own devices, children will tend to make poor choices with respect to health. It is as if, in relation to food consumption, as in many other spheres 'without parental constraint the life of the child is anarchistic' (James et al. 1998:11). Healthiness, on its own, is constructed as being an insufficient reason for children to consume food, and, to some degree, they need to be tricked into consuming healthy foods, or at least any healthy food needs to also be enjoyable and tasty – as if the two were not compatible, and healthiness was normatively associated with lack of enjoyment. As social scientists we should certainly try to avoid automatically reproducing these assumptions about competence, and about the respective automatic coupling of children with enjoyment rather than health. Certainly a lot of the literature concerned with so-called 'pester power' reproduces it, as I have already suggested, and this is unhelpful in attempting to understand the nuances of the relationship between contemporary childhood, food and identity. Moreover, it is potentially unhelpful for those interested in convincing children that eating healthily can itself be enjoyable!

Acknowledgements

Thanks to Margo Barker, the project's Principal Investigator, as well as Lynda Matthews who played in important role in assembling the initial corpus of magazines. I am grateful to everyone else from the Leverhulme-funded *Changing Families, Changing Food* Programme at the University of Sheffield (Award number F/00118/AQ). Special thanks to John E. Richardson for his comments on early versions of the chapter, and to Maria Patsarika for advising on some literature concerned with childhood. The editorial team also made important suggestions for improvement.

Notes

1. The list of other warrants is as follows: Gives Energy; Natural/Authentic; Gentle/ Delicate; Effectiveness; Gentle *and* Thorough; Brain Development; Charm; Vitality; Clear Skin; Training/Weaning; Build Reserves for Winter; Stimulate Appetite; Economical; Fast/Easy/Convenient; Quality; Helps Sleep; Bodily Well-Being; Balance; Growth (General); Strong Bones/Limbs; Strong Teeth; Good for the Blood; Non-Habit-Forming; Fitness; Variety/Change; Texture; Does Not Contain *X*; Not Messy; Bright Eyes/Eye Sight; Safe/Trustworthy/ Reliable; Suitable *and* Desirable; Offers 'Advantages'; Strength; Appearance of Food); Simple to Prepare; Problem-Solving (General); Comfort; Replacement/ Substitute; Disease Resistance/Illness Prevention; Modern; Controllable; Relieves Worry; Tempting/Appetising; Professionalism; Freshness; Magical; Geographical Origins; Easy Storage.
2. Permission to reproduce the advert was denied in line with Dairy Crest Limited's policy of only allowing their intellectual property to be used in matters directly relating to their company.

References

Billig, M., Condor, S., Edwards, D., Gane, M., Middleton, D. & Radley, A. (1988). *Ideological Dilemmas: A Social Psychology of Everyday Thinking*. London: Sage.

Burridge, J. D. (2008). 'The dilemma of frugality and consumption in British women's magazines 1940–1955'. *Social Semiotics* 18(3):389–401.

Charles, N. & Kerr, M. (1988). *Women, Food and Families*. Manchester: Manchester University Press.

Cook, D. T. (2003). 'Agency, children's consumer culture and the fetal subject: Historical trajectories, contemporary connections'. *Consumption, Markets and Culture* 6(2):115–132.

Cook, G. (2001). *The Discourse of Advertising*. London: Routledge.

DeVault, M. (1991). *Feeding the Family: The Social Organisation of Caring as Gendered Work*. London: The University of Chicago Press.

Dixon, J. & Banwell, C. (2004). 'Heading the table: Parenting and the junior consumer'. *British Food Journal* 106(3):181–193.

Dyer, G. (1982). *Advertising as Communication*. London: Routledge.

Edwards, D. (2000). 'Extreme case formulations: Softeners, investment, and doing nonliteral'. *Research on Language and Social Interaction* 33(4):347–373.

Gelperowic, R. & Beharrell, B. (1994). 'Healthy food products for children: packaging and mother's purchase decisions'. *British Food Journal* 96(11):4–8.

Giddens, A. (1991). *Modernity and Self-Identity*, Cambridge: Polity Press.

Herrick, C. (2007). 'Risky bodies: Public health, social marketing and the government of obesity'. *Geoforum* 38(1):90–102.

Hill, H. & Tilley, J. (2002). 'Packaging of children's breakfast cereal: Manufacturers versus children'. *British Food Journal* 104(9):766–777.

James, A. (1982). 'Confections, concoctions and conceptions', in Waites, B., Bennett, T. & Martin, G. (eds), *Popular Culture: Past and Present* (pp. 294–307). Buckingham: Open University Press.

James, A. (1990). 'The good, the bad and the delicious: The role of confectionery in British society'. *The Sociological Review* 38(4):666–688.

James, A., Jenks, C. & Prout, A. (1998). *Theorizing Childhood*. Cambridge: Polity.

Jeffries, L. (2007). *Textual Construction of the Female Body: A Critical Discourse Approach*. Basingstoke: Palgrave.

Lee, N. (2001). *Childhood and Society*. Buckingham: Open University Press.

Livingstone, S. (2005). 'Assessing the research base for the policy debate over the effects of food advertising to children'. *International Journal of Advertising* 24(3):273–296.

Machin, D. (2007). *Introduction to Multimodal Analysis*. London: Hodder Arnold.

Marshall, D., O'Donohoe, S. & Kline, S. (2007). 'Families, food, and pester power: Beyond the blame game?' *Journal of Consumer Behaviour* 6(4):164–181.

Mayall, B. (2002). *Towards a Sociology for Childhood: Thinking from Children's Lives*. Buckingham: Open University Press.

McDermott, L., O'Sullivan, T., Stead, M. & Hastings, G. (2006). 'International food advertising, pester power and its effects'. *International Journal of Advertising* 25(4):513–540.

Nicholls, A. J. & Cullen, P. (2004). 'The child-parent purchase relationship: 'Pester power' human rights and retail ethics'. *Journal of Retailing and Consumer Services* 11(2):75–86.

Parkin, K. (2006). *Food Is Love: Advertising and Gender Roles in Modern America*. Philadelphia: University of Philadelphia Press.

Turner, J. T., Kelly, J. & McKenna, K. (2006). 'Food for thought: Parents' perspectives of child influence'. *British Food Journal* 108(3):181–191.

Vološinov, V. N. (1973). *Marxism and the Philosophy of Language*, (trans.) Matejka, L. & Titunik, I. R. London: Harvard University Press.

Warde, A. (1997). *Consumption, Food and Taste: Culinary Antinomies and Commodity Culture*. London: Sage.

Wiggins, S. & Potter, J. (2003). 'Attitudes and evaluative practices: Category *vs* item and subjective *vs* objective constructions in everyday food assessments'. *British Journal of Social Psychology* 42(4):513–531.

Index